Shaping
Web Usability

Shaping
Web Usability

Interaction Design in Context

Albert N. Badre

♦♦Addison-Wesley

Boston • San Francisco • New York • Toronto • Montreal
London • Munich • Paris • Madrid
Capetown • Sydney • Tokyo • Singapore • Mexico City

The publisher offers discounts on this book when ordered in quantity for special sales. For more information, please contact:

Pearson Education Corporate Sales Division
201 W. 103rd Street
Indianapolis, IN 46290
(800) 428-5331
corpsales@pearsoned.com

Visit A-W on the Web: www.aw.com/cseng/

Library of Congress Cataloging-in-Publication Data

Badre, Albert.
  Shaping Web usability : interaction design in context / Albert N. Badre.
      p. cm.
  Includes bibliographical references and index.
  ISBN 0-201-72993-8
      1. Computer software—Development—Human factors. 2. Computer input-output equipment. 3. Human-computer interaction. 4. World Wide Web. I. Title.

  QA 76.76.D47 B338 2002
  005.2'76—dc21   2001056075

ISBN 0-201-72993-8
Text printed on recycled paper
1 2 3 4 5 6 7 8 9 10—MA—0605040302
First printing, January 2002

To Barbara and David

Contents

Foreword

This is an exciting book written by a pioneer in the field of human-computer interaction, or HCI as we often call it. It is exciting because the author applies the knowledge and practices that have evolved within the HCI field ever since our discipline started in the late 1950s and early 1960s. This book represents the application of about 40 years' worth of expertise to the human-computer interface to which millions and millions of eyeballs are glued each and every day: the World Wide Web.

This book is about an everlasting truth, a truth that many people, many companies, many organizations have learned the hard way. That is, when designing technological systems for people to use, one *must* take into account the characteristics of the users, the nature of the task, and the knowledge, experience, biases, strengths, and weaknesses that the users bring to the task. In the case at hand, the task is using the World Wide Web.

Badre nicely captures and explains this notion via his concept of *context*. Chapter 1 begins with an attention-getting story that dramatically captures the essence of context and why users matter. (Wait, please stay with me a bit longer before turning to page 1.)

A few years ago I taught a course on navigating and visualizing the Web. As was then in vogue, I made heavy use of the way-finding literature—drawing on maps, building and road signage, and 2-D spatial orientation as a way to design navigational aids—and now believe that approach not to have been particularly useful. After all, the Web, or more precisely, the network of inter-related Web sites and pages, does not have a real 2-D spatial organization.

I wish this book had been available at the time, as I find its concept of context to be a more useful way of considering Web navigation than the concept of way-finding. Context need not have a spatial organization, although it may, as Badre very nicely illustrates with several compelling series of grocery store shopping pictures. But it always has a conceptual or logical organization, and that is what matters.

The job of the Web designer is to take into account the users' many contexts while creating a Web-browsing experience that leverages the many contexts of use including the Web environment, user, genre, site, and page. Badre nicely shows how this can be done in a wide variety of ways that draw on his diversity of experiences and interests—many consulting assignments, teaching Web design to working professionals and students, understanding both computers and people, and doing research to back up his teachings.

I commend his book to you. Read on.

Jim Foley
October 2001
College of Computing
Georgia Tech
Atlanta, Georgia

Preface

I got great pleasure from writing this book. Most satisfying is knowing how readers can use the book and how it will help them in their work. I tried to put myself in the reader's place, considering possible questions and seeking the answers—not unlike the approach I recommend for the Web design process. The emphasis on users comes from my own experience. I provide arguments showing the need for a user-centered approach to Web design and present a methodology for the systematic consideration of users during design and development.

The reader will notice that I focus on design rather than implementation. Design principles and methods are long range, whereas implementation is tied to technology, which is often short-lived. This book is about designing *usable* Web sites—Web sites that are easy to use and that provide a pleasant, enjoyable, and successful user experience. It also examines the proposition that designing usable Web sites requires employing the Web-specialized methodology of designing for context.

In my daily life as a human interface researcher and practitioner, I am often asked by Web developers and site owners for solutions to their problems, for guidance about design, and for sound ideas to make a difference in approaching the users. End users have also come to me with questions about using Web sites and software systems. Their confusion could have been avoided if designers had employed a more careful process when developing Web sites and Web application interfaces. This book explains this careful process. It answers the questions of Web developers, provides solutions to a wide range of development problems, and offers specific guidelines to support design excellence at every step in the process.

Accordingly, this book draws heavily not only on research findings in the design and behavioral sciences but also on my own extensive experience as a Web usability consultant and practitioner. I target primarily Web developers who need to know about designing usable Web sites, but the general "Web-interested audience"—those who want to design their own Web sites—will also benefit.

This book is not written exclusively for Web designers and developers but is also geared toward reaching those who want to learn about human computer interaction as it is specialized to Web environments. Web researchers will also find the book helpful because it covers Web usability issues that must be considered for emerging technologies and environments where there are limited research and experience. These environments include mobile Web environments and wireless technologies. In general, this book is for anyone with a serious interest in making the human-Web interactive experience gratifying and productive.

The book is structured around the "Web contexts": treatments of the Web environment, the user, the Web genre, the Web site, and the Web page. A separate chapter is devoted to each. The book also does the following.

- Delineates a user-centered approach to Web design
- Tackles the usability issues of retrofitting Web pages for small-screen real estate as well as designing for mobile devices
- Takes up the challenge of the encounter between Web art and Web usability
- Discusses how to evaluate the usability of Web sites
- Addresses the cultural context of Web design

The book presents many Web examples that illustrate concepts, techniques, and guidelines. This clarifies the close relationship between theory and practice, and thus narrows the potential gap between the researcher's interests and the practitioner's needs.

Albert N. Badre
September 2001

Acknowledgments

The ideas and insights in this book have been enriched by my own teachers, wonderful professional colleagues, consulting clients, and the many students who have been part of my academic career. I thank only a few of them here by name, but I am grateful to all of them.

My mentor and friend, the late Manfred Kochen, inspired in me a passion for scholarship and interdisciplinary curiosity that remains to this day.

John Stasko, Mark Guzdial, Jay Bolter, and Gregory Abowd graciously reviewed one or more versions of the manuscript and provided constructive comments. I am especially indebted to my friend and colleague Jim Foley for providing constructive comments and for writing the Foreword. I want to acknowledge Wendy Rogers, the primary author on Chapter 5, and Kayt Sukel, who helped me write Chapter 10.

I am immensely grateful to freelance editor Marian Gordin. The first question that Marian asked me when I met her was, "Who is the audience for this book?" The moment she asked that question, I was confident that she spoke my language. When I began getting her detailed edits, I saw her remarkable ability to take lengthy, wordy sentences and turn them into succinct prose.

I am deeply indebted to Julie Shinabery for taking on the incredibly laborious task of securing permissions for some 65 figures. Also, with unwavering attention to detail, she made sure that all the figures, illustrations, tables, and screenshots were properly prepared for the publisher. I am also grateful to Sarah Craighill for preparing the illustrations for several of the figures and for commenting on early versions of some of the chapters.

My deepest thanks go to my son, David, with whom I had many early discussions, and who read and critiqued parts of the work, as well as to my wife, Barbara. She was my art adviser and drew the ballerina illustrations, and she also engaged me in discussions that helped to sharpen my presentation of key concepts. I would like to thank the Addison-Wesley team, including production, marketing, and editing people. They are not only highly skilled, but also extremely pleasant professionals.

Finally, I especially thank Peter Gordon of Addison-Wesley, a truly wise man, for his support and patience. He is a genuine friend of the author.

1

Human Computer Interaction for the Web

The billboards loomed over America's highways and byways, displaying three scenes. In the first, the frowning housewife holds up a pair of grubby trousers for all to see. In the second panel, she places the offending garment in the washing machine and then adds laundry powder from the sponsor's distinctive box. In the last picture, she displays the now sparkling clean pants, and her radiant smile, across the consumer landscape.

That housewife sold millions of dollars' worth of laundry detergent.

It was the middle of the 1950s, and billboard advertising was in its prime in the United States. The detergent promotion did so well that the sponsor decided to expand it to international markets, and it chose a Middle Eastern country to experiment with adapting the advertisement.

The billboards had been very successful, so the ad agency confidently prepared the new design, substituting in Arabic the name of the detergent. Ad executives bought their display space and launched the campaign. It was a resounding failure.

Why? When the designers moved into new territory, they ignored three important principles: designing for user characteristics, designing for the user experience, and designing for context.

They disregarded user characteristics when they failed to replace the image of the quintessential U.S. housewife with a face and clothes familiar to the Middle Eastern audience. They ignored user experience by maintaining the left-to-right orientation of the three pictures in the display. Unlike readers of English, Arabic readers scan from right to left. Consequently, Middle Eastern consumers saw the smiling woman use the sponsor's soap and end up frowning at a grimy pair of trousers.

Finally, if the designers had analyzed context, they would have found that billboards for advertising were not common in this Middle Eastern country at the time. They might have chosen to promote their product through the more popular medium of magazines and newspapers.

The lessons learned from this experience are at the heart of this book. The absolute requirements to design for the user and for context are the bases of usable Web design and the foundation of Web design's connection to usability engineering.

The practice of interaction usability engineering is rooted in the field of Human Computer Interaction (HCI), which itself combines three distinct methodological approaches. HCI methodologies derive from the science of behavior, computing technology, and design. The science of behavior emphasizes the quality of the empirical methodology used to discover important insights about interaction behavior. Computing technology models and invents technological solutions for human interaction problems. For design, methodological power resides in the designer's virtuosity of expression. It is from this methodological context—combining the methodologies of discovery, invention, and design—that the practice of interaction usability engineering emerged.

This book connects interaction usability practice to the design of Web pages, Web sites, and Web applications. Because Web usability design is grounded in HCI methodologies and principles, we will begin with a summary of HCI history and principles and how they are related to Web usability.

From Human Factors to Usability: A Short History of HCI

During the past two decades, both the number and diversity of people using computers have increased dramatically. Computers now mediate everyday activities in business, industry, education, entertainment, and the home, whereas until the early 1980s computer use was restricted to the technically sophisticated. This rise in use led to a flurry of interface research and design activities during the 1980s and 1990s, which produced the Graphic User Interface (GUI) and, eventually, the Web.

Origins

Scientific interest in the interaction between human beings and computers and user interface design is rooted in the more general area of human-machine systems, human factors engineering, and ergonomics. Systematic investigations of human factors engineering go back to the early time-and-motion studies of Frank Gilbreth (1911). These and all other studies conducted between the world wars concentrated on the operator's muscular capabilities and limitations. During World War II, the emergence of radar and the technology associated with aircraft cockpits led to a shift in emphasis away from physical interaction with machines to the perceptual and decision-making capabilities of operators.

Toward the end of the 1950s, interest in human-computer interfaces arose out of this system's engineering tradition and crystallized around Licklider's (1960) concept of symbiosis. Licklider described a relationship in which the human operator and the computer and its software form two distinct but interdependent systems. They cooperate to attain a goal because each component has unique abilities to bring to bear on a given task. The human component is more suited to engaging in tasks that require creativity, such as raising the "important questions," posing the "original problems," or making the "critical decisions." Computers, on the other hand, excel at performing such functions as rapid and accurate data storage and retrieval, as well as rapid aggregate analysis, calculation, and plotting of retrieved data. Human operators and computer systems could thus have a symbiotic relationship in which they augment each other's capabilities in performing complex, multifaceted tasks.

Throughout the 1960s and early 1970s, human factors researchers paid more attention to mapping out the information-processing and decision-making skills of the typical user than to engineering a symbiotic association between operators and specific systems. It was not until well into the 1970s that technological advances made real-time interaction common-place and with it made Licklider's idea of symbiosis feasible. As a result, the late 1970s and early 1980s saw a deeper interest in the now-blossoming field of cognitive psychology and adapting its findings to the design of user interface strategies. Of particular interest was the focus on interaction with data-bases (Reisner, 1977; Shneiderman, 1978; Thomas, 1977).

We also began to see the emergence of theoretical constructs of the interaction between users and computers. These included the keystroke-level and GOMS models of Card, et al. (1980, 1983). The GOMS model is specified by four components: a set of *g*oals, a set of *o*perators, a set of goal-achieving *m*ethods, and a set of *s*election rules to choose among methods. Another theoretical construct was the levels of interactions model, with its four inter-action levels of conceptual, semantic, syntactic, and lexical, initially proposed by Foley and Wallace (1974) and expanded by Foley and Van Dam (1982).

Focus on the User Interface

In the late 1970s and early 1980s, a flurry of psychological research, mostly carried out in industrial research laboratories, dealt with the user interface (Reisner, 1977; Thomas and Carroll, 1979; Gould, 1981). It was during those years that the field of HCI was officially "born." For the first time, books with the words "human computer interaction" in their titles were published (Badre and Shneiderman, 1982; Card, et al., 1983). The Association for Computing Machinery (ACM) Special Interest Group in Computer Human Interaction was established, and in 1982 the first conference on Human Factors in Com-puting Systems, which became the annual CHI conference, was held.

Along with the explosion in popular and personal computing in the 1980s, there arose a parallel emphasis on usability issues: how to make soft-ware and computer systems easy to learn and use. Until the mid-1980s the interface was embedded in application software. There were, however, some graphic utilities, and the interface began to emerge as a separate component. The introduction of the Xerox Star began a new generation of interfaces using the desktop as metaphor. These interfaces displayed high-quality graphics and used the point-and-click mouse to invoke actions and manipu-late screen objects. Thus emerged the GUI interface, which was popularized with Apple's computers: first Lisa, then the Macintosh.

As the GUI interface evolved, the new discipline of Human Computer Interaction matured. Key HCI principles of User-Centered Design (Norman, 1986) and Direct Manipulation (Shneiderman, 1982, 1983) emerged. We saw the first textbook—*Designing the User Interface: Strategies for Effective Human-Computer Interaction* by B. Shneiderman—and the first influential HCI design idea book—*The Psychology of Everyday Things* by D. A. Norman. This was followed in the 1990s by several textbooks (Shneiderman, 1992, 1998; Mayhew, 1992; Preece, et al., 1994; Dix, et al., 1998) and the introduction of the ACM HCI Curriculum.

User Interface Software

Other researchers during the 1980s worked to develop tools and methods for user interface design. This research arose from the belated recognition by computer scientists that the user interface is as vital a component of computing systems as an operating system or database. Those scientists and engineers were primarily concerned with inventing tools and systems of tools that help create interfaces, such as User Interface Management Systems (UIMS) (Coutaz, 1989; Siebert, et al., 1989) and User Interface Design Environments (UIDE) (Foley, et al., 1989).

Usability

In parallel with the research and academic evolution of HCI, the software industry focused on designing user-compatible interfaces and making software systems increasingly more usable. Starting in the mid-1980s and gaining strength in the 1990s, the interface development community employed usability engineering methods to design and test software systems for ease of use, ease of learning, memorability, lack of errors, and satisfaction (Gould and Lewis, 1985; Nielsen, 1993).

It was no longer enough for a designer to be sensitive to usability concerns or to adopt an intangible user-centered perspective. Designers must also set objective, measurable, operational usability goals. An operational definition of usability, in turn, must include some identifiable and measurable concept of effort. For example, the effort to complete a task may be measured in terms of both the time it takes a user to perform a task successfully and the number of observable actions taken in the process.

Usability practitioners of the 1990s considered two factors as measures of usability.

- *Ease of Learning:* We can measure usability by comparing the time it takes users to learn to do a job when working with an unfamiliar computer system to the time it takes them to learn to do the same job some other way. As measured by time, it takes the user more effort to learn a system that does not incorporate and build on the user's existing habits. The users will have to ignore what they already know about the job to develop a new collection of habits.

- *Ease of Use:* The minimum number of actions required to complete a task successfully becomes an increasingly important measure of usability for more experienced operators. For example, the number of mouse clicks entered per procedure is a good way to compare the ease of use of two designs. Other factors being equal, the design that requires fewer keystrokes per procedure will be more usable.

Focusing on the Web

At the same time that usability practitioners were becoming pervasive in the software development industry, the World Wide Web was becoming a force in information sharing and a popular medium for business advertising and transactions. Web usability became a particular focus of the HCI community during the late 1990s (Nielsen, 2000). This interest was heightened by the fact that Web developers were poorly designing corporate Web sites. The developer's training was limited to Web authoring tools and languages, which can be learned in a relatively short period of time. These early developers were not sensitized to the usability issues that had become an integral part of the software development culture. As the evolution in technology made it possible for "new media" style Web sites to be developed with graphics and animation, the number of usability problems increased, with a correspondingly greater negative impact on business revenues and customer retention (Manning, et al., 1998).

HCI Principles for the Web

The same basic HCI principles that govern software interface design apply just as effectively to designing Web sites and Web applications. Just as a badly designed user interface can doom a software product despite its complex functionality or the power of its technology, a poorly designed Web interface, despite its impressive graphics, can propel the user to another site with one click of the mouse. As user satisfaction has increased in importance, the need for reliable Web usability design methods has become more critical.

As the following chapters will demonstrate, the same usability design principles developed for designing user interfaces also apply to the design of usable Web sites. These principles include user-centered design with early focus on the user, early human factors input, task environment analysis, iterative design, and continuous testing. Let's examine some of these principles as they relate to new media technology on the Web.

User-Centered Design

Defining the user culture, including user characteristics, user types, levels of expertise, and user task descriptions, is a prerequisite to interface development and testing. Attention to individual differences will increase in importance and detail as the new media allows us to interact at more than simply the information-processing levels. For example, as the Web interface incorporates video technologies, we must pay attention to individual and cultural differences in facial expressions, gestures, and demeanor.

Early Human Factors Input

Considerations are given to the human factor aspects of design very early in the development process because it is easier and less costly to introduce human factor constraints at this stage. As new media technologies allow us to create artistic, immersive, and all-encompassing interactive experiences, developers need to consider and design for the emotional, affective, and psychomotor human factors.

Task Environment Analysis

Task analysis is used to determine functionality by distinguishing the tasks and subtasks performed. Particular attention is paid to frequent tasks, occasional tasks, exceptional tasks, and errors. Identifying goals and the strategies (combinations of tasks) used to reach those goals is also part of a good task analysis. By conducting a task analysis, the designer learns about the sequences of events that a user may experience in reaching a goal.

With the increase in the power of rendering and simulation technologies, metaphor-based Web designs will require us to become more environment specific, complete, and accurate in our task analysis. Task analysis based on time-and-motion studies, or that relates only to the cognitive and informational component, will no longer suffice. Analysis will need to cover all aspects of the Web task environment, including the physical, social, and aesthetic.

Iterative Design and Continuous Testing

The iterative design process for developing user interfaces stems from the experience that "first designs," no matter how well founded in experience and background, contain unanticipated flaws. In addition, because of the bias of visible experience, first designs often replicate the real world. With the new media available to Web designers, we can replicate real-world environments with much greater detail. This capability should not, however, confine us to the limitations of the real world if we can accomplish the same tasks using strategies that are more efficient, yet natural, to our human capabilities.

Several iterations of design and continuous testing are usually needed to take full advantage of the capabilities of the new media and allow us to come up with novel interactive environments to perform old tasks.

You can see an example of this kind of design problem in the design of Web newspapers. Available technologies let us simulate the newspaper reader environment in almost exact detail, but the same technologies can also be used to improve on the limitations of the current environment. For example, we can free the reader from the physical limitations of the paper page by the use of hypermedia. The end result of extensive iteration of such designs could lead to an environment that is much more compatible with the human natural systems of information acquisition, processing, and representation.

Web Usability

Although HCI principles apply equally well to both graphic user interfaces and Web interface design, there are significant differences between GUIs and the Web. There are several unique Web features to which GUI-experienced usability designers should pay particular attention. Among the more prominent are compatibility with device and browser diversity, user-initiated and -controlled navigation, and low cost of switching between sites. Other Web-specific factors include multiple points of page entry into a site, ease of being distracted with the enormity of information available, and the easy ability to personalize what visitors want to see.

In a course I teach to professional developers on Web usability, I asked a group of 15 participants, who were experienced in both GUI and Web design, to brainstorm about the differences between GUIs and the Web that should concern designers. Here are the ten most important differences the group identified.

1. The Web is less secure.

2. There is less privacy on the Web.

3. The Web is platform independent.

4. Web sites contain more dynamic content.

5. The Web has a broader audience.

6. Web devices and browsers have compatibility problems.

7. Users have different expectations for the Web.

8. Learning is expected with GUIs, but not with the Web.

9. There is more than one entry point into a site on the Web.

10. Navigation is user controlled on the Web.

In addition to understanding the differences between GUI and Web design environments, usability designers should pay particular attention to the predominant and recurring usability problems infesting the World Wide Web. In the same usability course, I asked participants to name the ten most important Web design problems. They were first asked as a group to generate a list of problems. Then the 15 participants voted on what they considered to be the *most* important problems.

1. The Web end user is not considered; the design is not user centered.

2. It is slow due to large multimedia files and useless Java scripts and plug-ins.

3. The information is disorganized and poorly structured.

4. There is a lack of standards and consistency.

5. "Design" consists of showing off technology.

6. Designers treat the Web as a brochure.

7. Pages are cluttered.

8. Developers do not maintain and update sites.

9. Pervasive banner ads are annoying.

10. Page layout is poor.

Designing usable Web sites requires more attention to context than designing usable GUIs. Sensitivity to the factors that surround user interaction with the Web takes on added importance because of the ease with which users can turn off one site and put on another. As Web usability designers, we must make sure not only that the interaction is simple but also that the user feels comfortable in the physical, mental, and emotional environment of the interaction. The Web interaction context can be as small as a page or as large as the physical, cognitive, social, and emotional surrounds of the user in the act of using the Web.

Furthermore, providing the right functionality forms the essence of a usable Web site. As designers we must recognize that the usability quality of a Web interface diminishes and becomes insignificant if the site does not support the tasks that users want to perform or does not provide the information for which visitors are searching.

Themes

This book focuses on two themes: (1) designing for context and (2) designing for the user experience.

Designing for Context

Designing usable Web sites and applications requires employing a contextual design methodology that is geared to the Web. This contextual approach to Web design includes treatments of the Web environment, the user, the Web genre, the Web site, and the Web page. A separate chapter is devoted to each of these "Web contexts."

Designers should keep in mind that users perform in a context, which includes the user's background, the location where he or she is performing, and the tasks being performed. Brown and Duguid (1994) refer to these contextual elements as "border resources."

For the best Web design outcome, we need to design contextually. That means when we design a human-constructed artifact, as opposed to a natural object, we must take into account the relationship between the artifact's core elements and the elements that surround the core. In the case of designing a Web page, it is important to consider tangible peripheral elements such as the site to which the page belongs and other sites to which the target page's site relates, as well as browsers and platforms. Intangible peripheral elements, which are much more difficult to discern, also come into play. These include elements such as the user's characteristics and habits, cultural practices and norms, and aesthetic appreciation. A chapter is devoted to each of these topics. I believe that designers who successfully integrate peripheral elements into their designs create Web sites that enhance the user experience.

Designing for the User Experience

Until now, the goal of usability design was to make technologies easy to learn and use. Although the definition of usability includes "user satisfaction," in practice, we have only considered efficiency as measured in times and actions or for operational problems revealed by a usability evaluator. Usability professionals tend to assume that efficiency and relatively smooth operation correlate positively with users' satisfaction, and they look no further. We seldom try to measure directly a user's comfort, preferences, or enjoyment when using a technology. Designing for the user's quality of experience (pleasant or unpleasant) means taking into account not only how well and easily users perform tasks but also their previous experience with similar tasks and technology, and their interests, needs, motivations, and expectations.

For Web user experience, we need to answer certain questions: Did users perform tasks as they expected to? Were they successful in achieving their goals? How did they feel as they were performing? Were they annoyed or satisfied, challenged or excited, hesitant or confident?

Usability scientists and engineers have for the most part operated out of the idea that if a technology is simple to use, people will like it and will focus on the functionality, not the technology. Usability designers addressing the user experience will anticipate why, when, under what conditions, and how a visitor is likely to interact with the Web. After designing with these questions in mind, the usability designer will evaluate the total user experience.

The pleasantness of a Web experience depends on several factors, including why the user is visiting the site, whether the user's expectations are met, the context of the user's visit, and the identity of the user. Collecting data and understanding these factors are prerequisites to designing for the user experience.

The inadequacies of interpreting subjective input from users can be somewhat ameliorated by using well-tested and reliable measuring instruments such as rating and ranking scales, as well as thinking-aloud methods. It is important to realize that feedback from users is not fiction but a valid expression of their experience. Optimizing the user experience should be the ultimate aim of the Web usability designer.

2

Web Usability Strategy

People often ask me either to design a "usable" Web site or to review one and make comments and recommendations on its usability. My first step is to generate all the realistic scenarios of use we can either construct or envision. In creating such scenarios, a designer specifies interface objects and actions for given contexts from the perspective of the user. Identifying relevant design objects for given contexts, as well as specifying user actions from a human-centered perspective, is at the core of what I call the "userview" process.

Specifying context is important to the Web design process because context helps us understand how objects within a universe of discourse relate to each other to form a coherent whole and provides us with a framework in which to relate objects to their surrounding environments. Focus on the user early in the design process produces user-centered Web design. Let's examine more carefully the three design concepts of *scenario, context,* and *userview*.

Scenarios

To create successful scenarios, we first must answer four questions.

1. Where and under what conditions will the Web site be used?

2. For what purpose will the site be used?

3. Who will use the site (the target audience)?

4. How will the site be used?

There may be many answers to each question. The permutations of the different combined answers constitute all the possible scenarios. Some combinations are naturally more realistic than others. A good designer is able to weed out the unsuitable ones.

As an example, let's say you want to design a Web site for a museum. Two different scenarios for the site are (A) a kiosk situated in the museum's entrance lobby to be used by visitors to get information, survey special exhibits, and print out spatial directions, using touch screen and 3-D spatial navigation, and (B) a Web site for local people who can use Web TV remote controls at home to get information on museum exhibits. For scenario A, these are the answers to the preceding four questions.

1. Kiosk in the museum

2. To get information and print directions

3. Museum visitors

4. Touch selection and VRML spatial navigation

For scenario B, the answers are the following.

1. Television at home

2. To get information on exhibits

3. Families at home in the museum's locale

4. Selection and navigation using TV remote control

Of course, by changing only one of the answers each time, many other scenarios are possible.

Context

Scenario development helps us envision the objects and actions needed for design. Context is the relationship of these objects and actions to each other and to their environments. "The weaving together of parts into a coherent whole" describes the object's relationship to other objects. This is an important sense of context in Web design because it addresses the issue of how information should be organized. For example, it determines the placement on a Web page of a label relative to a field or a header to text—that is, the spatial placement of objects that are semantically close (similar in meaning) to each other.

A second essential way in which to define the context of an object for Web site design is to view context as "that which surrounds the object." In this sense, context can be either cognitive or physical. For example, cognitively, the context of a word is a function of the sentence containing the word. An example of physical context is a book on a shelf of books in the library. The other books and the library are both contexts in that they surround the target book. As we will see in Chapter 3, the union of physical and cognitive contexts is quite important to Web design.

In Web site design we must also consider an object's relationships to many environmental levels, which can be represented as ever-larger concentric circles. Figure 2.1 is a graphic example of the environmental context of a jar of Folgers decaffeinated coffee. The Folgers jar is in the section of decaffeinated coffees, which is in the coffees section. The coffees are on the aisle containing coffees and teas, which is in the dry foods area, which is in the supermarket.

A cognitive example of context as "that which surrounds" an object is the selection of words to convey meaning. Here we need to consider the relationship of the word we select to the sentence, the paragraph, the document, the topic, the field of specialization, and the reading audience. Each of these environments, starting with the sentence, is a successively larger context in which to consider the choice of words to use.

In our design philosophy, the largest context is assigned the highest precedence for consideration. For example, to convey the meaning, "an area of cleared, enclosed land used for pasture," we should not use the word *field* if the Web site audience is primarily athletes. For an athletic audience, the predominant meaning of the word *field* is "an athletic or sports area." We know

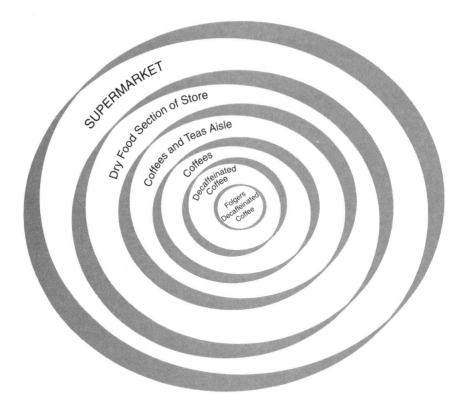

Figure 2.1: *Context as that which surrounds*

that when we read a sentence, we process predominant meanings first and then consider secondary meanings (Foss, 1970; Cairns and Kamerman, 1975). If a word has a meaning other than the predominant one for members of the intended audience, then it will take longer to process the sentence. The point of this example is that there are costs associated with not considering the environments in which the objects of design reside.

Using a contextual strategy to design Web sites requires us to consider five levels of design context:

- The environment context
- The user context
- The genre context
- The site context
- The page context

Designing contextually for each level means considering not only how objects relate to each other on any given level but also how the contexts relate to each other generally.

Figure 2.2 shows levels represented as concentric circles where design decisions made in the larger circle supersede those made in the smaller ones. This order of supersession is fundamental to the strategy of contextual design. The extrinsic design context refers to the actual physical and cognitive spaces in which users visit a Web site. The user context refers to the audience requirements, such as Web user cultural constraints or a user's physical limitations. The genre context specifies the type of site, such as news media, tourism, or shopping. The site context refers to the user, or human, interface relating to characteristics such as site navigation and organization. The page context addresses design constraints inherent in a single page.

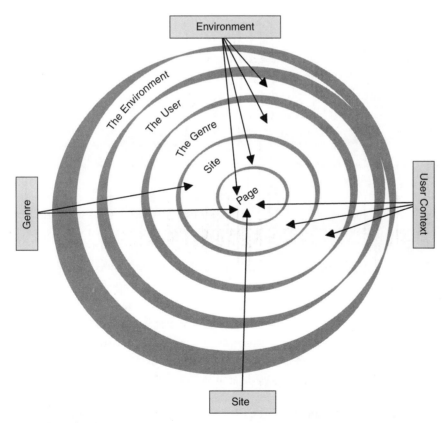

Figure 2.2: *Contextual order of supersession for design decisions*

Design decisions made at higher levels supersede decisions made at any lower level. Let's say we are designing a tourism site. In the tourism genre, the proportion of graphics to text is high on a given page. If we are designing for a culture where information is usually conveyed textually, then this user constraint of textual pages would supersede the tourism genre characteristic of a high proportion of graphics.

Using another museum scenario example, we start by considering design decisions relative to the location where the Web site will be used. If we determine that the site is intended to be used mostly in K–12 classrooms, then the environment context suggests that the visitors to the site will be groups of children rather than individuals. This "group" characteristic carries with it a certain set of constraints that will impact how to design interaction and navigation at the site level. Under such constraints, the designer may have to consider using voice, video, audio, and possibly a remote control. The "group usage" characteristic will also require that pages be designed with relatively large objects that can be seen from a group distance. The museum genre context will call for a site with color graphics and possibly spatial navigation, even though for the sake of simplicity we recommend that the designer avoid 3-D elements for navigation at the site level and avoid graphics at the page level. Here the design decision at the genre level supersedes those at the site and page levels.

The Userview Process

The contextual approach to Web design is concerned mainly with how successively larger, more encompassing contexts relate to each other and to design objects. Within any given context, we need a systematic strategy that allows us to specify design solutions. That strategy is grounded in the human-centered approach (Norman, 1986) to designing usable interactive systems. The general methodology consists of a sequence of tasks that a designer performs in defining the Web user interface and implementing site usability. It also involves iterative modifications and compromises. The process derives from the following set of accepted usability design principles of practice (Gould, 1988; Whiteside et al., 1988).

User-centered approach. Defining the user culture—including user characteristics and types, a user level of expertise, and user task descriptions—is a prerequisite to Web interface development and testing. Methods for user-centered designs range from user interviews and observations to videotaping users as they work and administering attitude and information surveys.

Early human factors input. Consideration should be given to the human factors and user interface design guidelines very early in the process. Usability guidelines come from three sources: results from experimental human behavior research, accepted conventions of practice, and consensus of experts. It is easier and less costly to introduce human factors and user interface design constraints in the early stages of development.

Iterative design. The iterative design process for developing Web interfaces (see Figure 2.3) stems from the knowledge that "first designs," no matter how well founded in experience and background, contain unanticipated flaws. Iterative interface designers start by profiling the audience and performing task analysis. Developing and implementing a prototype of the design, based on guidelines, principles, and examples, follows. Depending on the environment, the

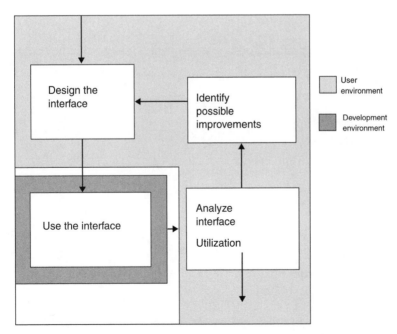

Figure 2.3: *The iterative development cycle*

prototype is presented to the user for testing and feedback. During subsequent testing rounds, the interface is refined and changed according to the results of the analyses.

Continuous testing. Usability evaluation should begin very early in Web site development and continue throughout the process. In the early phases, testing involves focus groups, interviews, and questionnaires. This stage is followed by storyboard paper designs, simulations, and prototypes. In later stages, usability evaluations involve lab tests, field testing, and sequential data analysis.

Integrated design. Certain questions need to be considered simultaneously at the very start of the process and on a continuing basis because of their interdependency in formulating a cohesive usability design. Designers should focus initially and concurrently on the following questions: (1) What functions does the user need to perform the tasks? (2) How should the user be allowed to invoke those functions? (3) How should we tell the user how to invoke the functions?

Figure 2.4 depicts the structure of the systematic and repeatable userview process. We start by generating four Web design documents. The first is

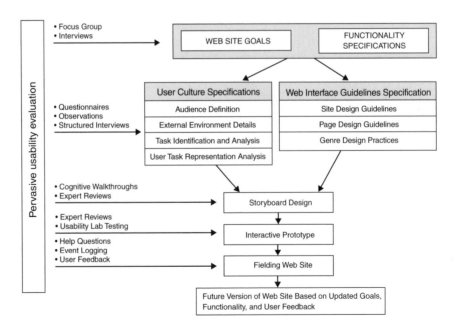

Figure 2.4: *The userview process for Web site design*

a discovery document, which specifies the Web site's projected functionality and goals. The results of this discovery will help us generate a second document that specifies the user culture and a third that establishes Web interface design guidelines and human factors principles specific to the Web application under development. The fourth document, which defines a comprehensive usability plan, comes early in the userview process. This document takes established usability evaluation techniques, data collection methods, and measuring instruments and adapts them to the current development project.

The next sequence of steps uses the generated documents to specify a storyboard representation of the design, construct an interactive prototype, and build the first version of the Web site. Throughout this process, we will implement the specialized usability evaluation plan, which will be detailed in Chapter 12. As you can see in Figure 2.4, we collect data and conduct usability evaluation using different techniques for the different stages of the userview process.

Goals and Requirements

Each Web site development project begins with a goal in mind: for example, to gain exposure, to increase efficiency, or to do something better via the Internet. Coupled with this motivation is a set of perceived needs that the Web site could fulfill. The transformation of these vague needs to a requirements specification document for the Web is a complex process.

Our initial task of scenario making is an informal activity of specifying goals, functionality, audience, and conditions of use via discussions with the Web site procurer or owner. Then, in a more formal process, we develop the requirements discovery document needed at the outset of the userview process. A requirements definition is a statement in a natural language of what user services the Web site should provide. We call this goals and functionality document a discovery document because, as designers, we have the task of discovering client objectives and what the client would like Web site visitors to accomplish. The document should be geared to the customers (users) of the Web site to facilitate corrections and additions. It is a formal statement specifying user services and Web site functionality in more detail than what is in the scenario specification and with enough precision to serve as a contract between system procurer and Web site developer.

As we know from software engineering practice, the need for a functional requirements specification arises from the lack of verifiability of natural language documents. Although as Web designers we should make every effort to write complete, consistent, and unambiguous requirements definitions, there is no formal way to verify the adequacy or correctness of the result. Functional requirements specifications, on the other hand, rely on a formalism that we can validate by checking consistency, completeness, and correctness. Both documents, natural language and formal, should only specify external behavior. In other words, at this point in the userview process, the requirements specify *what* the system should do, not how it should do it. We deal with the *how* issues as we specialize Web interface design guidelines to user culture.

Requirements, which we must be able to test to ensure that they are met by the final Web site implementation, fall into two major categories: functional and nonfunctional. Functional requirements specify what the Web site should do, such as what services it should provide. Nonfunctional requirements set constraints and standards for the system. For example, a nonfunctional standard could be a requirement that the maximum system response time be no more that two seconds.

As an example of defining goals and requirements, consider being commissioned to develop a Web site for a fast-food business with delivery service. This is a regional chain of brick and mortar hamburger restaurants that wants to establish an online order and delivery service via the Internet. The goal for the Web site is to enlarge the customer base by making it more convenient for customers to order food. This high-level goal can be broken down into subgoals in two categories: general goals, affecting the operation of each store as a whole, and user-specific goals, designed to meet the needs of different user groups.

General Goals
General goals affect the operation of the virtual restaurant as a whole or the relationships between entities in the restaurant. Here are some examples.

- To provide consistent information for all users of the Web site
- To provide accurate and reliable information to all Web site users
- To provide reliable and continuous access to information for all the Web site users
- To provide Web site users with a communication tool that is effective for the tasks performed in the actual store
- To optimize the resources (time, staff, or others) used to perform an operation in the store
- To promote activities and operations that, without a Web site, are not possible, feasible, or practical in existing stores

User-Specific Goals

Such goals are set to meet the demands of different user groups. The concept and assessment of these demands are covered in Chapter 4, but let me point out here that the needs of different user groups for a given Web site may sometimes conflict. For example, it is reasonable to assume that there are at least two kinds of fast-food consumers: health-aware people and those who only want speed and convenience. Within those groups there are repeat customers, who know what they want and are looking for a fast text index search, and people interested in meandering through a visual, graphic presentation of the various foods. Conflicting needs among users have to be identified during the audience definition and task analysis stages, then solved by a decision process that will affect the design of the final product.

Requirements are the basis for the development of a system and are defined after a study of the goals of the system. Although a task analysis or a complete audience definition may not be necessary for the requirements definition, requirements should be set forth with end users and tasks in mind.

Functional Requirements

These describe the desired functions of the Web site. Not every type of user needs to perform every function. For example, customers need not, and should not, set the prices of products offered by the store. We start by listing some high-level functional requirements. Here are some of the functions for the fast-food ordering Web site.

1. Indicate the location of a store in the user's zip code area.

2. Give navigation directions for people who want to go to the store to order or pick up in person.

3. Identify specials of the day.

4. Offer orders by groups of items (a meal).

5. Allow a user to browse through the entire selection of individual foods and order any single item or combination of items.

6. Allow users to select delivery to a specific location or pick up at the store.

7. Handle the complete purchase transaction process, from information to selection to payment.

8. Permit advance ordering, specifying time and date.

9. Look for sales and promotional offers.

10. Announce new stores in various locations and changes in existing stores.

11. Announce the past or future closing of stores.

12. Allow store managers to enter information about their products, prices, sales, and promotions.

The preceding requirements are only high-level requirements and are meant to illustrate the types of functions available on the Web site. In an actual requirements definition document, much more detail would have to be provided about each requirement, which should be made complete, consistent, and nonambiguous. Terminology in the requirements document should be clearly defined in a glossary. Box 2.1 outlines the features of a requirements document. In this brief requirements presentation, my goal is simply to provide you with an overview of the system requirements and to emphasize the importance of the need for the development of a good requirements document. For further details on the elaboration of a good requirements document, see Davis (1993).

The preceding functional requirements are not needed by or meaningful to all users of the Web site. The matrix in Table 2.1 indicates which of the 12 functional requirements are important for each of two user categories. The principles illustrated by the use of these two user categories are generic ones that hold in other situations.

Nonfunctional Requirements

Nonfunctional requirements express constraints to be imposed upon the final system. Although they are important, and a good definition of nonfunctional requirements is key to a successful system design, their importance is often downplayed because of the difficulty in transforming nonfunctional requirements into design features using a procedural process.

Nonfunctional requirements for a fast-food ordering site are numerous. The following brief list gives an idea of the types of nonfunctional requirements at play.

- Users must feel that they are deriving a benefit by using the Web site.
- The costs of developing and maintaining the operation of the Web site should not exceed the benefits derived from its introduction.
- The Web site should be easily accessible by customers.
- The site should be accessible from a home or office computer, a PDA, and an in-store kiosk.

■ ■

Box 2.1: A Web Site Goals and Functional Requirements Document

A requirement document should have the following structure.

Introduction: This section should describe the motivation, need, and objectives for the Web site. It should place the Web site in context, briefly describing its functions and presenting a rationale for it. It should describe how the system fits into the overall strategic objectives of the organization commissioning the Web site.

The Web site model: This section should set out the contextual model showing the relationships between the Web site components and its environment.

Functional requirements: The functional requirements of the system should be described in this section.

Hardware: The hardware and its interfaces should be described here.

Information structure requirements: The logical organization of the data used by the Web site and its interrelationships should be described here.

Nonfunctional requirements: This section describes the nonfunctional requirements of the Web site.

Maintenance information: This section should describe the fundamental assumptions on which the Web site is based and describe anticipated changes due to hardware evolution, changing user needs, and so forth.

Glossary: This section should define all the technical terms used in the document.

Index: A variety of indices (alphabetic, functions, etc.) is desirable.

■ ■

These nonfunctional requirements, though general, should encourage Web site developers to consider such constraints early on when designing and building a Web site.

Table 2.1: *Functional Requirements and User Groups*

Requirement	Customer	Manager
R1: Locate store	✔	
R2: Provide directions		✔
R3: Search for an item	✔	
R4: Compare prices	✔	✔
R5: Browse	✔	
R6: Order and purchase	✔	
R7: Advance ordering	✔	
R8: Window shopping	✔	
R9: Looking for sales	✔	
R10: New stores	✔	✔
R11: Closing stores	✔	✔
R12: Data entry		✔

User Culture

Knowing the users, their environment, and the activities or tasks is crucial to the design of Web sites. Also, understanding how users represent the activity in a brick and mortar context is prerequisite to designing that activity for the Web. We collect information about users, tasks, and user environment by conducting structured interviews, administering questionnaires, and observing users engaged in similar real-world activities. Chapter 12 covers the elements of Web site usability evaluation, including how to collect, validate, and apply user culture data.

Audience

Designers should not rely on their own preferences and experiences when designing Web sites but should identify the target users of the site and design with their needs and characteristics in mind. The audience definition should identify the appropriate characteristics, as well as specific individual differences, that may impact the interface design. Identifying the target audience also facilitates the selection of representative samples for evaluating the usability of the site. Important differences exist in people's experiences, abilities, backgrounds, motivations, personalities, and work styles. A well-designed Web site should accommodate this inherent heterogeneity, a topic treated comprehensively in Chapter 4.

Writing an audience definition starts with considering general categories of user characteristics and requirements and general questions that apply regardless of the Web application at hand. As an example, for the category of "user experience," standard generic questions deal with issues such as computer experience, Web experience, past use of various interactive technologies, and application domain experience. In addition, for any specific Web site, we need to specialize the general categories. In the case of the fast-food ordering site, the "domain experience" user category leads to answering questions such as these:

- What frequency of customers are first timers versus repeaters?

- What do customers order?

- How often do they change what they order?

- Is there a relationship between customers' orders and repetition frequency?

- Who orders lunch, breakfast, and dinner?

- Do people eat in the restaurant or take out?

- Do people order individually or in groups? When in groups, are they mostly adults, adults with children, for lunch, dinner, and so on?

- Are they office workers at lunch and families in the evening?

- Do customers of a rural store have requirements different from suburban or urban customers?

These are only some possible questions dealing with the "user experience" category as applied to the domain of fast-food ordering. We collect information of this kind via focus groups, structured questionnaires, and field observations.

Environment

As part of specifying the user culture, we need to understand the details of the user's external environment. Designers should specify constituents based on the environment from which the users access the site. The home, the office, and mobile environments are very different ones, potentially leading to different uses of a given Web site and therefore different interface designs.

For the fast-food ordering site, customers logging on from home in the evening are most likely interested in dinner foods. Under these conditions the design should highlight the dinner aspect of the Web presentation. A midday order from a customer in an office may call for designing a Web interface that facilitates group orders. An order from a mobile customer in the morning might mean that the customer will stop and pick up the order on the way to work. Unlike an office order, a midday home or mobile order may mean the customer will be coming in to eat at the restaurant. In that case, a menu tailored to sit-down customers should be made available as a first priority on the Web page.

The kind of user interface may also be affected by the location of the customer. From home, people may have the time to browse a visual presentation; from the office, where the pace is faster, we may need to provide a text-only option; from the car, an auditory interface is desirable. Chapter 3 contains a comprehensive treatment of the Web environment.

Task Analysis

Defining user culture depends, along with other components, on identifying and understanding user tasks. Designers should know what tasks or activities the users will perform and how, as well as how often they perform each task. The purpose of task analysis is to determine the functionality of the Web site by decomposing functions into tasks and subtasks that the user performs while using the site. Designers should pay particular attention to the categories of frequent tasks, occasional tasks, exceptional tasks, and errors. The process of conducting this analysis educates designers about the sequences of events that a user may undergo to accomplish a task. An identification of goals and the strategies (combinations of tasks) used to reach those goals is also part of a good task analysis.

We perform task analysis with varying emphases and detail. A transaction-oriented task analysis is intended to identify times and other statistics associated with different components of a transaction. On the other hand, a user-oriented task analysis takes into account the various cognitive aspects of interaction, attempting to identify specific problems associated with Web interaction. Whether the analysis is transaction-oriented or user-oriented, we typically perform it in two stages. First, we identify goals, strategies, and the activities performed. Second, we give structure in order to analyze the information to uncover deficiencies and sources of inefficiency and to suggest improvements.

Task Identification. We usually design Web sites either to create a new service or to augment or replace a set of activities now being done in a physical environment, so it is important to start by identifying and analyzing how people perform similar tasks in equivalent or related environments. Techniques a designer can use include automatic event logging, verbal protocols, video, natural observation, and other methods. To illustrate task identification and analysis using the fast-food Web site, here is a brief description of the observation technique.

The goal of observation is to isolate and identify the components and structure of a task in situations relevant to human interaction with the Web site under development. A good selection of real-world environments and tasks to observe is critical to the success of the task identification and ideally should include all of the following.

- People performing the same or similar tasks manually
- People performing the same or similar tasks using other Web sites or computer systems
- People using other Web sites that they visit frequently
- People using systems that share common properties with the new Web site
- People working in an environment similar to the one where the new Web site will be installed

Natural observation of how people order fast food means using the actual fast-food restaurant to identify and study the tasks. The first step is to do on-site videotaping of customers' food selection and ordering activities with the customers' knowledge. We can do this by installing a video camera in the ceiling above the counter where customers place their orders. The tasks are then decomposed and identified. Task sequences and frequencies from the videotape are transcribed, and the data is then analyzed using statistical analysis routines.

We conduct a transaction-oriented task analysis to obtain, for example, such information as average times, percentages, and perhaps distributions related to task performance. We correlate the information with data collected from customers via questionnaires and from store workers via structured interviews. For instance, from the questionnaires, we can find out how often a customer orders from the restaurant. Then the frequency of repetitions can be correlated with order content or with the time it takes to perform the ordering task, information that we derive from an analysis of the videotape. Using these findings, we can make decisions about a look and feel as well as an interaction style to accommodate different levels of customer experience.

Task Structuring. The second stage of task analysis is structuring the information we identified in the first stage. A range of techniques exists to accomplish this, from less restrictive and informal methods to highly organized and structured formal ones.

Hierarchical decomposition of tasks into subtasks is by far the most popular representation of tasks. High-level tasks are decomposed into tasks of a lower level, which, in turn, are further decomposed until no more decomposition is necessary (atomic actions). A "tree" structure of tasks is created in this way, and, though simple and strong, this representation fails to account for important features such as decisions, individual differences, and errors. Figure 2.5 shows a hierarchy example for a portion of the fast-food ordering task.

The Users' Task Representation Analysis
Once we have gained an understanding of the target audience, the next goal is to use those findings to determine what tasks the Web site should perform. Our focus remains on the target audience, however, because it is crucial to understand what our target users think the Web site should do and how they model those processes mentally. Several activities are necessary to accomplish this goal. First, the functional needs of users must be ascertained and analyzed. Specifically, we need to answer the question "In what way and in what sequence are customers most likely to use the Web site to perform tasks?" For fast food ordering, for example, do they first look at a menu, or do they just order what they already had planned?

The second step is to understand how users model these tasks. How do they describe the tasks? What common terms or analogies do they employ? Even if their models are difficult to implement, they should be incorporated into the design. Essentially, we want to design a metaphor for the Web site that our users will recognize and understand. For instance, at shopping Web sites, a common metaphor is the shopping cart or shopping bag. In the case of the fast-food customers, do they think of the food items as a menu of single items, or do they represent the items as a selection of plates of food or meals? An understanding of the most likely mental model could affect how we present the items on the Web page.

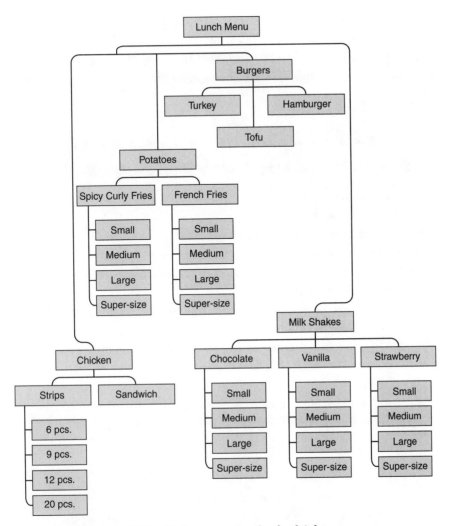

Figure 2.5: *Task structuring for foodrightnow.com*

To gain an understanding of how potential site visitors represent the tasks at hand, we use techniques that include controlled experimentation, thinking-aloud methods, and structured interviews where the users are encouraged to describe the tasks they are performing. We should pay particular attention to their terminology and analogies and incorporate these into our designs.

Web Interface Guidelines Specialization

Usability guidelines for Web interface design come from three main sources: psychological research, convention, and consensus of expert practitioners.

These can be found in style guides, Web design handbooks, professional and trade journal articles, textbooks, and usability Web sites. Guidelines are usually general and need to be specialized to the particular application and predefined user culture. Box 2.2 shows examples of some Web usability guidelines.

Box 2.2: Selected Web Design Guidelines

- Page layouts should be consistent.
- Minimize the need for scrolling.
- Use text links for easy navigation.
- Users should be able to reach goal in minimum number of clicks.
- Provide links to navigation aids such as content, index, site map, and home page from every page in the site.
- Navigational buttons should be available on both the top and bottom of every page.
- Make sure there is a distinction between a list of contents on a page, links to other pages, and links to other sites.
- All links of a given type should have the same default characteristics such as color, underlining, type, font, and so forth.
- Minimize the use of graphics for sites where the purpose is to complete a transaction; graphics are too slow to download.
- Provide a text-only option.
- If graphics must be used, use small images, and repeat them if possible.
- In using graphics, minimize the number of colors.
- Do not use more than six colors for information coding on a single screen.
- A home page should fit on one screen. Avoid the requirement to scroll.
- On a page where reading is necessary, do not use flashing or motion because this can interfere with reading.
- Patterned backgrounds make it difficult to read text.
- Use consistent terminology.
- Provide on every page navigational aids for returning to previous page and to home page.

The use of guidelines is an important first step in the iterative design process. Specializing general guidelines in the context of a specific Web site reduces the number of potential iterations required to finalize the design of a Web site before fielding it. Let's consider the fast-food example for the guideline that users should be able to reach their goal in a minimum number of clicks. If in studying the audience and the users' task representation we discover that the frequent customers' mental model of their order is a meal representation instead of a menu of individual items, then by designing for clusters of items we reduce the number of clicks.

Constructing Storyboards and Interactive Prototypes

There are a variety of ways to model a hypothetical Web site. One approach that I advocate and use is the storyboard, a device that is common in many fields such as filmmaking and choreography. Specific plans—whether for a film or play scene or a dance sequence (Andriole, 1988)—are represented in a succession of sketches. We use this sketching technique in user interface and Web site design to show the prototypical content of pages and how these relate to each other in a site representation. We also use the storyboard to represent the navigation options available to site users. We use static storyboards to conduct walkthroughs, as we will explain in Chapter 12. Also, constructing static storyboards is a prerequisite to building an interactive storyboard or prototype on which we can do usability testing. Figure 2.6 is an example of a storyboard for a segment of the fast-food Web site.

Metaphor Design

Web technology is still relatively new. When people visit a Web site, they draw from previous knowledge and expectations, gradually building a mental model of how they think the Web operates. When the Web site's behavior clashes with the model, the user will most likely become confused and annoyed. A well-designed interface will help the Web user to form a consistent and usable model. One way of developing such a model is metaphor design.

A metaphor is a representation of a real-world environment that depicts real-world actions, concepts, and objects (Carroll, et al., 1988). Metaphors are powerful techniques for making a Web site less imposing to new users. It also can decrease the learning curve because the user can take advantage of previous knowledge and is not forced to learn everything from scratch. Designing a good metaphor is not a simple task. A poorly designed metaphor is much more damaging than the lack of a metaphor because it will mislead the user,

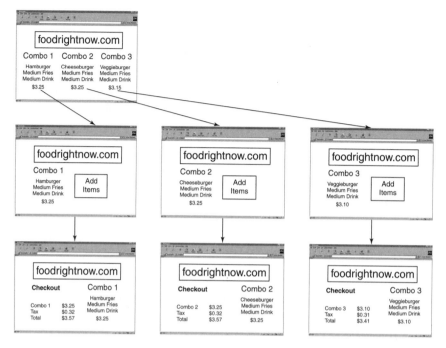

Figure 2.6: *A partial storyboard*

undermining his or her trust in the system, and, therefore, confidence in using it. The following are guidelines for metaphor design.

Design a metaphor for the naive user. Because people learn how to use computers by building on previous knowledge and expectations, the metaphor should be meaningful for beginning users. It is important to realize that beginning users will form some mental model while using the Web site. Therefore, we should present the metaphor in a way that is clear and takes advantage of common beginner activities.

Choose metaphors that are congruent with the Web site behavior and that encompass most (if not all) aspects of the site. Make sure not to mislead the user when selecting an explicit metaphor. Exclude aspects of the site that do not follow the metaphor.

Ensure that the emotional tone of the metaphor is sympathetic to the emotional attitude of the user. It is possible to design a metaphor that convincingly models the Web site but that is entirely inappropriate in its emotional resonance.

When one metaphor cannot model all aspects of an entire system, use a set of metaphors that follows a certain theme. Choose metaphors drawn from a single real-world domain, but do not choose objects or procedures that are exclusive alternatives from within that domain. A popular example is the desktop metaphor where the individual metaphors (files, trash cans) all fall within the domain of the office environment. When choosing sets of metaphors, it is also important not to use objects that have similar meanings in the real world to model different aspects of the Web site.

Ensure that metaphors do not encumber the expert user. Metaphors designed for the novice will often hinder an intermediate or expert user. Allow more experienced users to remove the metaphorical shield and use accelerated navigational and interactive schemes. Another potential solution is to replace the metaphor with a series of new, more sophisticated metaphors that will encourage users to learn more about the system. New metaphors continue to make the system interesting.

3

The Web Environment

There are two senses in which I use the word *environment* in this chapter: the user environment and the site environment. The user environment consists of the actual physical and cognitive spaces in which the user interacts with the Web. The school, the office, home, and a public venue are different actual environments in which users may engage in Web activity. The site environment is the real-world metaphor(s) used to design the Web site's structure, look and feel, and permissible activities. For example, a brick and mortar bookstore environment can be a metaphor for a book shopping Web site.

Designers should consider the user environment to anticipate those features and cues of the environment that may trigger biases, thought processes, and decisions impacting the user's Web actions. Designers also should consider people's behaviors and actions in real-world environments when using them as metaphors to design Web sites. What follows is a discussion of issues that a designer should keep in mind when designing for user and Web environments.

The User Environment

Designing suitable Web sites requires an understanding by the designer of the user's Web ecology—that is, the totality of relations between Web users and their environments. The user's Web ecology is composed principally of two spaces: physical space and cognitive space.

The Physical Space

The physical space of Web users is the actual physical environment in which Web users function, perform, and make and execute decisions relative to a selected Web site. Their environment can be the office, the home, school, or a public venue. The physical environment of Web users can have a direct impact on how the user interacts with the Web. Users take action with a perspective and a mental model that is partially biased by their physical environment. The elements of the physical space that can affect the user's interaction with the Web include the following.

- Physical space objects
- Interrelationships of objects
- Characteristics of objects
- Physical location

Physical space objects. Physical objects are items in a Web user's real-world environment, which the user perceives as discrete items, independent of the physical location in which they exist. Furthermore, an object either has a useful function or conveys information meaningful to the user, irrespective of location. For example, the object "chair," in a living room, is for sitting. If it is moved into an office, the chair is still for sitting. A picture conveys information regardless of what wall it hangs on. Of course, the user's interpretation of the function of the chair or the information that the picture conveys can vary or be influenced by the user's perspective. Objects in physical space are potential cues that can trigger thought processes as the user navigates the Web.

Interrelationships of objects. How objects are positioned relative to each other defines the morphology (structure and use) of the environment. For example, the morphology of a grocery store is related directly to how grocery items are organized relative to each other. How items are organized influences how a person perceives the use of the environment. Of course, Web users do not necessarily use the items in the physical environment to perform

Web tasks. How these objects are organized, however, can influence how users perceive their Web tasks.

The importance of the environment in learning and problem solving has long been recognized (Godden and Baddeley, 1975). Students who learn and then recall material in the same environment perform better than students made to recall in a different environment. Embedded in any context are cues and clues that guide the process of observation, interpretation, and meaning making. Different organization of groceries in the aisles of two supermarkets leads to two different strategies of approaching the shopping task.

Characteristics of objects. Every object has physical characteristics by which we can describe it, recognize it, locate it, classify it, and distinguish it from other objects. Examples of physical characteristics are color, shape, size, location, and volume. Given the influence of environmental cues on thought processes, an object with one set of descriptors can have an impact different from the same object with slightly different characteristics. For example, two jars of coffee that are the same size, shape, and brand but have different colors, green and red, trigger two different thoughts: decaffeinated and regular.

Physical location. The actual location where the user accesses the Web may have a direct impact on the user's state of mind, immediate needs, and purpose for using the Web. It is important to keep in mind that people are often driven by the current requirements of where they are at a given time. A visitor to New York City may have a need to access New York information about the weather, entertainment, or flight schedules out of the city. Therefore, in this case, New York–related information should be more readily Web accessible at this time than information related to some other city.

The Cognitive Space

While multiple users can share a single physical space, each of those users has a unique cognitive space. A user's cognitive space is composed of many factors, such as individual thought processes, impressions, perspectives, plans, goals, and concerns that are specific to that individual. Given any set of cognitive factors, in interacting with the physical environment, a user can have a set of Web needs and actions that are different from those that would surface as a result of another set of cognitive conditions. The user's cognitive space consists of the following.

- Thoughts triggered by the physical space
- Current situation-induced thoughts

- User intentions and goals
- Information processing

Thoughts triggered by the physical space. There is some evidence that physical cues in the user's environment can trigger mental processes such as memory for associated concepts, ideas, and attitudes. The idea of learning and recall being associated with environmental cues goes back to the British associationist philosopher John Locke (1690). There have been many early controlled studies supporting the hypothesis that contextual stimuli affect recall (Greenspoon and Raynard, 1957; Godden and Baddeley, 1975). For example, Sue has just arrived in her workplace office from her home, where she was doing comparative Web shopping for window shutters she wants to install as part of the renovation on her house. She enters the office and sees a draft of a manuscript chapter on her desk. Seeing the chapter reminds her that she needs to find a reference to a cited author, which leads her to searching a bibliographic database on the Web. Notice that even though she was already logged on at home to perform activity related to the house, that physical environment did not trigger her other need for a citation reference.

Current situation-induced thoughts. These are thoughts triggered, not by a physical object in the environment but by an intangible condition. Let us say you are presenting a position paper in a workshop and the computer you are using to make the presentation is Internet connected. Someone in the audience asks a question, and you believe an example would be the best way to answer the question clearly. You don't have an illustrated example with you, but you can show one by accessing a specific Web site. Your thought process triggered by the question leads you to the need for Web access. Just as location awareness is important for Web site design, so is situation awareness.

User intentions and goals. Intentions and goals are important components of a person's cognitive space. People's intentions and goals are defined by their current activities, which provide a framework in which actions and behaviors take place. For example, Dan, a student in an English literature class, has the goal of learning more about Shakespeare's play *Julius Caesar*. Dan's particular goal will lead him to access English literature or Shakespeare sites. On the other hand, if Dan were a student in a history class and needed information about Julius Caesar as a historical figure, then history and Roman sites would be more relevant. Designers should be aware of how environments and situations can shape goals and intentions and how goals and intentions can lead to specific kinds of Web activity. For English literature classrooms, Web designers should make literature sites more easily accessible than history sites because students in that environment are more likely to have literature search goals than history goals.

Information processing. To properly consider the processing of information by the interactive Web user, we must take into account a few key distinctions that cognitive psychologists have identified and developed relating to selective attention and human memory. We will focus briefly on the constraints of selective attention, short-term memory/working memory, and long-term memory. A more comprehensive treatment of cognitive processing can be found in such psychology books as Sternberg (1996) and Ashcraft (2002).

The human information processing system is like a central processor operating on a multistore system that includes the selective attention register, short-term memory, and long-term memory (Shiffrin and Schneider, 1977; Norman, 1970; Atkinson and Shiffrin, 1968; Waugh and Norman, 1965; Broadbent, 1963). Other plausible approaches, such as the "levels of processing" view (Craik and Lockhart, 1972), which considers information processing in terms of depth that distinguishes between syntactic and semantic processing, have also been advanced. More recent modifications and elaboration on the early theories include the emphasis on attention processes, the emergence of working memory (Baddeley and Hitch, 1974), and the distinctions within long-term memory (Squire, 1993). Figure 3.1 shows a schematic of human memory, including a selective attention register, the working memory/short-term memory component, and long-term memory. The central processor contains mechanisms (programs), such as ones for attention, retrieval, organization, and recognition, which operate on information in the various memories.

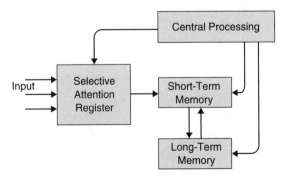

Figure 3.1: *A schematic of human memory*

The important distinctions here are those relating to selective attention and memory. When a person tries to ignore sensory data, messages, or events in the immediate environment to focus on a specific piece of information, that mental process is *selective attention*. Because the Web environment is full of such distracting stimuli, understanding a few key issues about this process by designers of Web interaction is vital.

In early studies (Cherry and Taylor, 1954; Broadbent, 1952), subjects wearing headphones heard two different messages, one in each ear, and were asked to repeat, or "shadow," the message coming into the designated ear as soon as they heard it. It turns out that any physical differences between the two messages helped the listener attend to the target message (Johnston and Heinz, 1978). Comparable results were found for visually presented stimuli. Treisman (1960) found that subjects made accurate shadowing based on message content. Her attenuation theory says that all messages receive some kind of consideration, but the informational importance of the unattended ones is reduced.

Norman (1968) proposed the useful and practical "pertinence" modification on the Treisman attenuation theory. He suggested that attention to a given piece of information is a function of two factors: sensory activation and pertinence. Sensory activation refers to the feature that is most salient, such as the loudest sound or the brightest color. Pertinence refers to the target information component most important to the person at that time. This component could include words, pictures, or objects that relate to a person's background, goal, or context of use. Consider the example of a travel Web site: To visitors looking for information about air travel availability, a word such as *reservations* is pertinent. If the designer combines sensory activation and pertinence by having the word *reservations* flash briefly, then the word will most likely be selected for attention.

Next in considering the processing of information by human beings comes short-term/working memory. Short-term memory (STM) is the older term, referring mostly to short-term information input and retrieval. Distinguishing characteristics of STM are a limited capacity and a rapid recall and decay rate. Working memory (WM) refers to a mental workplace where conscious information processing occurs.

As Figure 3.1 shows, information enters STM from either the attention register or long-term memory (LTM). It remains there in a buffered state for a short period (Reitman, 1970) until it is either processed further into the system or replaced by new, incoming information. Short-term memory carries five to nine chunks of information (Miller, 1956). A chunk is a unit of information that has meaning to the individual processing the information. When the buffer is full, each new entering chunk will cause the oldest non-rehearsed chunk to be lost from STM.

While the capacity of STM does not vary beyond the seven plus or minus two chunks, the size of a chunk can vary relative to what is processed as a "meaningful chunk." Consequently, the amount of information retained in STM varies as a function of chunk size. A four-by-four array of 16 randomly placed letters will be impossible to retain in STM when the size of each chunk is one letter. The 16 letters can be retained, however, if each row of letters constitutes a familiar word. Figures 3.2a and 3.2b illustrate the difference. The random letters in Figure 3.2a must be retained in one-letter chunks. The same letters in Figure 3.2b have been reorganized so that the individual needs to retain only four chunks of four letters each.

The strategy that an individual uses to combine, or chunk, information may very well determine the size of a chunk and, hence, the amount of information retained in short-term memory. There is ample evidence to suggest that chunking strategies are a function of a person's experience or level of expertise (Badre, 1982a, 1982b; Reitman, 1976; Chase and Simon, 1973). In designing Web pages for tasks that require rapid processing, it becomes important to consider user expertise and associated chunking strategies.

Working memory (WM) is the newer designation to use in dealing with the processing of information in short time spans. It is the place where information is consciously available for processing. It is called a "working memory" because it is our mental workplace where not only information requiring immediate, conscious manipulation and effort is stored but also where reasoning, language comprehension, visual processing, and other conscious information processes take place (Baddeley, 1992).

a. More and smaller chunks   b. Fewer and bigger chunks

L	A	F	L
E	T	X	T
I	S	T	L
A	S	T	L

F	A	L	L
T	E	X	T
L	I	S	T
S	A	L	T

Figure 3.2: *Number of chunks by chunk size*

The third type of memory we should consider is long-term memory (LTM), which has a probably unlimited capacity, a much slower recall rate, and an unknown (if any) decay rate. Long-term memory is distinguished from the other two stores in that it can retain more information for extensive time periods.

It is generally agreed that long-term memory has the capacity to store (encode) vast amounts of information. What is not agreed upon, however, are the issues of how the deposited information is organized and represented in LTM and why certain information is more readily retrievable than other encoded information. The major competing theoretical views of memory organization revolve around different representations (Anderson, 1983; Collins and Loftus, 1975; Smith, et al., 1974; Anderson and Bower, 1973; Tulving, 1972; Collins and Quillian, 1972, 1969; Schaeffer and Wallace, 1969). These representations range from the "hierarchical node-link" constructs to the "associative semantic distance" structures. Squire (1993) proposes a taxonomy that distinguishes between declarative memory of retrievable knowledge, which can be consciously manipulated, and nondeclarative memory of knowledge that impacts behavior without involvement of conscious processes. Memories of events (episodic) and facts (semantic) are declarative. Skills and habits are examples of nondeclarative memory.

While it is important to understand how information is represented in memory, it is even more pertinent to Web usability design to understand the relationship between the processes of encoding and representing information on the one hand and retrieval effectiveness on the other hand. There may be a relationship between how the information is presented at the time of encoding and how effectively it can be retrieved at a later time. Indeed, there are indications that long-term memory is contextual and encoding-specific. This means that retrieving information from LTM is a function of the availability of the context of the learned information at time of retrieval (Thomson and Tulving, 1970). The potential association between "context" and "retrieval" leads to the postulate that a person remembers by reconstructing associated information.

Information is encoded in an acculturated context (Cole, 1997). For example, if you asked a person from Western society to respond as quickly as possible to the command "Name something that is not a dog," the answer will most likely be "cat." The reason is that "dog" and "cat" belong to the same semantic category culturally.

We can use the distinctions in human cognitive processes previously discussed to explain the processing of information by the interactive Web user. However, in constructing such a model of the interactive user—a model intended to form a basis for design guidelines—we should keep in mind that memory processing takes place in a "task/action" context. Hence, a model of the interactive user, while focusing on memory processing, should also consider the user as an actor and a problem solver. Such a model should notice selective attention behaviors, such as drawing a user's attention to a particular screen location. It should heed the rules governing selective attention, drawing a user's attention to particular screen locations and thus optimizing the ease of search. It should also take into account behaviors at the elementary response-association levels in tasks such as transcription data entry. The model also should be able to explain interactive behaviors at levels of task complexity requiring creative problem solving by experts, such as the writing of "macros" for data analysis.

Any consideration of how an interactive Web user processes and manages information is inseparable from a consideration of the environment in which the processing takes place. In this environment, information is stored in either an insalient form (for example, core memory, hard disk, offline documents) or a salient form (for example, on a display screen). The user relationship to this information storage environment is one of information management. Users manage information not only by encoding it in the different locations but also by organizing it and retrieving it. The user's information management relationship to the Web-stored information can be represented in parallel to the central processor's management of information in working memory (WM) and long-term memory (LTM). Indeed, we can think of WM as the temporary workplace of salient information and LTM as the store of insalient information. Figure 3.3 is a representation that combines the memory schematic presented earlier with external environment storage.

If we define *salient* storage as the location of information with which a person is presently "working," then for the interactive user, salient storage consists of both working memory and the display screen. Both the Web display and WM can be considered the focus of current work. To regain information from *insalient* storage often requires conscious retrieval strategies, routines, and heuristics (problem-solving techniques), and the processing cost (time plus effort) is usually longer than that associated with salient storage.

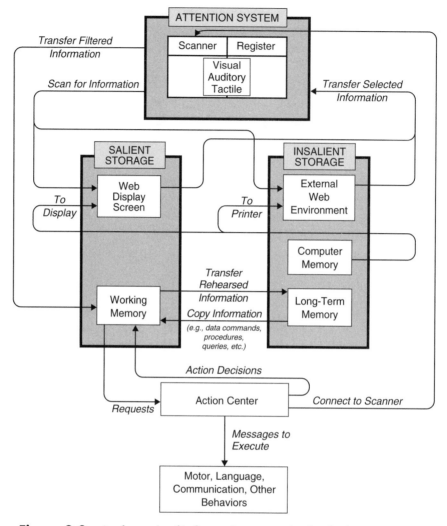

Figure 3.3: *A schematic of information processing by the interactive user*

Visual access of displayed information is certainly less costly and less time consuming than retrieval from long-term memory or the World Wide Web, which often involves a procedural approach of some kind. In LTM (both semantic and episodic), remembering an event or object may require the evocation and reconstruction of associated events and objects. For example, remembering which year you first learned that Abraham Lincoln was the sixteenth U.S. president requires reconstructing an associated set of events. Likewise, for the Web, accessing specific information would normally require executing one or more command or link procedures. Searching for specific information in a document may require using reference aids such as an index, a table of contents, or a road map. Thus, for the interactive Web user, insalient storage can be considered to consist of LTM and Web documents.

The information-transfer relationship between the user and a Web site is a symbiotic one. Salient storage is short-term memory extended by the display screen; insalient storage is long-term memory extended by the Web site and the Internet. It is in the context of extending memory that we conceptualize the design of effective user-Web interaction.

The Site Environment

Designers should pay particular attention to users' expectations of how a Web site is organized and how they can use it. These expectations are related to users' stored knowledge based on previous experience with real-world settings. The representation of knowledge based on previous experience can be expressed in terms of schemata, scripts, and mental models. A schema is a mental representation of general knowledge about events, actions, and objects. A script is a fixed instance of a schema leading to specific outcomes. To express a schema, we store and use scripts. We use a script to describe a fixed schema in a specific environment (Schank and Abelson, 1977). Mental models allow us to adapt our schemata and scripts to novel and slightly different environments.

Understanding users' mental models requires specifying how users represent both structural and functional knowledge about their environment. For example, using the subway system in Munich requires a structural representation of the system that orients the rider to key Munich locations. Figure 3.4 is an example of a structured knowledge representation that shows the complete system with various locations and directions, plus the fact that there are two main lines—the S-Bahn and the U-Bahn—each of which has several sublines that intersect at various points.

In addition to having a structural mental model of the subway system, users need to have a functional model, one that allows them to map how they can use the system to go from one point to another. Figure 3.5 is an example of a functional representation of the system. What is being shown here is the path that the rider should take to get, for example, from Universitat to Deisenhofen station. It shows that the rider must start by boarding the U-6 and then change to the S-2 at the Marienplatz.

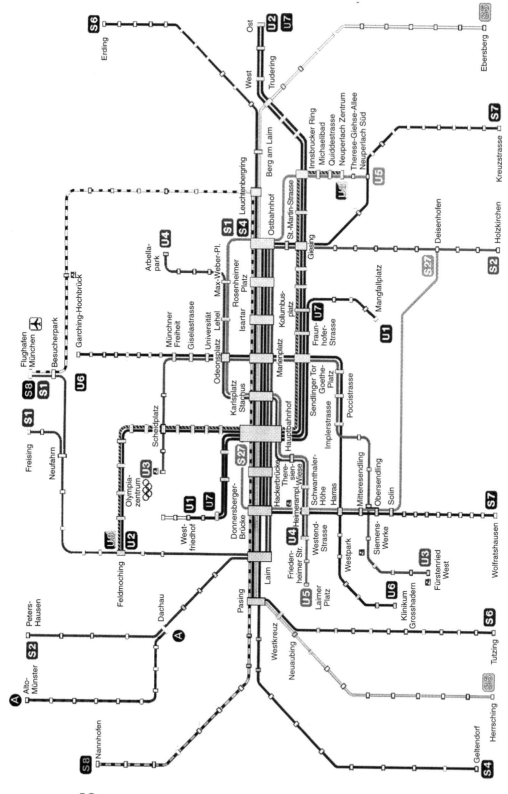

Figure 3.4: *Structural representation of the Munich subway system*

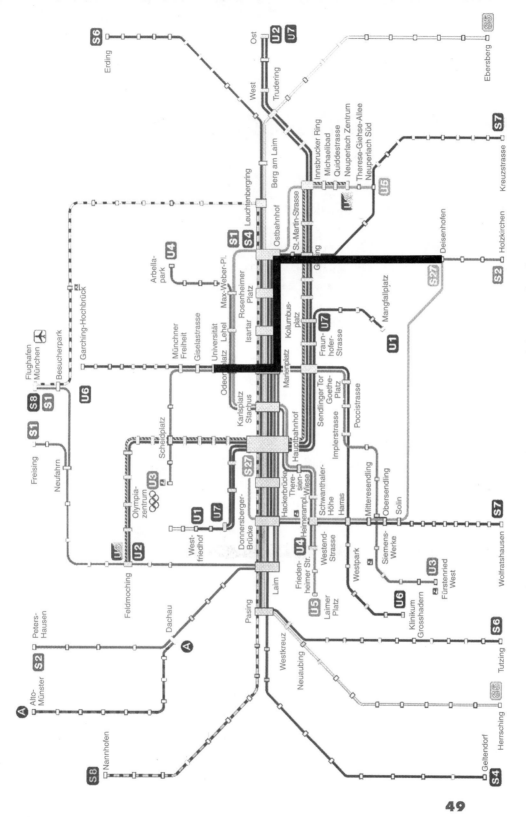

Figure 3.5: *Functional representation of the Munich subway system*

Through mental modeling, people are able to learn and adapt. The learning and adapting processes can be much less difficult for the users if they can build on previously learned representations and knowledge of how to perform familiar tasks. For example, designers of a book shopping Web site can benefit from taking into account how people use bookstores, even while being cognizant of the constraints of Web interaction. Because Web environments cannot be exactly the same as brick and mortar ones, understanding the users' mental models for real-world environments will allow designers to incorporate familiar elements into Web site design that make the site easier to navigate and use. Indeed, the users' mental models of Web environments require merging a script for using the real-world environment with a script for using and navigating Web sites. The design of Web sites has to take both scripts into account.

Designers need to understand the mental models of the users to reconcile the users' scripts of the real world with that of the Internet world. Success requires an understanding of how users organize their knowledge of the real-world environment—their structured mental model—as well as their knowledge of how they perform tasks in that environment—their functional mental model. By the same token, we must also understand the users' structural and functional mental models of the site environment that we plan to design. Such an understanding helps us design a more usable Web site. Let's consider the example of a site for grocery shoppers.

We start with the likely assumption that an e-supermarket shopper has knowledge and experience buying groceries in a brick and mortar supermarket. His structured mental model of grocery shopping on the Internet is apt to be influenced by his real-world experience. In the actual store where he goes grocery shopping, categories of items are organized and located in various areas of the building. For example, the fresh vegetables and fruits are located together in a section on the right side of the store, while the frozen vegetables are on the left side. What is important about this information for simple site design is the categorization of groceries with which the user is familiar. Location becomes important for an "enriched environment design," as I discuss later in this chapter.

Scripts this user has stored for supermarket shopping influence his functional mental model. For example, to get fresh vegetables, he walks to the right aisle of the store. Then he goes to get milk from the dairy products section in the rear of the store before he starts walking the aisles to get the rest of the items on his list. This sequence of familiar steps could influence how a user would expect to shop for groceries on a Web site.

Scenarios

Let's consider the mental model and scripts available to four hypothetical users of a real-world supermarket. We will describe four scenarios and then analyze script elements that would need to be incorporated into the design of a Web supermarket site.

- *Scenario 1:* Shopper new to store and searching for a single item
- *Scenario 2:* Shopper new to store who has a list of items
- *Scenario 3:* Shopper familiar with store and searching for one item
- *Scenario 4:* Shopper familiar with store who has a list of items

Scenario 1. Denise wants to buy a jar of Folgers coffee. She walks into what looks like the main entrance of the store. Once inside the entrance, she pauses to look around at the scene before her. She notes the store environment, the special kiosks displaying items on sale, which direction other shoppers go when they enter the store, and which direction the store encourages her to take first.

Based on her collective knowledge of what other stores have been like—her structural mental model—Denise decides to look for the aisle with coffees and teas. Her experience is that the coffee aisle is usually not the first, so she moves toward Aisle 2 and studies the navigation signs hanging from the ceiling, looking for the word *coffee.* Not seeing *coffee,* she moves on, walking from aisle to aisle, pausing briefly to read the navigation signs, and at the same time noticing the colors, shapes, and patterns of each aisle. Because of Denise's experience with other supermarkets, these properties of supermarket objects serve as cues to the shelf contents of aisles. For someone who has never been to a supermarket, colors, shapes, and patterns are contextual learning cues, which are used at higher levels of experience. At last Denise spots the *coffee* sign and enters the coffee aisle. Her task is now to look for Folgers coffee. If her experience with buying coffee is minimal, Denise will look for the words *coffee* and *Folgers.* If on the other hand, she is an experienced coffee shopper, she will start by reducing the search space with heuristics such as shapes of objects and colors—for example, red for regular. Box 3.1 contains a script for the first scenario shopper. Figure 3.6 (see also Plate 1) shows what the shoppers in the first scenario see as they navigate the store, influencing their functional mental model of supermarket shopping.

■ ■

Box 3.1: Script for Scenario 1

Shopper new to store and wants to buy a jar of Folgers coffee

Step 1: Shopper walks into main entrance of store.

Step 2: She walks to left perpendicular to aisles.

Step 3: She moves toward second aisle.

Step 4: She looks at the navigation signs hanging from the ceiling.

Step 5: She walks from aisle to aisle, pausing briefly to read the navigation signs.

Step 6: She assimilates colors, patterns, and shapes in different aisles.

Step 7: She spots the *coffee* sign and enters the coffee aisle.

Step 8: She looks for the words *coffee* and *Folgers*.

■ ■

Scenario 2. Salvatore has a list but no experience with this particular store. He will proceed with a combination of random steps and expectation-based behavior. He walks into what looks like the main entrance of the store. Once inside the entrance, he pauses to look around at the scene before him. He notes the store environment, the kiosks displaying items on sale, which way other shoppers go when they come inside the door, and which direction the store encourages him to take first.

He then consults his shopping list, which includes bread, coffee, and lettuce. Based on his collective knowledge about the layouts of other stores, Sal decides that lettuce is the first thing he will find in this store. He turns toward the first aisle, notes that this aisle is for vegetables and fruits, and moves toward the lettuce.

After selecting the lettuce, Sal moves toward Aisle 2. He reads the navigation sign hanging from the ceiling. This aisle has bread, and he walks down the aisle toward the bread on the shelves. He first notices the loaves of bread on the shelves that are at eye level. He prefers wheat bread, but he does not prefer any particular brand. He compares prices and qualities of breads and selects a loaf.

Figure 3.6: *What Scenario 1 shoppers see* (see also Plate 1)
(Photos courtesy of Harris Teeter, Inc.)

Salvatore again consults his list and realizes that the only thing left to get is the coffee. He walks from aisle to aisle, pausing briefly to read the navigation signs. As he gets to the aisle with cereals, he remembers that he needs corn flakes, which he forgot to put on the list, and he picks up a box. Continuing to search, he finds the coffee aisle and selects the particular type of coffee he likes.

With all of the items on his shopping list selected, our shopper decides to check out. He assumes that the cashiers are at the front of the store and takes his items there. His assumption is correct, and he purchases the items and leaves the store. Box 3.2 contains a script for the second scenario shopper. Figure 3.7 (see also Plate 2) shows actual scenes from Harris Teeter for the Scenario 2 shopper.

Scenario 3. Roger stops at his regular store to buy a jar of Folgers coffee. He walks into what he knows is the main entrance to the store. Without paying much attention to other shoppers, the store environment, or kiosks that are displaying special items, he heads directly to the group of aisles on the right side of the store. While he does not remember the exact

---

■ ■

Box 3.2: Script for Scenario 2

Shopper new to store who has grocery list that includes bread, coffee, and lettuce

Step 1: Shopper walks into what looks like the main entrance of the store.

Step 2: He pauses to look around at the scene before him.

Step 3: He consults his shopping list and decides to look for the lettuce.

Step 4: He turns toward Aisle 1 and moves toward the lettuce.

Step 5: He moves toward Aisle 2 and finds the bread.

Step 6: He walks from aisle to aisle looking for coffee.

Step 7: He gets to the aisle with cereals and remembers that he needs corn flakes.

Step 8: He takes a box of corn flakes from the shelf.

Step 9: He reaches the coffee aisle and picks his brand.

■ ■

Figure 3.7: *What Scenario 2 shoppers see* (see also Plate 2)
(Photos courtesy of Harris Teeter, Inc.)

aisle number, Roger knows from considerable experience that the coffee aisle is somewhere in that group.

As he walks perpendicularly to the aisles, he looks down a couple of aisles. Because of his experience, he no longer raises his head in order to read the hanging signs. Instead, Roger uses the cues available on the shelves in the aisles, such as patterns, colors, and shapes, to determine which is the correct aisle. Figure 3.8 (see also Plate 3) shows a comparison of how cues lead to different aisle looks. When he recognizes the cues of the coffee aisle, he enters that aisle and looks at the shelves for the jar shape and the red color of regular coffee. Box 3.3 contains a script of the third scenario shopper.

Scenario 4. Irina walks into what she knows is the main entrance to the store. Without paying much attention to other shoppers, the store environment, or kiosks that are displaying special items, she consults her list: lettuce, apples, wheat bread, hamburger buns, coffee, tea, and soup. She moves directly down the first aisle to select a head of lettuce and inspect the apples.

Irina also needs bread, which she knows is in Aisle 2. She moves toward the bread, noticing first the loaves of bread on the shelves that are at eye level.

■ ■

Box 3.3: Script for Scenario 3

Shopper is familiar with store and looking for a jar of Folgers regular coffee

Step 1: Shopper walks into what he knows is the main entrance to the store.

Step 2: He heads directly to the group of aisles on the right side of the store.

Step 3: He walks perpendicularly to the aisles on the right.

Step 4: He looks down each aisle, noticing colors, shapes, and patterns.

Step 5: He recognizes the cues of the coffee aisle and enters that aisle.

Step 6: He searches for the jar shape and the red color of regular coffee labeling.

■ ■

Figure 3.8: *What Scenario 3 shoppers see* (see also Plate 3)
(Photos courtesy of Harris Teeter, Inc.)

She prefers wheat bread, but she does not have a particular brand that she likes. She looks for the section with darker breads. While in this aisle, she looks for and finds the buns.

Next Irina goes to the soup aisle because it comes before the coffee aisle. She walks down the soup aisle, looking for her favorite brand of chicken soup that she knows comes in a red and white can. To locate the can, she looks specifically for a combination of the words *chicken soup* and the red and white colors.

The last items on the list are coffee and tea. Irina knows from experience that they are in the same section in a nearby aisle. Ignoring the navigation signs hanging from the ceiling, she moves directly toward the coffee aisle. She cues on patterns, shapes, and colors to find her brand of coffee and favorite tea. Box 3.4 contains a script of the fourth scenario shopper. Figure 3.9 (see also Plate 4) shows actual scenes for the Scenario 4 shopper.

Designing from Scenarios

Remember that we start with the premise that designers of a supermarket Web site can benefit from taking into account how people use the real-world environment of supermarkets to incorporate familiar elements into Web site design. Designers must understand two scenario components as reflected in user mental models: (1) the users' organization of their knowledge of the real-world environment—their structured mental model—as well as how they perform tasks in that environment based on their schemata for routine events or (2) scripts—their functional mental model. Starting with the assumption that the vast majority of people who would e-shop for groceries have had extensive experience in supermarket shopping, we will use as an example the fourth scenario, shopping from a list by an experienced shopper who is familiar with the store.

It is clear here that this experienced shopper starts with a definite categorization of groceries in a store. Her organizational knowledge tells her that each of the pairs, vegetables and fruits, wheat bread and buns, and coffee and tea, belong together. Her expectation, therefore, is that when she goes to shop in a store, be it an e-supermarket or a different brick and mortar one, her mental model for this familiar organization will hold true. The designer of a supermarket Web site must take this knowledge into account in terms of both organizing the site and providing the corresponding appropriate look and feel for the organization. In arranging the site grocery items, we need to make sure that items such as lettuce and apples are in the same category. In

■ ■

Box 3.4: Script for Scenario 4

Shopper is familiar with store and has a list: lettuce, apples, wheat bread, hamburger buns, coffee, tea, and soup

Step 1: Shopper walks into what she knows is the main entrance to the store.

Step 2: She consults her list.

Step 3: She moves directly down the first aisle.

Step 4: She selects a head of lettuce and inspects the apples.

Step 5: She goes to the next aisle for wheat bread and buns.

Step 6: She first looks in the general shelf area where the wheat bread is located.

Step 7: She gets the wheat bread.

Step 8: She looks at bottom shelf where she remembers the buns are and gets a package.

Step 9: She goes to the soup aisle.

Step 10: She looks specifically for a combination of the words *chicken soup* and the colors red and white.

Step 11: She goes to the last aisle to get the coffee and tea.

Step 12: She scans for colors, shapes, and words to select the desired items.

■ ■

providing visual cues, we need to make sure that the colors, patterns, and shapes of links (such as icons) to categories are similar to those familiar to the experienced supermarket shopper.

The script for the fourth scenario shopper defines a sequence of grocery shopping actions. This sequence should inform the designer of how to sequence links leading to certain "Web aisles." If, in studying shoppers' scripts, we discover that a large percentage of the time they go to the produce section first, then that should be the first available link for "list shoppers."

Shoppers who have never or very infrequently shopped in a supermarket and do not have enough knowledge for building a viable mental model will do a random aisle walk. It is possible that they will use scripts from shopping at small grocery stores or other types of retail establishments. It would

Figure 3.9: *What Scenario 4 shoppers see* (see also Plate 4)
(Photos courtesy of Harris Teeter, Inc.)

be useful to find the most common generalities for shopping to use in designing for the totally novice user. On the other hand, shoppers who have considerable experience in other supermarkets but not in this particular one will bring their expectations with them. People's mental models are often a function of their expectations based on what they know in addition to their real experience (Carroll and Olson, 1988).

Simple versus Enriched Site Environments

In using physical-world environments to model the design of Web sites, we must decide to what extent the environment should be mirrored. On a scale of simple to enriched design, we need to set the appropriate level of enrichment.

There are those who have the opinion that the simpler the site design in mirroring the environment, the more usable the site (Nielsen, 2000). The notion that simple is better is probably an overgeneralization that is not supported by solid empirical evidence and does not necessarily apply equally for all Web usage. The purpose of the site and the goals of the users play decisive roles in whether a simple or enriched site is more usable. If efficiency is our usability goal, then simplicity is important in Web site design. If, on the other hand, a site is satisfying and usable if it provides an enriched experience, then simplicity may not be the only or main consideration for designers. It may be that "experiencing" an environment, enriched with detail, is as important to the user as performing the task efficiently.

In an attempt to determine if a site environment's usability is related to enrichment level, Badre and Jacobs (1999) conducted a study of the relationship between performance and satisfaction and site enrichment. The questions at hand were: To what extent should the usability of a Web site include the requirement that site visitors "feel" they are visiting an actual physical site, so the site visit experience becomes more like a real experience? Furthermore, does providing an "enriched" environment using 3-D image representation result in a more satisfactory experience for the visitor than providing a simple link-click navigation environment?

For the study we developed two versions of a museum Web site. Using the Atlanta High Museum's permanent exhibit, we designed two navigational metaphors. The first was a book index metaphor, where visitors click key words organized in an index format. The second was an enriched, 3-D spatial navigation representation using Quick Time VR to give the visitor the "feeling" of moving through the actual museum. Participants were given three tasks to accomplish in the form of answering three questions: (1) Which collection is the Punch Pot from? (2) Who painted *Homage to Hoffman*? and (3) What is the name of the [pictured] object? (*The Walking Tiger*). Figures 3.10, 3.11, and 3.12 show the art pieces in the three tasks.

Forty-two participants were divided into two groups to answer the questions, either for a school report or in preparation for a visit to the actual museum. Each participant performed two out of the three tasks in both Web versions. The order of tasks performed was both permuted and counterbalanced over participants of each group. The time to complete each task and the number of clicks to completion were collected as indicators of performance. A Lickert scale questionnaire was administered to score and evaluate level of satisfaction.

Overall, the index method was superior on the performance measures of time to completion and number of clicks. See Figures 3.13 and 3.14. On the satisfaction preference scale, visitors preferred the enriched version overall. Figure 3.15 shows the difference in scale ratings, and Figure 3.16 compares the overall percentage. Those who were looking for museum objects for a

Figure 3.10: *Punch Pot, ca 1765–1775*
(High Museum of Art, Atlanta, GA; Frances and Emory Cocke Collection, 1988.38)

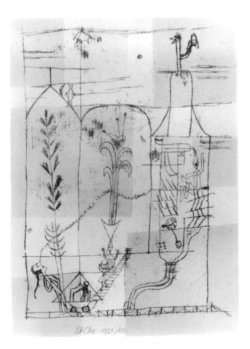

Figure 3.11: Homage to Hoffman by Paul Klee
(© 2002 Artists Rights Society (ARS), New York/VG Bild-Kunst.Bonn.
High Museum of Art, Atlanta, GA. Purchased with funds from the Lawrence and
Alfred Fox Foundation for the Ralph K. Uhry Collection, 49.43)

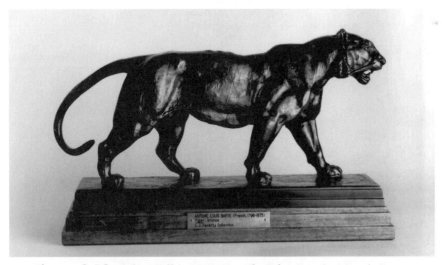

Figure 3.12: The Walking Tiger, 19th C, by Antoine-Louis Barye
(High Museum of Art, Atlanta, GA; J.J. Haverty Collection, 49.43)

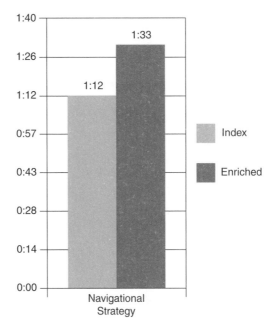

Figure 3.13: *Overall average time*

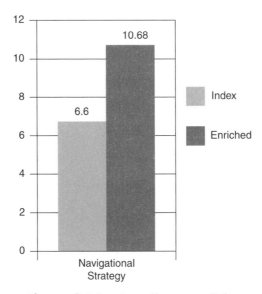

Figure 3.14: *Overall average clicks*

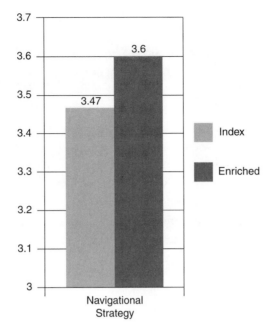

Figure 3.15: *User preference ratings*

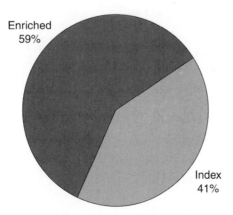

Figure 3.16: *Preferred strategy*

school project preferred the index strategy to the enriched version 72 percent to 28 percent. Those whose objective was to plan a visit to the museum preferred the enriched strategy 75 percent to 25 percent. This result suggests that what is usable to Web site visitors is a function of their Web usage goal. There are situations where enrichment is preferred and, therefore, more usable than simplicity.

When participants were asked to remember other art objects they may have seen by pointing them out in a display of art objects, the index search participants were able to identify zero objects, while the spatial navigation participants remembered an average of 2.5 objects. This result suggests that spatial navigation provides a different experience with different results from that of a simple index navigation approach. The enriched site design will be preferable and, therefore, more usable and useful if the purpose is to give users the experience it can provide.

4

The Web User, Part 1:
The Audience

W eb sites have two audiences: the target audience for whom the Web site is
intended and a potentially larger group who visit the site because they
can access it. Our purpose should be to design for the target audience, but we
should take into account the general Web user.

Understanding the Web User

People who visit Web sites are most likely experienced computer users who
have probably been using other Internet services such as e-mail, chat rooms,
virtual communities, or file transfer. Currently, the average Web user is highly
educated, having obtained at least one degree. Male users have been in the
majority, but there is a decisive trend toward an increase in female users worldwide, particularly among new and young Web users. Of course, such statistics
will change drastically over the long run as the Web becomes more accessible
worldwide, especially through the use of cell phones and handheld devices.

To understand who the general Web user is in a given period of time, designers must stay current with the latest data. We should use nationally published data collected by surveys such as the GVU WWW survey and the NUA Internet surveys, *www.horus.com,* or *www.statmarket.com.* As an example of statistical changes, Table 4.1 summarizes the GVU's ninth and tenth WWW surveys' data on age as a function of location, gender, years on the Web, and skill level (Kehoe, et al., 1999). It is in the context of this general profile that we define the target audience for a given project. Keep in mind that the GVU data is relatively old, given the growth rate on the Internet. It is presented here only as an example of the kind of data designers could gather from such surveys.

Table 4.1: *Average Age for Different Categories*

		GVU10	GVU9
Entire Sample	All	37.6	35.1
Location	USA	38.5	34.4
	Europe	30.9	35.5
	Other	34.4	36.0
Gender	Female	37.6	28.8
	Male	37.5	30.9
Years on the Web	< 1 Year	41.4	36.9
	1–3 Years	38.0	35.0
	>3 Years	36.3	34.3
Skill Level	Novice	41.1	
	Intermediate	39.5	
	Experienced	36.3	
	Expert	34.1	

Defining an Audience

Defining an audience is an essential prerequisite for designing a Web site. The user profile will influence the way we design and evaluate the interface. The experiences, characteristics, needs, skills, and requirements of the user can affect design decisions at both the site and page levels. We consider Web users in terms of both individual and group differences. Individual differences include characteristics such as skill and personality factors, while group differences include characteristics such as national language and cultural factors. Recognizing these differences and identifying the predominant audience characteristics enable us to place appropriate constraints on interface design and interaction style. Successful usability design practice also takes into account people's cognitive limitations and capabilities, including the abilities to assimilate, retain, and retrieve information. For user interface evaluation, it is easier to select test participants who are representative of the intended audience if we already know the predominant and important audience characteristics.

To generate an audience profile, we need to perform the following tasks.

1. Identify the relevant individual differences.

2. Identify and specialize the cognitive processing capabilities and limits.

3. Generate audience definition and categorization.

Individual Differences

The first task is to determine what factors affect how an audience uses the Web site. People differ on an individual level. These differences may include differences in mental abilities, temperament, and motivation. It is important to characterize the users in terms of these differences to place constraints on the interface design. In addition to these differences, frequency of Web use and overall computer experience will result in different levels of sophistication corresponding to different user needs. For example, experienced users may find help and other support intended for novices to be annoying and prefer to interact in a style that takes advantage of their accumulated knowledge.

Individual differences can be grouped into four categories: (1) knowledge, experience, and skill; (2) personality factors; (3) physical and demographic attributes; and (4) user levels. The relative importance of these factors is determined by the projected Web site that one plans to build. For example, knowledge and problem-solving skill would be important for a complex system encompassing many transaction-oriented and decision-making tasks, but personality differences would have a greater effect on the success of an entertainment-oriented Web site. Physical and demographic attributes, on the other hand, would be highly important for a Web site designed for the visually impaired. In all cases, however, the complete set of factors must be examined.

Knowledge, Experience, and Skill

Individual users may differ in level and type of education as well as in their knowledge, experience, and skill levels. There are several key factors in this category that are determinants of a user's performance. These factors describe the cognitive abilities and styles of projected users as well as their knowledge and experience of the projected Web site's domain. Not all factors are necessarily applicable in every Web design situation, but there will be situations in which they all have direct implications for designing the constituents of the interactive environment.

Education Level and Type. The education of intended users directly affects usability design issues such as training, mode of presentation, and textual content and style. The user profile might include questions such as How much formal education (high school, college, graduate) have users had, and how long ago did they have it? What type (science, engineering, liberal arts, vocational, trade) of formal education did users have? Did they acquire skills needed for their current job through formal schooling or via on-the-job-training? How well has schooling prepared them for their career? What were their best and worst subjects?

Reading Level. For Web sites requiring text browsing and reading, it is important that text is written at a level appropriate for user comprehension. Reading-level indices are obtained by measuring the difficulty of written text comprehension using formulas that count the number of words per sentence and the number of syllables per word. The higher the index, the more difficult it is to understand the text. There are various specialized tests to determine the average reading level of the text (Flesch, 1975; Fry, 1977). Text should be written to accommodate the user's education level. By improving the readability of a document and making the text easier to understand, we improve the overall usability of the Web site.

The general user population is on a literacy scale that ranges from those who read at college level to those who are functionally nonliterate and illiterate. While the current Web user is highly literate, this may not be the case in the future as the Internet reaches underserved American and Third World populations. If the user profile for a specific application has an equal mixture of levels, then the general rule is to accommodate the lowest level. Higher-level readers easily use text written at lower indices, but people at lower levels are at a distinct disadvantage when trying to read and understand text written above their level.

Knowing the users' approximate reading/education level also helps the usability designer to select appropriate interaction strategies. For example, if users are judged to be at lower levels on the scale, or if the audience consists of individuals who are not technically trained, the designer should select appropriate vocabulary and avoid using technical jargon in help messages and other textual presentations. When a significant audience segment is illiterate, functionally illiterate, or non–English speaking, the designer should provide nonverbal interaction styles (for example, iconic) and pointing devices. This example shows how a user context characteristic of illiteracy requires a design decision that supersedes the site design constraint of conveying information in simple text.

Skill Level. The user skills that should be considered in Web design depend to a great extent on the task requirements of the intended Web site. These might include job-related, typing, motor, verbal, quantitative, and troubleshooting/mechanical skills. To develop a profile of audience skills, the designer should ask questions such as What jobs has the user held and for how long? What were the primary accomplishments on the job? Does the user touch-type or hunt and peck? How many words per minute? Is the user mechanically skilled? In addition to such questionnaires, standard tests on representative audience can measure many job-related typing and other skills and aptitudes.

Knowing user skills helps the designer to select appropriate interaction strategies. For example, skilled typists, with a typing rate of 135 words per minute (Card, et al., 1987), can use the keyboard as the primary input device. For unskilled typists, those who hunt and peck at a rate of 10 words per minute, a mouse, touch screen, or some other device may be more appropriate. If an application requires quantitative operations and audience quantitative skills are low, a high priority must be placed on automating quantitative operations. For audiences with specialized skills, the designer should make sure those skills are accommodated, and even taken advantage of.

Problem-Solving Strategies. Background and experience often shape how an individual will go about solving problems (Badre, 1974). While it is very difficult to predict the exact strategy that an individual would use, it is generally understood that people tend to rely more on trial-and-error, heuristic methods than on procedural, algorithmic ones. Learning and remembering procedures and rules of procedures take more effort than most people are willing to invest. People prefer to use resources such as rules of thumb, hints, and cues to solve problems. These strategies have implications for the Web interface designer. Applications with complex tasks should allow the user to experiment and to practice trial and error, with low failure risks, by providing visible and easily accessible hints, prompts, and guidance.

Knowledge and Experience. Knowledge of subject matter, computer system and application knowledge and experience, and familiarity with the task domain or related domains are important determinants of user performance in the interactive environment of the projected Web site (Mackay and Lamb, 1991). Consequently, user knowledge and experience have many implications for interactive system design. Designers should provide conceptual models and metaphors of the user interface consistent with (1) the task and (2) real-life experience (Carroll, et al., 1988). Features such as interaction styles, presentation formats, and command names should be compatible with the features of interfaces familiar to the audience. For example, the default format design for fill-in forms should be similar to the format of forms that already exist and are familiar to the user in the brick and mortar environment. Of course, an easy tailoring option should be available for user groups with different experiences. If designers are familiar with the users' previous experience, then they will avoid inconsistencies with other interfaces familiar to the audience. For example, an internal link with the same name in two Web sites should not have different functions or lead to different types of information.

Learning Style and Experience. Learning styles and experiences play an important role in defining the audience for interface design. Of particular interest to the designer are questions relating to habits of learning and knowledge acquisition. Are members of the audience in the habit of using drill and practice methods to acquire new concepts and skills? Do they rely on audio-visual methods? Are they comfortable with textual/book learning styles, or are they more adept at hands-on, learn-as-you-do techniques? Answers to such questions feed directly into design considerations. For example, in the case of hands-on learners, the designer may need to provide an automatic tutorial session in which the system presents an interaction sequence and the user presses keys only to continue or exit the sequence. An alternative design strategy would be to encourage browsing and a "trial-and-error" approach to learning by providing menus, prompts, and other such facilitators.

Task-Related Factors. It is important to specify user attributes that are related to the job and task(s) to be performed. These include activity duration, frequency of actions taken in a given time period, complexity of tasks, and user responsibility. Other task-related factors include a characterization of the environment of use (public or private), part-time or full-time employment, turnover rate for job type and user's job turnover history, and individual history of the specific job.

User Types. Unless a site is to be used by a very small and select group of people, there is bound to be variety within the user population. It should, however, be possible to divide the users into important and helpful categories. This division could be made along task lines—for instance, where some users will be using the site to accomplish one particular set of tasks and other users will have a different set. Audience members could be categorized according to levels of expertise. Frequent users will have different needs from those of occasional users. When forming these categories, it is useful to attach associated percentages of the population. For example, 70 percent of the expected user population could be performing daily data-entry tasks with the site, such as entering information into the Yahoo calendar, while 20 percent occasionally use the site for report generation, and 10 percent use it for research and market analysis.

Groups of Web users can often be identified and categorized by important cultural characteristics that can influence naming conventions, methods of accomplishing tasks, and communication protocols. Understanding the dominant culture of an audience will help the designer choose appropriate symbolism and metaphors for the interface. Most software products are marketed in many countries, not just the one where they were developed and produced. Creating or retrofitting software for different countries requires attention to technical detail that goes beyond mere translation. This is particularly true of designing for the Web because it is literally a worldwide phenomenon. Anyone connected to the global Internet can access a Web site.

As designers, we should first explore and understand how cultural influence leads to variations in people's behaviors and practices and how such variations affect interactions with the Web. These findings help us to design culturally sensitive interfaces. For example, colors have different meanings in different cultures. In Japan white is not the color of purity but the color of death. Variations in language and vocabulary should be incorporated into the interface. How pictorial information is presented and organized for scanning on a display is related to the script direction of the user's first language. Cultural context of Web design is covered more comprehensively in Chapter 11.

Personality Factors

Personality factors affect the ease of user acceptance for interacting with and navigating a Web site. Such attributes as tolerance level and motivation should indicate how much time users will spend trying to use the new Web site to perform a transaction before giving up. The following personality factors should be taken into consideration.

Tolerance Level. Tolerance for time and novelty, as well as for working with other people, should be considered when designing Web sites for usability. Assuming that we are designing the site to be accessed as part of the user's daily job, questions such as the following can help develop an audience profile. Are workers under time pressure in their job? Do they often work overtime, and how do they feel about it? What is their tolerance for routine work? How comfortable are they with new task assignments, technologies, and procedures? Physicians, for example, who have very little time to learn a new technology or navigate to perform a task, will need to be accommodated with interaction strategies that require no extra time to learn to interact or navigate. If they are used to voice-recording their patient record entries, then a speech recorder should be made available as part of the interface design. It should also be made possible for them to replay their recording by selecting the appropriate object on the screen. (On the other hand, for users who work in the same room with other users, voice recording and annotation may not be tolerable.) Do users prefer working with others or by themselves? An answer to this question may determine whether we should design the site for access by groups or by individuals.

Affective Factors. Affective factors to consider when designing Web usability encompass attitudes and morale; interest in being challenged; trainability for change, motivation, work values, fear of computers; and related personality factors such as reflective/impulsive and introverted/extroverted. A key number of questions have important implications for design. What are user strengths and weaknesses? How would users describe their standards of performance? What influences their productivity and satisfaction? Aside from money, what do they want most in a job? What are they doing currently to achieve their career objectives? How do the users feel about computers?

Even though there is very little empirical research to support definitive guidelines in this area, designers should create and test possible solutions related to affective factors. For example, impulsive people who are likely to attempt more actions resulting in errors may find it helpful to have an "undo" function to cancel the result of the last operation. For reflective individuals, the interface should provide ample tutorials and instructions. For extroverted personalities, designers can include alternative strategies to keep them interested. Individuals who have a fear of failure will benefit from an interface design that includes considerable guidance, such as menus and prompts, to avoid situations in which the user is unsure of what to do next. To achieve user satisfaction and diminish the potential for alienation, the design should provide timely feedback and speedy responses, a correction mechanism for data entry, and a spelling checker.

Cognitive Style. Cognitive style encompasses several dimensions of the different ways that people think about and perform tasks. Some individuals mainly verbalize their ideas about problems and solutions, while others tend to visualize the problem. Also, some people are analytical, while others are intuitive. Specialized tests may be administered to identify these characteristics. There is evidence that spatial ability is another cognitive factor directly related to performance in a user interface task (Vincente, et al., 1987). Because any given audience encompasses all possible cognitive styles, a designer should consider designing flexible interfaces that accommodate different dialog styles.

Demographic and Physical Attributes

The following demographic and physical attributes will place constraints on interface design as well as indicate the relative likes and dislikes of projected users.

Demographic Attributes. Among the demographic attributes with implications for the design of Web site usability are age, gender, salary, and mobility. For example, the designer should avoid small point sizes of fonts when the audience consists of a significant segment of individuals over the age of 50, since visual acuity decreases with age. Likewise, because memorization skills decrease with age, interactions for older audiences should not depend on retention and recall. Also, research shows that for users over the age of 35 designers should use high-contrast colors. When the audience is composed of people of different age groups, the designer may need to avoid vocabulary or phrasing that might aggravate generation differences. Avoid language in text that demonstrates bias toward one gender or another, unless the audience consists of only one gender.

Physical Attributes. An audience definition statement should take into account factors related to physical capabilities and limitations. Issues that might affect design include the use of glasses (nearsightedness, bifocals), left- and right-handedness, auditory devices, and other visual and motor aids. If the audience has a very high percentage of male users, color should not be the only coding device because 8 percent of males have some form of color blindness.

User Levels

The designer should take into consideration the users' varying levels of expertise with the Internet and the Web. Schneider (1982) proposes five such levels: parrot, novice, intermediate, expert, and master. Each level is characterized by the user's ability to combine, or "chunk," the information he or she needs to process when performing a task. There is ample evidence in the research literature that the larger the chunk size of the user, the more advanced the user is (Chase and Simon, 1973; Badre, 1982a). For the purpose of Web usability design, we will consider three levels of expertise: novice, experienced, and expert.

As users progress up the scale of expertise, their level of comfort with interaction and navigation styles changes. The novice is usually more comfortable with recognition-style interactions and the use of links to search and navigate. Experienced users are more likely to use search options and engines. Chunk size ranges from simple actions for the novice to action sequences by the expert. Experts are more competent in the tasks that are frequently performed and have deep knowledge of additional functionality available within the Internet, on the browser, and on the Web site. They can perform tasks such as Web customizing or changing "cookies" irrespective of their level of experience with a given Web site. Keep in mind that a person may be experienced with one Web site and a novice to another.

The novice has very little knowledge of the Internet, the browser, or Web interaction. Novices process information in small chunks: a single word or single action. They understand a collection of isolated concepts about the

Internet and the Web. They begin to associate meaning with specific actions, but they have not begun to explore the Internet system for unknown functionality. Web site design should provide unobtrusive assistance features for novice users by incorporating contextual help functionality and site maps.

The experienced user focuses on the task rather than its components. The chunk size of experienced users is at the task level as opposed to the keystroke or single-action level. They have begun to notice the more subtle features of the Web site and are beginning to get familiar with, but not yet fluent in, more general Internet or browser features and capabilities. The experienced user has achieved knowledge and "knowhow" in a specific Web site domain.

Practically speaking, the expert is capable of using any function offered by the Internet and the World Wide Web. Experts recognize how tasks, actions, and data are interrelated, and they use the Web for multiple types of tasks, ranging from making an online purchase to creating a Web page. Experts search for ways to be more productive.

In the GVU WWW survey, the level of expertise is defined in terms of the number of activities performed on the Web. Box 4.1 lists the activities.

In their report on the tenth edition of the GVU WWW User Survey, Kehoe, et al. (1999) define the level of expertise by the number of activities as follows.

Novice: 0–3 activities

Intermediate: 4–6 activities

Experienced: 7–9 activities

Expert: 10–12 activities

The definition of *expertise* in the Kehoe report does not take into account the type of activity performed. However, the researchers do report that, on further analysis of type of activity by level of expertise, some activities are found to be more popular with novices, while experts perform other activities more frequently. For example, more than 41 percent of novices had used an online directory, but only 10 percent had created a Web page. On the other hand, 98 percent of experts had created a Web page. While more than 90 percent of expert users had performed more advanced activities such as creating and customizing Web pages, changing cookie preference, and listening to radio online, the percentage of novice users performing these advanced activities ranged between 7 and 14.

■ ■

Box 4.1:
Activities Used to Define Skill Level

In the General Demographics questionnaire, one question is "Have you ever performed any of the following activities online?"

- Ordered a product/service from a business, government, or educational entity by filling out a form on the Web
- Made a purchase online for more than $100
- Created a Web page
- Customized a Web page for yourself (for example, My Yahoo, CNN Custom News)
- Changed your browser's "startup" or "home" page
- Changed your "cookie" preferences
- Participated in an online chat or discussion (not including e-mail)
- Listened to a radio broadcast online
- Made a telephone call online
- Used a nationwide online directory to find an address or telephone number
- Taken a seminar or class about the Web or Internet
- Bought a book to learn more about the Web or Internet

■ ■

When determining the sophistication of projected Web site users, in addition to knowing about their Web experience, it is helpful to assess their overall experience with computers. It is also important for designers to acknowledge how sophisticated they expect and want their users to be. Questions that could be used to determine an initial profile of the user population's expertise include the following: Have you used a personal computer (for example, PC, Macintosh)? Which of the following devices have you used (mouse, keyboard, touch screen)? Have you ever used a system that used pictures in addition to words? Do you play computer games? Do you have a home computer? Have you been a programmer? If so, what languages? For how long? What is the largest program you have ever written?

Cognitive Processing Capabilities and Limits

The Internet clearly has emerged as the predominant tool of the information culture. In this culture, information is a commodity, and efficiency in storing, organizing, transmitting, and managing information is required for acceptable productivity levels and competitive advantage. In all sectors of this information culture, whether in business, education, leisure, or government, the Internet is becoming a central information-processing tool. Consequently, we should view the Internet and Web user primarily as an information processor. The usability effectiveness of designs depends in great part on their compatibility with the user's information-processing capabilities and limitations (Allen, 1982; Badre, 1980). As designers, we must take into account the users' cognitive and perceptual limits and how people are likely to process information in an interactive environment.

Although there is great diversity in individual intelligence, education, and experience, there are some basic universal human information-processing characteristics, which were discussed in Chapter 3. These characteristics, both capabilities and limits, affect the way people store, remember, and manipulate information, which in turn have implications for Web design.

In the case of selective attention, this means both creating designs that draw user attention to a particular screen location and optimizing the ease of locating displayed information. For example, using a unique bright color to draw attention to a displayed link can increase the chances that it will be noticed before other links.

For short-term memory, capacity is traditionally considered to range from five to nine chunks of information. This limitation suggests that organizing Web page information to accommodate the capacity of short-term memory is key to ease of assimilation for tasks requiring rapid information processing. Another example of a short-term memory situation is one where a Web user is interrupted from interacting with a page to answer the telephone for a period of 15 seconds. The ease with which the user can continue after the interruption depends on the extent to which the information on the screen mirrors the user's short-term memory of meaningful chunks and how well the design makes the chunks readily noticeable.

Users' mental representation of the Web and Web interactions and, therefore, how they would initially approach a Web task, is influenced by information stored in their long-term memories. Consider the case of frequent users of a specific travel Web site. Here the users acquire a memory of patterns of interaction and navigation relative to that Web site. If those same users have to access and use a different travel site, the memory of their frequently used site can either aid or hinder in navigating the new site, depending on the new site's design features and how users are allowed to perform their transactions.

For example, because inquiries about flight availability and reservations are the most frequent transactions, travel/airline sites usually place this category on the top of the first page. Users, therefore, have a memory of where and how to search for this information, and they employ this memory when they access different travel sites. A design that does not account for the placement of the availability category on the top of the home page would be a poor usability design because it does not accommodate long-term memory.

Generating an Audience Profile

Defining the target audience for a given Web site means generating a document that specifies the relevant characteristics, the range and frequency values of the identified characteristics, and how this specified information might impact design decisions. If we are unable to define how an identified user characteristic relates to some design decision, then that characteristic should not remain part of the user profile. Box 4.2 shows an audience profile document with a few examples of frequency and design impact.

Once we generate an audience profile, the next step is to classify the audience on the basis of the most likely categories. This categorization, in turn, should be based on some key characteristic such as age range, experience level, job responsibility, national language, or culture. We should then select from the audience profile document a subset of characteristics that are most relevant to the category. The type and size of each audience category will help us determine the types of interface styles required for the Web site. For example, if the target audience is 50 percent English speaking and 50 percent French speaking, then the site will need to be available in two languages and designed for two different cultures.

To identify the set of characteristics for generating an audience profile, we need to apply the appropriate methodology to collect data. Audience definition involves a combination of existing studies, on-site interviews, and surveys. We can obtain a substantial amount of information about the characteristics of users from demographic studies. We can learn about information processing

Box 4.2: Audience Profile Document with Select Examples of Frequency and Design Impact

Characteristic	Range	Frequency	Design Impact
		A selected sample of Frequencies	A selected sample of Design Impacts
Personal Data			
Age	18–65	18–50 (30%) 51–65 (70%)	High contrast colors; large fonts
Gender	Male/female	75% female	Visual navigation
Handedness	Left/right	10% left; 90% right	None
Color blindness code	Complete/partial	8% of male	Redundant
Population	Cognitive style	20% Verbal/Analytic; 80% Spatial/Intuitive	High proportion graphics
Learning style	By reading/By doing		
Attitude	Positive/neutral/negative		
Motivation	High/moderate/low		
Income	High/medium/low		
Mobility	High rate/Low rate		
Length of time on job	1–2 years/3–5/6–10/over 10		
Adaptability to change	High/medium/low		
Computer/ Web Experience			
Frequency of use	Low/medium/high	10% low; 20% medium; 70% high	Implement accelerated mode
Total use time	Weeks/months	30 weeks	Online learning
Computer interaction experience	GUI/WEB/DOS/Fill-in	100% GUI & Web	Direct manipulation; contextual help
General computer experience	None/1–2 years/over 2		
Web navigation time	None/one year/over a year		
System experience	Expert/moderate/novice		
Domain/ Product Experience			
Knowledge of subject matter	Expert/moderate/novice	90% novice	Online help for subject-matter content
Domain skill level	High/medium/low	90% low	Online help for domain functionality

(continued)

Box 4.2: Audience Profile Document with Select Examples of Frequency and Design Impact *(cont.)*

Characteristic	Range	Frequency	Design Impact
Domain/ Product Experience			
Time of domain experience	Zero to several years	Average, one month	
Frequency of domain work	Low/medium/high	90% low	
Application experience	No similar apps/one similar/many similar		
Education			
Education level	High school/college/ advanced/vocational/ liberal arts/science/ engineering/MBA	100% high school	Text for 6th- to 8th-grade reading level
Skills and Aptitude			
Reading level	Less than 5th grade/ 8th grade/higher than 8th	100% 8th grade	8th- or lower-grade reading level
Typing skill	Low/medium/high	80% low	Minimize keyboard requirements
Verbal	High/medium/low		
Quantitative	High/medium/low		
Job/Task Characteristics			
Experience level	Novice/intermediate/expert		
Frequency of performance	High/medium/low		
Primary training	None/elective formal/ mandatory formal		
Job categories/ responsibilities	Administration/clerk/etc.	90% clerical	Make frequently used clerical commands/ functions visually visible
Turnover rate	High/medium/low	90% high	No offline learning
Task importance	High/low		
Task type	Browsing/transacting/etc.		

and cognitive abilities directly from studies on cognition. We collect data on the audience's experience via the use of surveys.

Initially, designers need to follow three steps to determine which characteristics must be analyzed.

1. Meet with a representative audience sample.

2. Observe current operations.

3. Conduct structured interviews and focus groups.

The first real insight into the user population comes from meeting with a small group of prospective users. Designers should record perceived similarities and differences about individuals as they talk to the group about the projected Web site and then determine which characteristics they think will be important in designing for the target audience.

If the site is to replace a current operation for carrying out some set of tasks, observe the current method under normal conditions. How are the tasks performed? What kind of ordering is incorporated? Are paper forms or other materials used? What terminology is used? How do the users ask and receive assistance while doing their tasks?

Following these activities, designers should prepare a prototype questionnaire to be used in a structured interview format with a sample of projected users. It is important to ask the respondents what they think is missing in the prototype questionnaire because the document should be continually revised and administered until the designer and the respondents are satisfied with its content. Based on these results, the designer develops a survey questionnaire aimed at obtaining responses about important user characteristics such as education, preferences, skills, work, and environment. Whenever possible, questions should be in the form of multiple choice with a free-form response added at the end of a question or section of questions. Boxes 4.3, 4.4, and 4.5 contain examples of questions about the various categories.

■ ■

Box 4.3: Education and Task Questions for an Audience Survey Questionnaire

Here are examples of questions about the user's education level and type that would be appropriate for a more complete questionnaire.

What is your highest level of education (check one)?
❑1 ❑2 ❑3 ❑4 ❑5 ❑6 ❑7 ❑8 ❑9 ❑10 ❑11 ❑12
❑13 ❑14 ❑15 ❑16 ❑graduate

Education level is important for the assessment of the cognitive styles and reading abilities of the users. Therefore, the choices of levels of education that are present in the questionnaire are those that are relevant for the population being queried. Multiple choice allows for a simple classification of the responses in a formal way that can be analyzed statistically.

What was your major field of study?
In college   _____
In graduate school _____

As level of education is important, so is the field of study. Someone with an engineering background is trained to think differently from someone from a social sciences or management background. Domain-specific knowledge will also be different based on the user's education. One-line free-form responses are recommended here because a multiple-choice answer would have to be too extensive and still might be incomplete. An additional question is provided to indicate the type of education received.

What form of education did you receive?
___ Liberal Arts
___ Science/Engineering
___ Trade
___ Vocational
___ Other

What were your most favorite and least favorite courses in school? Why? (free-form answer)

(continued)

This question serves more than one purpose. First, it gathers information about the types of classes preferred by the user, leading to possible answers to questions such as "Do you like math?" The free-form answer can serve to evaluate an individual's ability to construct an answer. Those who do not answer this question will reveal something about their willingness to devote time to activities that may not give them any direct benefit.

The designer should consider a number of factors about all these questions. First, some of them may not apply to all subjects. If the questionnaire is conducted orally or by computer, questions that do not apply should be skipped or modified. Second, the format for the answers may be given in two or more alternative forms because people may have the information available immediately in different ways. The question below is an example of this situation.

How did you rank in your graduating class?

_____ of _____   or   top ___%

The alternative to this multiple-answer format would be a free-form answer, but a free form would not give structure to the answer and would possibly complicate encoding for statistical purposes.

Another important set of questions pertains to the user's task experience and skills. Here are some examples of these types of questions.

Please outline your employment history, describing positions held and time on the job.

Position:_____   From:_____ To:_____
Position:_____   From:_____ To:_____

What do you like most in your current job? What do you like least?

How do you feel about group work?

___ I enjoy working with others.

___ I prefer to work by myself.

What factors most strongly affect your productivity?

(free-form answer)

What influences your job satisfaction?

(free-form answer)

Who do you answer to? Describe your relationship with your immediate supervisor.

(free-form answer)

(continued)

Box 4.3: Education and Task Questions for an Audience Survey Questionnaire *(cont.)*

How many employees are you responsible for? Describe your relationship with your staff.

(free-form answer)

Do you like to have direct contact with the public? If so, what do you like most and least about it?

(free-form answer)

Would you like to have more or less direct contact with your customers? Why?

(free-form answer)

What styles of writing do you enjoy reading? (Check all that apply)

___ a novel or long prose

___ a poem

___ a cartoon or comic book

___ a newspaper article

___ a newspaper editorial

___ a well-organized reference manual

___ a letter

■ ■

■ ■

Box 4.4: Skill and Experience Questions for an Audience Survey Questionnaire

Questions about the user's skills are also important to determine what capabilities to build into the interface and to help prescribe the interaction. For example:

What is your typing style?

___ Touch typist

___ Hunt and peck

___ Cannot type

A section on self-assessment in the questionnaire is often useful because it gives the respondent an opportunity to express opinions not covered in

(continued)

other categories. Answers should be in free-form. Though hard to encode for statistical analysis, these responses may reveal some important characteristics not otherwise identified. If a common thread is identified that would affect the design of the system, a second questionnaire may be needed.

What are your strengths?
What are your weaknesses?
Do you have any special abilities or skills?
How would you describe yourself in ten words or less?
How do you think your employees think of you?
Would you say you are an approachable person?
Some people like all instructions to be explicit; others prefer to do things on
     their own.
How would you describe yourself?
What types of customers irritate you?

Experience in using the Internet and other computer systems is an essential audience characteristic to determine. Current and previous user experience with Web sites translates into expectations for future sites. User frustrations with previous sites may hinder using the whole or parts of future sites. These problems should be identified and addressed in the development of a new site or a new site interface. Questions appropriate in this category include the following. Notice that explicit metrics ("at least once" or "at least two hours a day, three days a week, for two weeks") are given to allow respondents to know exactly how to classify themselves.

Have you ever used any of the following systems or devices at least once before?
___ Windows-PC or compatible
___ Apple Macintosh
___ Mainframe computers
___ Other business computer. Specify: _____
___ Other personal computer. Specify: _____
___ Cash register
___ ATM (automatic teller machine)
___ Voice mail systems or telephone answering machines
___ Voice menu systems (press 1 for xxx, press 2 for yyy, etc.)
___ Touch screens
___ Mouse
___ Light pens

(continued)

Box 4.4: Skill and Experience Questions for an Audience Survey Questionnaire (cont.)

Have you used any of the following over the last two weeks?

___ Windows-PC or compatible

___ Apple Macintosh

___ Mainframe computers

___ Other business computer. Specify: _____

___ Other personal computer. Specify: _____

___ Cash register

___ ATM (Automatic Teller Machine)

___ Voice mail systems or telephone answering machines

___ Voice menu systems (press 1 for xxx, press 2 for yyy, etc.)

___ Touch screens

___ Mouse

___ Light pens

Have you ever used for work (at least two hours a day, three days a week, for two weeks) any of the following systems?

___ Windows-PC or compatible

___ Apple Macintosh

___ Mainframe computers

___ Other business computer. Specify: _____

___ Other personal computer. Specify: _____

Have you used any of the following systems for more than four hours during the last two weeks?

___ Windows-PC or compatible

___ Apple Macintosh

___ Mainframe computers

___ Other business computer. Specify: _____

___ Other personal computer. Specify: _____

Which of the following types of software have you ever used regularly for business purposes?

___ Word processor

___ Spreadsheet

___ Data base

___ Communications

(continued)

___ Project management
___ Inventory control
___ Time management
___ Other. Specify: _____

Some additional computer-related questions are incorporated into the questionnaire. Due to the variability in the responses, the answer is left in free form to allow subjects to express themselves.

Do you own a personal computer? What kind? What do you do with it?
Do you play computer games?
Have you used computers in the military? What kinds?
What frustrates you most in using the software you use for your work? Please describe the problems and the software and hardware involved.
Have you ever been a programmer? If so, what languages? For how long? What is the largest program you have ever written?

■ ■

■ ■

Box 4.5: Demographics and Identification Questions for an Audience Survey Questionnaire

Even though demographics may be obtained from census data, it is important to develop a specialized questionnaire to collect individual and demographic data on the target audience. The target audience may not have the same characteristics as the general population. A sample of demographic questions follows.

Your age: _____

Gender:
___ Male
___ Female

Ethnic group:
___ White (Caucasian)
___ African American

(continued)

Box 4.5: Demographics and Identification Questions for an Audience Survey Questionnaire *(cont.)*

___ Asian
___ Hispanic
___ Native American
___ Other: _____

Marital status:
___ Single
___ Married
___ Divorced
___ Widowed

Your annual income: _____

Annual household income: _____

Are you
___ Right-handed
___ Left-handed
___ Ambidextrous

Do you wear glasses or contact lenses to correct your vision?
Are you color blind? To what extent?
Do you have hearing disabilities?
Do you have any physical limitations or challenges?

Finally, there should be an identification section in the questionnaire. This should appear at the end of the questionnaire and answering each question should be optional to maintain anonymity, if desired by participants. Questions in this section would include the following.

Your job title: _____
Your work hours: _____
Your name (OPTIONAL): _____
Business telephone number (OPTIONAL): _____

■ ■

5

The Web User, Part 2: Older Adults

When we are determining user context, we must also consider whether the target audience represents a demographic population segment, such as women or men, the disabled, children, students, or older adults. Designers should use the research literature on demographic audience segments to drive their design decisions. In this chapter we present a case of using state-of-the-art research to help us design Web sites for the older adult segment of our population.

The population is aging. There are more individuals today in the United States over the age of 65 than there have ever been before, and the number is expected to grow. Figure 5.1 (see also Plate 5) shows the data for two groups:

* This chapter is coauthored by Wendy Rogers and Albert Badre, both at the Georgia Institute of Technology. During the preparation of this chapter, Wendy Rogers was supported in part by grant PO1 AG17211 from the NIH (NIA).

ages 65–84 and age 85 and above. These age groups represent tens of millions of people in the United States alone, and increases are projected for other countries worldwide. Consequently, this is a user population whom Web designers must accommodate.

There have been several studies focusing on older adult users of the Web. (References to "older" adults, users, and so on refer to those aged 65 and over unless otherwise noted.) We will review specific studies of age-related differences in Web usage patterns and usage difficulties. To foreshadow, older adults are interested in using the Web, and many of them do. However, evidence suggests that older users, compared with younger users, have more difficulty finding information, are slower, make more errors, and are likely to get lost while navigating. To understand the potential source of these difficulties, we will elucidate the characteristics of older adults that must be considered in the context of Web design. The focus will be on age-related sensory, motor, and cognitive changes that may influence interactions with computers in general and the Web in particular. The chapter concludes with specific guidelines to aid in the effective use of the World Wide Web by older adults.

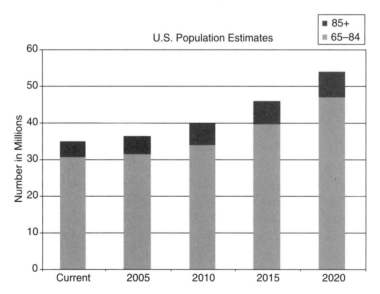

Figure 5.1: *Projected population estimates* (see also Plate 5)
(Source: *http://www.census.gov/population/www/projections/natsum-t3.html.* Reprinted with permission.)

Older Adults and the World Wide Web

The potential of the Web to benefit the lives of older adults is tremendous. Social ties with family and friends can be facilitated; purchases can be made for everything from prescription medications to books to groceries; health-related information can be easily obtained. Moreover, older adults as consumers either have purchasing power or, if they are on fixed incomes, can do comparison-shopping. Therefore, it is in the interest of companies and service providers involved in e-commerce to ensure that their sites are easy to use for this segment of the population.

Do older adults currently use the Web? Yes, although, of course, not all older adults are Web savvy. However, the number of older adults online is increasing. SeniorNet conducts usage surveys to track such numbers for individuals over the age of 50. In their 1995 research, 29 percent of the older adults surveyed used computers, and 17 percent of those older adults with computers at home reported regular use of the Internet (SeniorNet, 1998). By 1998, this latter number had increased such that nearly 70 percent of older adults with computers at home reported accessing the Internet. Moreover, a recent report by the U.S. Department of Commerce (2000) indicated that the age group "over 50" is the fastest growing population segment in terms of Internet use, with a 53 percent growth in use rate from 1998 to 2000.

People who do not currently use the Web give ignorance of how the Web works as their primary reason. Other reasons are lack of access and unfamiliarity with what they can do on the Web (Morrell, et al., 2000). An encouraging finding is that nonusers reported interest in and willingness to learn how to use the Web, contrary to popular stereotypes about older adults' antipathy toward new technologies.

The research indicates that older adults use the Web for a variety of activities (SeniorNet, 1998; Morrell, et al., 2000). The most frequently mentioned activity was using e-mail. However, in the SeniorNet survey of people over 50, the second most frequent activity was using the Internet as a research tool to find information on a particular topic. Respondents to that survey also reported frequent visits to news sites, current-event sites, and financial-related sites. This pattern of Internet use was comparable for the Morrell, et al., survey of adults aged 40–92. In addition, these participants reported using the Web to obtain information about travel, weather, and health, as well as hobbies.

Older adults are using the Web, but questions remain about the difficulties they encounter in their efforts. Though there are very few empirical studies, the available evidence suggests that older adults do have more usability problems than younger adults. In one study (Mead, et al., 1997), older and younger participants searched a simplified, 19-page version of a Web site to find specific pieces of information. Older users followed many more links per task than younger users, particularly for the more difficult search tasks. Older adults were significantly less likely to finish the tasks in the time allowed. They were more likely to return to the "home page" to begin a new task, even when this was not the most efficient path to the next target. Older adults were also less likely to recall or recognize previously visited locations and more likely to return to a page within a single search task. Therefore, keeping track of the previous path and the current position in the hierarchy appeared to be more difficult for the older individuals.

Age-related differences in Web searching were assessed by Kubeck, et al. (1999). Participants were given questions to answer via the Web using the Yahoo search tool (for example, name five herbs used for medicinal purposes and what each is used for). For simpler tasks, which required 6 to 9 steps to find the answer, there were minimal performance differences between the younger and older adults. However, for the more difficult searches (requiring 13 to 16 steps), there were age-related performance differences. Older adults either were less efficient than younger adults or found lower-quality answers. Similar navigation and searching difficulties were recorded for older adults searching an online library database (Mead, et al., 2000).

Characteristics of Older Users

Certain characteristics of older users can give us some insight into the source of age-related difficulties in using the Web. Age-related changes in motor movement, perceptual processing, or cognitive functioning may contribute to usability difficulties.

Movement Control

There is a general consensus that as people age, motor behaviors slow down. Compared to younger adults, older adults take longer to make similar movements, their ability to maintain continuous movements declines, coordination is disrupted, and movements are more variable (for a review, see Vercruyssen, 1997).

Older adults experience difficulties with fine motor coordination, such as using a computer mouse to navigate through a site or positioning the cursor on a desired target. Research has suggested that when older adults use a mouse, they are slower and less accurate than younger adults (Walker, et al., 1996). For a very small target item (3 pixels), older adults had difficulty hitting the target, with accuracy of only 75 percent for this target, compared to more than 90 percent for the other targets (6, 12, and 24 pixels). These data suggest that there may be a critical minimum target size, below which older individuals will be unable to use a mouse to accurately position a cursor.

Perception

Although age is associated with alterations in all sensory abilities, the changes most relevant to Web site design involve declines in eyesight and hearing. Additional information on age-related sensory declines is available in a recent review by Schneider and Pichora-Fuller (2000).

Color Vision

Color vision is the ability to discriminate among lights differing in spectral composition. For older adults, discrimination between colors is difficult, particularly for the shorter wavelengths of the spectrum. Consequently, designers should not require older users to discriminate between colors that are close in hue, especially those with short wavelengths as in the violet, blue, and green range.

Contrast Sensitivity

Contrast sensitivity refers to the ability to distinguish between adjacent areas that differ in light intensity and patterns that vary in width. Making discriminations such as these becomes more difficult with age, especially when alternating patterns are broad to very narrow. To compensate for contrast sensitivity declines, the text and background on Web sites should be of high contrast. Critical text information will be easier to process if designers vary the size and boldness of the type and increase the foreground-background contrast.

Temporal Resolution

Temporal resolution refers to the tracking of changes in stimuli, and age-related declines are evident for this ability. Older adults have difficulty perceiving flashing stimuli in the range of 10 to 45 Hz (cycles per second). Therefore, the temporal frequency of a flashing light may need to be slower than 10 Hz for older adults and others who experience difficulty in perceiving distinct flashes instead of a continuous light. Consequently, Web site text boxes or graphics that flash may be problematic if the temporal frequency is too high.

Visual Acuity

Visual acuity—the ability to resolve details—also declines with age. To compensate for acuity problems, warning text should be presented in 12- to 14-point type as a minimal standard to increase performance. Smaller type sizes may be readable by older adults, but they may take longer to encode. Type compression (condensed type) may also be difficult to read.

Hearing

The presentation of auditory information via the Web may be a useful method to compensate for age-related declines in visual functioning. However, it is important to consider age-related auditory changes when implementing auditory display of information. Age differences in hearing acuity include loss of both absolute sensitivity and differential sensitivity. Older adults have the most difficulty with sounds of high frequency and may also have more difficulty detecting changes in pitch. Hearing problems are particularly relevant to speech recognition. Speech perception is relatively stable between ages 20 and 50, but by age 80, discrimination loss is about 25 percent. In terms of speech comprehension, however, older adults benefit more from contextual cues. Similarly, older adults have more difficulty when contextual cues are distorted or removed. Thus, older adults are most impaired under stressful listening conditions, such as distorted speech or interruptions. Although synthetic speech is demonstrably more difficult to understand than natural speech, it seems older adults can comprehend it as well as those under 50 (Smither, 1993). Evidence of this, however, is very limited.

Cognition

Studies of cognitive aging have revealed a great deal about the basic cognitive changes that accompany the normal aging process. Some abilities do decline, yet other abilities remain intact well into the seventh or eighth decade of life. Of course, there are substantial individual differences in both the rate and amount of decline. In general, aspects of memory (such as keeping a lot of information active in working memory), online reasoning ability, and aspects of attention, such as attending to more than one source of information, all show age-related declines. Abilities that tend to remain intact into old age include some aspects of memory (such as recalling well-learned information), verbal abilities such as vocabulary and reading, and some aspects of attention (such as focusing on a single source of information). Designers must recognize and accommodate those abilities that do decline while capitalizing on the abilities that remain intact. For recent reviews of age-related changes in cognition, see Craik and Salthouse (2000) and Park and Schwartz (2000).

Attention

Attention is a multifaceted construct that includes selecting information, as well as focusing, dividing, and maintaining attentional resources. Most relevant to Web site design is selective attention. Selective attention involves choosing from the environment the information that will receive further processing. It is the ability to select and process relevant information while rejecting irrelevant information. Older adults have greater difficulty selecting target information in a stimulus display (visual search) when the number of items to be searched increases (see Rogers, 2000, for a review of age-related differences in attention). Visual search may thus become more difficult when sites contain clutter or irrelevant information. Age differences have been reported for laboratory-based selective attention tasks along with the encouraging finding that older adults can benefit from cues to the relevant information. Thus, informational cues such as color or highlighting might prove especially helpful to older adults.

A related ability to visual search is the useful field of view (UFOV). The UFOV denotes the size of the visual field area from which an individual can briefly discern target information (Ball and Owsley, 1991). The UFOV declines dramatically with age. Consequently, the central placement of important information on a Web page is critical for older individuals, since they may be more likely to miss information presented on the periphery.

Memory

One of the primary cognitive declines observed in older adults involves working memory capacity, which is the ability to keep information active. For example, consider a task in which multiple steps must be performed to access a particular Web page. The older user may have difficulty maintaining all of the information active in working memory when many steps are involved in the process. Consequently, older users may get lost in the site.

Although the exact reasons for age-related declines in working memory capacity have not been established (for example, is the reduced capacity due to slower processing speeds of older adults or to an inability to inhibit irrelevant information?), age differences do exist. The designer's primary concern should be with the consequences of the decline. In particular, reduced working memory capacity means that there are limited cognitive resources available to store new information and to retrieve previously stored information.

Web Design Features to Avoid

There are more than 21 million Web sites on the World Wide Web (Netcraft, 2000). Unfortunately, many of these sites were not developed with the user in mind, regardless of whether the user is young or old. Web usability problems for existing sites are so prevalent that the design errors are pointed to as illustrations of what *not* to do when designing a Web site (Flanders and Willis, 1998).

A similar approach to learning from design errors is taken by Mead, et al., (2002) with a focus on older users. They reviewed sites that provide health information, presumably targeted to adults of all ages. Figure 5.2 (see also Plate 6) represents an amalgamation of the design issues they found that would make such sites difficult for an older adult user. Their mock site was designed to illustrate interface elements commonly found on Web sites that should be accessible to older adults but that may pose problems for older users. Many existing Web sites have characteristics that would make them virtually unusable by average older adults and many younger adults as well.

Look at these particular features in Figure 5.2. The small, serif font would make the page difficult to read considering age-related reductions in visual acuity. The patterned background reduces text contrast and makes distinguishing information arduous. The scattered, highly salient advertisements and large amount of information presented may interfere with visual search efficiency. The menus provide link names but no description of what information to expect when the link is followed.

Figure 5.3 (see also Plate 7) shows the improved version of Figure 5.2, taking into consideration the specific needs and requirements of older adults.

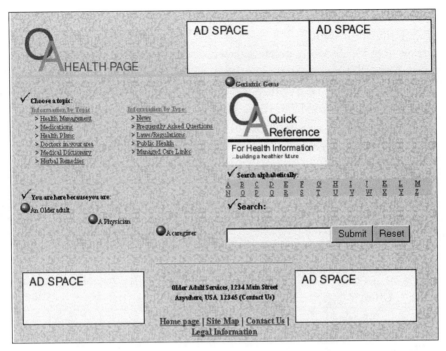

Figure 5.2: *Sample home page of a fictitious health Web site* (see also Plate 6)
(Source: Mead, Lamson, and Rogers, 2002)

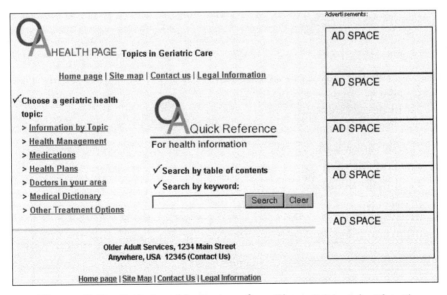

Figure 5.3: *Redesigned home page from Figure 5.2* (see also Plate 7)
(Source: Mead, Lamson, and Rogers, 2002)

As Mead, et al., (2002) point out, even the improved version of the site would require usability testing to ensure that older adults would not have specific, unforeseeable difficulties in using the site to accomplish their goals.

Figure 5.2 was created explicitly to illustrate Web design features that would likely cause user difficulties for older adults. Figure 5.3 illustrates how the fictitious site could be improved based on an understanding of the characteristics of the user population. In actuality, many Web sites have both good features and bad features that affect usability for older adults. For example, the Association for Senior Citizens home page *(http://www.asc50plus. org/)* is presented in Figure 5.4 (see also Plate 8). This page provides high contrast for the main text and uses a font that is clear and readable. However, the links on the left would be very difficult to see—given the nature of color vision changes that accompany aging—because users are required to

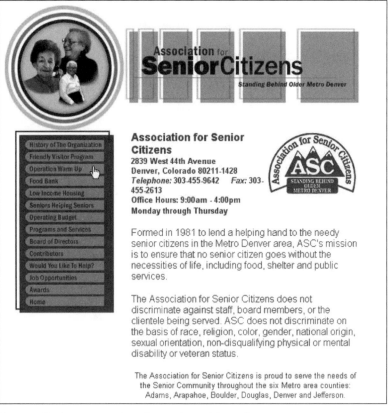

Figure 5.4: *Association for Senior Citizens home page* (see also Plate 8)
(Reprinted with permission.)

differentiate the colors of blue text on a blue background. Another potential design issue on this site concerns whether users would be familiar with such links as "Operation Warm Up." The answer to this question could be resolved through user testing.

Another site that would likely be of interest to older adults but potentially difficult to use is shown in Figure 5.5. This is the home page of the International Osteoporosis Foundation *(http://www.osteofound.org)*. The links on the top of the page are of high contrast (white on a blue background), but the links on the left are of relatively low contrast (black on a blue background) and would be difficult to see by many older individuals. Moreover, the point size of type used for these links is quite small.

Figure 5.5: *International Osteoporosis Foundation home page*
(Reprinted with permission.)

The sites in Figures 5.4 and 5.5 both require scrolling (as do most sites). A page up/page down option visible at all times might assist users who have difficulty manipulating a mouse for scrolling. An indication that more information was available (but not visible) would be especially helpful for the site in Figure 5.5, where all of the available options are not shown on the first screen. Note that the immediate visibility of all of the options is a positive design feature in Figure 5.4.

The issues of low contrast and difficult color discrimination are also illustrated in the home page of the Justice Store *(http://www.thejusticestore. com)* in Figure 5.6 (see also Plate 9). Notice that the background illustration reduces the contrast of the text and is also distracting, requiring the user to selectively attend to the relevant information and ignore the irrelevant information of the text in the background. This type of display would likely be especially problematic for older users. A positive aspect of this site is the well-marked links that are spaced sufficiently far apart to ease selection of the targeted link.

The benefits of removing distracting background illustrations are clear in Figure 5.7, a National Institutes of Health page that provides information about diabetes and periodontal disease *(http://www.nidcr.nih.gov/news/pubs/ diabetes/menu.htm)*. All of the text is presented with high contrast (blue on white or black on white), and all of the critical information (such as the links)

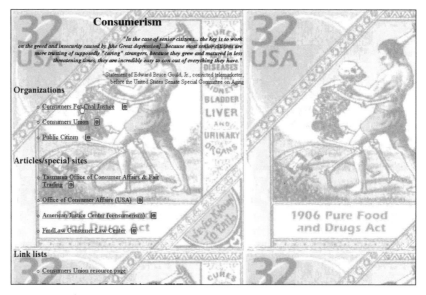

Figure 5.6: *Justice Store home page* (see also Plate 9)
(Reprinted with permission.)

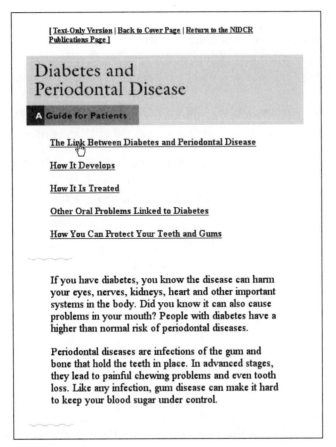

Figure 5.7: *National Institutes of Health page*
(Reprinted with permission.)

is centered on the page. There are no distracting blinking elements; the links are evenly and widely spaced; and the link names are long enough to be informative.

Design Guidelines

To maximize the usability of Web sites for older users, designers must capitalize and stay current on the existing knowledge base about age-related motor, perceptual, and cognitive changes. The preceding research provides the basis for the following design guidelines.

Age-related declines in movement control may be minimized with an adaptive interface. For example, older adults benefit from having a lower mouse movement ratio (Walker, et al., 1996), suggesting that adjusting the acceleration of the mouse would be an easy way to improve computer usability for older adults.

Other interface design solutions to compensate for age-related declines in movement control have been recommended by Worden, et al. (1997).

1. Area cursor—the cursor becomes a large square, which makes it easier to see and requires less movement precision. If the cursor covers two items or buttons, the default is the center of the square where a crosshair is presented.

2. Icon "stickiness"—the mouse-to-cursor gain (ratio of mouse movement to cursor movement) is dynamically adjusted when the cursor moves over an icon or button. Thus, as the mouse approaches the item, the gain ratio is lowered, enabling fine control and allowing the user to more easily stop the mouse on the icon or button.

3. Dynamic velocity-based gain adjustment—the stickiness of the icons is adjusted when the cursor is moving below a set speed. Thus, an icon or button will only slow the movement of the cursor if the cursor is moving slowly.

A combination of these variables yielded the best performance for older adults. An area cursor with sticky icons with adaptive gain control can improve older adults' performance up to 40 percent. An important by-product of attending to age-related issues is this interface can also improve young adults' performance up to 20 percent.

Limiting the need for mouse movements altogether may increase older adults' performance when browsing the Web. Mead, et al. (1997) discovered that while younger adults would scroll down the Web pages, looking for information, older adults would search for information one Web page at a time. This finding suggests that although a long Web page of information is acceptable design for younger adults, short Web pages, where less scrolling is required, would be a superior design for older adults and would ultimately lead to improvements in their performance.

Recommendations to accommodate the hearing loss experienced by older adults include control background noise, increase volume of important sounds, and incorporate supplementary visual cues (Charness and Bosman,

1990). In addition, high-frequency sounds (greater than 4,000 Hz) should be avoided and preference given to sounds with reverberation in the range of 1,000 Hz to 2,000 Hz.

Human factors guidelines for making speech more comprehensible to older listeners also exist: (1) Avoid the need for high-frequency detection and discrimination; (2) improve the discrimination of acoustic cues by maximizing their pitch, spectral, and location differences; (3) enhance signal-to-noise ratios through volume adjustment and by minimizing background noise and reverberation; and (4) foster accurate speech perception through the use of clear, reasonably paced, redundant, and context-rich messages (see Kline and Scialfa, 1997; Tun and Wingfield, 1997). These guidelines provide the basis for the initial development of messages to be transmitted to older individuals.

Specific guidelines for text presentation may be found in Echt (2002), but they can be summarized as follows.

- Use sans serif fonts like Arial or Helvetica.
- Strive for 14 point font size for body text and 18–24 point for headers. Provide a text sizing option on your page.
- Use boldface; avoid italics.
- Use upper and lower case; avoid using all capitals.
- Use left-justified text; avoid centered or full justification.
- Increase leading (the space between lines of text).
- Keep line lengths between 50 and 65 characters.
- Use headings and subheadings.
- Use negative contrast (black text on white ground).
- Use active white space.
- Place text on unpatterned backgrounds.
- Use consistent placement of page elements.
- Increase the size of peripheral elements.
- Separate the steps of a procedure using numbers or bullets.
- Use a minimum number of hypertext links in a single line of text.
- Avoid multicolumn format or frames.
- Avoid flashing or blinking text.

To improve visual search efficiency, designers should reduce the number of information sources per page and group advertisements in the periphery to facilitate searching for relevant information.

Given age-related changes in both visual search and UFOV, Kline and Scialfa (1997) recommend that the object of focus should be presented with consideration to the primary fixation point, be made prominent by reducing competing stimulus clutter, and be of high contrast. Although these recommendations were not made specifically for Web sites, they are directly applicable to the design of Web sites. In addition, the standardization of sites to include specific colors, formats, and text styles may be especially critical for older adults when they are searching for information. A consistent presentation format may ease their visual search.

Age-related reductions in processing speed and sensitivity to high temporal frequencies (very rapid flashing or movement), paired with minimal Web experience may prevent older users from taking full advantage of some new interface technologies. Rapidly presented visual feedback, such as controls that highlight when the cursor passes over them (rollover displays) and time-limited splash screens (Web pages that contain logos or warnings but no content), may come and go too quickly to allow older adults (and many younger adults) to respond appropriately. Use displays that stay on the screen for several seconds.

A challenging goal of Web site designers is to aid user decision making by providing intuitive menu and link names and informative descriptions of the information the user will access by following each link. Brief descriptions of the contents of each destination page can help, albeit at the cost of increased screen clutter. Informative link names are ideal, and their meaningfulness to older users can be determined during usability testing.

Consistent placement of interface elements (for example, placing the navigation bar at the top or on the left side of every page) can help users learn to recognize them, allowing maximum benefit from experience using the site. Consistency is only one of the usability guidelines developed by experts such as Nielsen (1997a) and Shneiderman (1997) that are applicable to Web site design and will benefit both older and younger users.

One way to reduce age-related differences in working memory is to provide environmental support (see Craik and Jennings, 1992). According to this research, older adults benefit from environments or contexts that provide meaningful cues for remembering information. For example, age-related differences in memory are typically smallest for recognition tests and greatest for free-recall tests. Based on the environmental support framework, recognition tests provide a meaningful context that supports the memory process. From a design standpoint, environmental support might be provided by ensuring that critical information is prominently located on the main page, rather than on separate pages.

Indexes and tables of contents may reduce the impact of age-related changes in working memory. Users need not learn topic lists or locations. Properly labeled and readily accessible links to topics within a Web site, or even within a page, remind users of what information is available and where it is located. Users should not have to think about where they are in a well-designed site.

Usability Testing with Older Adults

In the Human Computer Interaction literature, there is a name for the tendency of designers to believe that they are representative of the user population and will be able to rectify any design problems themselves: the "Egocentric Intuition Fallacy" (Landauer, 1997). Research shows that it is actually very difficult to foresee the usability problems that individuals will have when attempting to interact with a system. The idea that user input is not needed until after the initial design phase is incorrect (and inefficient) for users of all ages, but perhaps it is even more critical when the designers are aged 20 to 40 and the users are aged 60 to 80. These designers cannot intuitively imagine the goals of these users, their motivations for accessing a site, their previous Web experience (or lack thereof), or the age-related physical and cognitive changes that may affect their performance.

Interviewing users to gauge their preferences is a good starting point in Web site design, but designers should keep in mind that what users say they want is not necessarily what will enable them to best use the system. Reported user preferences should always be empirically tested by observing the performance of users. To illustrate, Ellis and Kurniawan (2000) found that older adults expressed a preference for Web sites with fewer but longer pages. Such a design would require them to scroll down Web pages to obtain the information they were seeking. Although the older adults claimed that they preferred this feature, they found it difficult to scroll down a Web page, and they did not realize that there was more information off-screen (see also Mead, et al., 1997). Testing found that it was easier for them to click a link than to scroll down a page in terms of the motor skill required. Thus, although older adults verbally expressed the notion that longer pages would suit them better, their performance was enhanced by shorter pages that would decrease scrolling. It is imperative that designers recognize that, when considering design issues for any user population, performance may carry more weight than preference.

Formative evaluation (during the design phase) and summative evaluation (at the prototype stage) are both critically important for ensuring that the final product, in this case the Web site, is usable and useful for its intended target population (Landauer, 1997).

To illustrate this concept of participatory design, consider the development of the Michigan Aging Services System (accessible at *http://MASS.iog. wayne.edu*) (Ellis, et al., 1998). Ellis, et al. started the development process by building bridges of communication between the intended users of the site and the design team. Then they developed a user model to represent the users' capabilities and limitations and held brainstorming sessions with prospective user groups to map the possibilities for their system. Based on these initial steps designers developed a prototype that they used to conduct usability testing via questionnaires, discussions, and online feedback from users. Based on this research, the site developers were able to improve the design of the prototype. Because their site is operational, they are able to continue gathering input from users to make design improvements. This development approach provides an excellent example of how formative and summative usability testing contribute to the design of usable sites.

The basic guidelines for designing any usable Web site are early and continual focus on users, empirical measurement and user testing, iterative design, and integrated design that incorporates all aspects of usability (Gould, et al., 1997). Our goal in this chapter has been to provide insight into the most relevant characteristics of the older adult user group and to provide guidance for designers who want to accommodate this target audience.

6

Designing for Web Genres

Designers of Web sites often draw on well-established brick and mortar practices to decide what should initially constitute the content, expression, and form of their sites. They do so, whether intentionally or not, in an attempt to accommodate the expectations people bring from their physical-world experience—experience that can be categorized into "genres." For example, people visiting news Web sites would expect the pages of that site to incorporate many of the structural and layout features of newspapers. Tourism sites might resemble travel brochures. Shopping sites might incorporate many retail features, such as aisles and shopping carts. The home page of an entertainment site might be designed to look like a colorful poster for a game or a show, or whatever the particular entertainment topic is. The benefit of this approach to design is usability. Visitors immediately feel comfortable in the site's environment.

News, shopping, entertainment, and information sites are each a genre that can be identified and distinguished from other categories by the content each provides to its intended audience. But designers should be aware that, perhaps more importantly, in addition to content, each genre has its unique, culturally established expression and form that define and distinguish the genre. For users to immediately feel comfortable with the content and to find

109

the site easy to use, they need to recognize the styles and formats to which they are accustomed in the physical world. Then visitors can gradually assimilate new Web features unique to the given genre.

Each of these genres has several subgenres, as shown in Table 6.1. Some supply information, some sell products, and others exist strictly for entertainment. Designers should consider genre and subgenre issues of content, expression, and form, and the "border" issues associated with each, before starting to make site or page design decisions (Brown and Duguid, 1994).

While a visitor can recognize a genre by its content, recognition via content alone would take longer than recognition by expression or form. Expression and form are recognized at the sensory-processing level. For example, text density or flashing elements can be detected by visual noticing—simply looking, not reading. Textual content, on the other hand, requires processing at a deeper, semantic level. Processing meaning takes longer than just looking. Therefore, visitors gauge what kind of site they are visiting by its expression and form. Then they use content to reinforce or correct their initial judgment. Accordingly, as we will see later in this chapter, it takes longer to verify a site's genre if its content, expression, and form are incongruent. In other words, a site is most user-centric, or usable, when content, expression, and form are compatible.

Table 6.1: *Web Genres and Subgenres*

Genres	News	Shopping	Information	Entertainment
Subgenres	Broadcast TV Newspaper Magazine	I. Product Sites II. Service Sites a. Travel b. Consulting c. Real Estate	Tourism Education Career Web Site Development Hobby Government City/Local Medical Business Intranet	Online Video Games Casino Games Sweepstakes Fan/ Celebrities Movie Music

Genre Content

Content gives a genre its uniqueness. The content of a news site is some kind of current or archived news. Because most Web visitors who browse news sites are aware of current events, they would immediately recognize a site as a news site simply by reading a current event headline. Thus, content designers should ensure that the home page of a news site provides headlines of the major current stories on topics important to the audience. International news, national news, financial news, sports, breaking stories: Any one of these content headlines tells visitors that the site is a news site. Notice the headline format for news of the day on the *USA Today* page in Figure 6.1. The headlines of featured stories are in the middle and top of the page in large text that serves as links to the full stories.

Information genre content covers topics reflecting the theme of the site. Depending on the nature of the information, content is presented as stories,

Figure 6.1: *Headline format on* USA Today *page*
(© 2001 *USA Today.* Reprinted with permission.)

news releases, essays, editorials, listings, data, statistics, and so forth. When people see such topical content, they can conclude that the site belongs to the information genre. For example, a university site would have content on topics such as curriculum, course descriptions, students, libraries, and faculty profiles. Figure 6.2 is the University of Michigan home page, showing clearly its topical content. By reading the text, without even viewing the word *university,* a visitor would immediately conclude that this is an information site in the academic institution subgenre.

The content of an entertainment site depends on the kind of entertainment the site carries. For example, a card-playing game site, such as the Leads

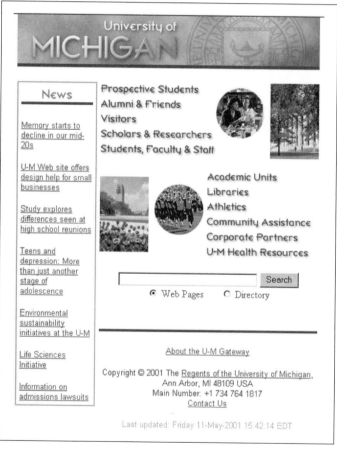

Figure 6.2: *University of Michigan home page*
(Reprinted with permission.)

University Union Bridge Club *(http://www.leeds.ac.uk/union/sports/bridge/)*, shown in Figure 6.3 (see also Plate 10), might have playing cards on its home page. Because the cards are placed on the top of the page, a visitor notices them immediately and can infer without further inspection that this is a site related to card games. Interspersed with the pictures are words like *Bridge.* So pictures and words make it clear that the site deals with the card game of bridge. See Figure 6.4 (see also Plate 11) for another example of how entertainment-related pictures and words define the content of an entertainment site.

The most visible content of the shopping genre, which distinguishes it from other genres, is the product or service that the site is selling. Included in the content is information on goods and services delivered online, as well as goods and services delivered in a brick and mortar operation. In addition, product and service information, such as reviews, testimonials, and pricing, is a predominant feature of the shopping genre content. Related to product and service purchasing are instruments required for transactions, such as credit card and account information. Figure 6.5 shows an example of a pricing information page for a perfume site, content that leaves no question in the visitor's mind that this is a shopping site.

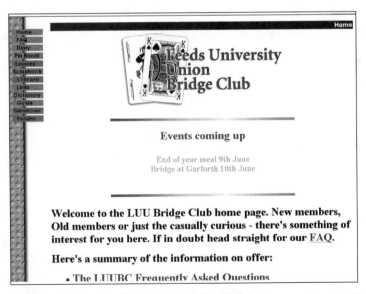

Figure 6.3: *Leeds University Union Bridge Club home page* (see also Plate 10)
(Reprinted with permission.)

Figure 6.4: *Gambling.com home page* (see also Plate 11)
(Reprinted with permission.)

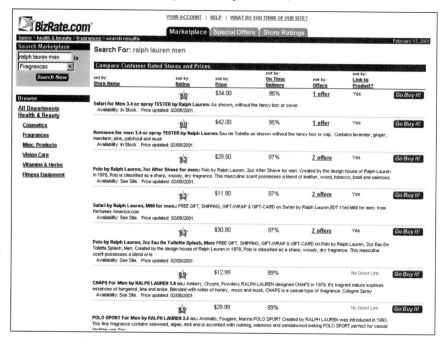

Figure 6.5: *Pricing information for a perfume site*
(Reprinted with permission.)

Genre Expression

The expression of a genre is the way content providers communicate with their target audience. Content may be "expressed" via text, graphics, sound, voice, animation, or other modes. In thinking of a specific genre, one of the first properties to come to mind is the style of expression. How is the content being expressed? Is the information expressed through pictures or by text? If pictures are the means of expression, is the depiction one of stylized images, abstract drawings, or photographs?

How a person expresses his or her ideas in communication venues such as lectures or conversations defines that individual's "communicating character." A speaker's face, gestures, and voice intonation represent some of the external behavior that the audience assimilates as part of the expressive component of the speaker's message. The expression embodied in the person's external behavior, not just the spoken words, is what creates a unique identity.

The same is true of Web genres. What distinguishes one genre from another is the combination of elements that define their expressions. Designers should pay attention to these elements to put together the most usable Web site for the intended genre. For example, designers of news Web sites should be aware that the expressive essence of a news page is the textual presentation. Attention would therefore have to be given to the details of what makes a good textual presentation. Supporting the text are informative photographs. Figures 6.6 and 6.7 are examples of the news genre showing the relative predominance of text and photographic pictures. Figure 6.6 is an example of the newspaper subgenre, and Figure 6.7 is an example of the broadcast news subgenre.

Now, consider the e-shopping genre. This genre has little text and is characterized by stylized pictures, bright colors, and iconic graphics as types of expression. Product sites often show objects such as shopping carts. Also, a permanent feature of a shopping site is the transaction page with its fill-in forms and purchase or submit buttons. Based on such features, visitors would immediately recognize the home page of a shopping site and would not confuse it with a news site. For contrast with news sites, look at the stylized pictures and iconic graphics of the products and services shopping subgenres in Figures 6.8 (see also Plate 12) and 6.9 (see also Plate 13).

Likewise, information and entertainment genres and subgenres have their own unique modes of expression. Information genre sites, for example, tend to use images and words in their links that hint at the kind of information

Figure 6.6: *Newspaper subgenre*
(©2001 *USA Today*. Reprinted with permission.)

Figure 6.7: *Broadcast news subgenre*
(Reprinted with permission.)

Figure 6.8: *E-shopping products subgenre* (see also Plate 12)
(© 2001 Lands' End, Inc. Used with permission.)

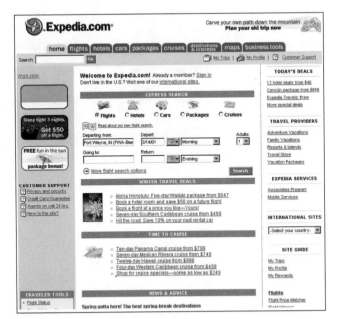

Figure 6.9: *E-shopping services subgenre* (see also Plate 13)
(Reprinted with permission.)

being conveyed. Their links tend to be topical. For example, some information genre sites such as education sites tend to be highly textual, with leading words that are used as links to the detailed content. Also, when information genre sites use photographs, they tend to be about a topic that is also presented textually. Photos in news genre sites usually depict some aspect of a current story and are not thematic or topical. For example, photographs in university sites would show campus buildings, classrooms, labs, or education landmarks. Each of these is a lead to the topic under consideration. Museum sites would have images of artwork.

Designers should make sure that domain words and images are present as genre expressions on the links of the home page for information sites. Examples of domain expressions in information sites are the education and medical subgenres in Figures 6.10 and 6.11.

Entertainment sites are expressed by their focus on stylized, bright, and colorful images that frequently use animation and flashing to suggest "fun activity." The home page of the gambling site in Figure 6.4 contained more

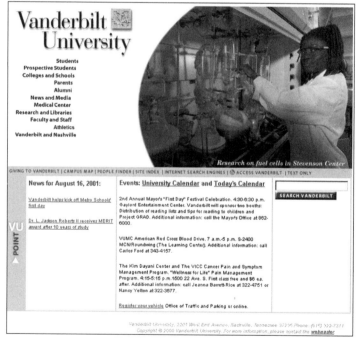

Figure 6.10: *Education subgenre*
(© 2001 Vanderbilt University.)

Figure 6.11: *Medical subgenre*
(University of California–San Francisco Comprehensive Cancer Center [*http://cc.ucsf.edu*].)

than 30 flashing or changing components. Later, you will learn that the use of flashing items on a screen can overburden a user's information load and interfere with the focusing of attention. However, keep in mind that genre constraints supersede page context design attributes. While a count of 30 flashing items is excessive even for an entertainment site, a large amount of animation and flashing may be important to allow visitors to "feel" the entertainment genre. A designer might choose to violate some human factors guidelines to create a stronger genre identity.

Genre Form

Genre form means the way the elements of the genre's site are arranged. How information on a site's page is organized is often a clue to the identity of the site. Certain structures or element arrangements tend to be prevalent on the majority of the sites of a given genre. These act as signature identifications for that genre. For example, in a news site, the placement of the featured story at the top and in the center of the page, with links to other current stories in a column on the right of the page, is a signature for that genre. The *USA Today* page in Figure 6.1 is an example of this prevalent form feature. To view a similar layout in the broadcast news subgenre, see the CNN.com home page in Figure 7.3 of Chapter 7.

Another form characteristic for news sites is the length of a text line. Line length is based on whether the text is meant to be read or scanned. Notice that text excerpts to be scanned, under headlines, are in a column format with lines of no more than 35 characters. For full length, an in-depth article is most frequently in full-length lines of up to over a hundred characters.

In a shopping site, the arrangement—or form—often mimics the layout of a store, or the way shoppers traditionally shop for the products offline. Tabs may represent "aisles," for instance. More recently, as designers of shopping sites have studied the habits of e-shoppers, layouts on some sites are shifting to accommodate the unique characteristics of online shoppers. One change is to feature special products or information goods in the center of the page.

It is important for designers to understand that genre form—more than content or expression—is likely to change as information about user habits increases. As a result, the original design should facilitate the easy rearrangement of elements on a site. For example, the products featured on the home page of a shopping site are likely to change as more is learned about the audience's purchasing habits. For the entertainment genre, an arcade games site would change the collection of games it displays on its home page in response to the frequency of games played over a period of time. On information genre sites, topics featured and the order in which they are listed on the home page can change as it is determined which particular topics are accessed most frequently over a period of time. This brings us to the concept of the evolving genre.

Genre Evolution

There is evidence that as a site of a given genre matures, it gets transformed from one that has many borrowed features of its real-world equivalent to a site that gradually incorporates its own unique features. As a result, it evolves its own genre identity, which becomes well recognized by its target audience (Eriksen and Ihlstrom, 2000). What is important is that it continues to have its own unique genre identity. Table 6.2 gives a sample list of characteristics that include both physical-world genre characteristics as well as evolved Web-specific ones.

Table 6.2: *Sample of Genre Characteristics*

		Characteristics		
		Content	**Expression**	**Form**
Genres	**News**	Traditional news programming and newspaper categories including: Current news International news National news Sports news Financial Breaking stories Archived stories Multimedia enhancements (video or audio clips)	Highly textual information Textual links Photographic images Conservative colors—navy blue, whites, gray, pages are dense, little white space Time and date determine importance, older stories toward bottom of the page	Feature story in top center Maximized for easy reading, black text on white Long pages Sites are medium to large (# of pages.) Necessary to scroll Grid with regular columns
	Shopping	Information and product goods Product information Multimedia content Transaction pages Customer service information Advertisements Categories model traditional shopping environment	Iconic images Not textual Unified design (branding prominent) Bright colors, pastels Model welcoming quality of traditional shopping environments More white space	Select goods featured in center of the page Maximized for easy browsing Short pages Sites are full range, small to very large (# of pages) Limited scrolling required
	Information	Tips or articles Tutorials Stories Releases Data Statistics	Highly textual information Textual links Photographic images Dense pages Little white space	Maximized for easy reading, black text on white background. Long pages Sites are full range, small to very large (# of pages) Necessary to scroll

(continued)

Table 6.2:   *Sample of Genre Characteristics* (*cont.*)

		Characteristics		
		Content	**Expression**	**Form**
Genres	**Entertainment**	Large multimedia files Graphic images Transaction pages Advertisements Limited HTML text	Iconic and photographic images Not textual Bright colors, more design focused Animations Sales pitch language	Main "feature" centered and highlighted Short pages Sites are full range, small to very large (# of pages) Limited scrolling required Banner advertisements prominent

Such an evolution has occurred on many news sites in the location of the featured story. Newspapers place the lead story on the right side at the top of the first page. At first, news Web sites copied this practice, but the size of a computer screen and the fixed position from which a seated user views displayed information made it necessary to change that. It became clear that to draw the reader's first attention to the featured story, the headline had to appear in the center at the top of the display. Today, most news sites have the featured stories centered at the top of the home page, presented as large, text headlines or thematic title links to the full story.

A number of other evolutionary forces are at work. Technologies that are unique to the Web have caused genre sites to take on characteristics that are not necessarily in the original physical equivalents. Examples include the availability of Web-specific features such as scrolling or hypertext capabilities such as linking, which do not exist in brick and mortar practices. Another spur to genre evolution are designers who want to exercise their creativity by using multimedia presentation technologies in ways not applicable to the real world. For example, it is possible to use voice clips in stories on news sites but not in printed newspapers. Also, Web developers often borrow features from other World Wide Web innovations, which takes Web sites further away from their original models.

Even as genre sites evolve, they continue to possess genre constraints. It is important for designers to rely on these constraints to distinguish genres in the eyes of their target audiences.

Genre Mixing

Web genres differ sufficiently in content, expression, and form that the effort it takes to recognize them and distinguish between them is relatively small. As mentioned earlier, two genre styles that we can easily distinguish from one another are online news and e-shopping. Both have special properties borrowed from their physical-world equivalents that permit their visitors to identify them.

A number of studies have investigated the usability of Web page designs (Borges, et al., 1998; Grose, et al., 1998; Vora, 1998; Gehrke and Turban, 1999), and the Web genre that has most often been the critical focus of usability studies and guideline recommendations is the shopping genre (Weise, 2000; Hurst, 2000; Nielsen and Tahir, 2001). Nielsen and Tahir propose 222 usability guidelines for designing a shopping site, including some based on real-world equivalents.

Barber and Badre (1998) found that cultural design attributes, which are those associated with the environment and the user, supersede genre attributes in existing Web sites. For example, if the culture prefers textual representations to pictorial ones—such as is generally true of the Arabic culture—but the genre usually expresses its content pictorially—such as is generally true of the tourism subgenre—a tourism site developed for an Arabic target audience is designed, whether intentionally or not, to be predominantly textual. This study by Barber and Badre suggests that, in the design of real Web sites, general cultural practices often take precedence over the practices specific to a given genre.

The chances are that designers veer from a given genre's practices more often because they are copying a design they liked or because they are innovating. Would site usability improve if designers relied on widely accepted cultural expressions and forms associated with one genre to design the properties of a site of another genre?

Badre and Laskowski (2001) studied this and related questions. How strongly should designers adhere to the culturally established attributes and practices of the real world when designing for the Web? Can designers successfully pick and choose among genre expressions and forms as they construct their Web sites? Up to the time of this study, these questions had not been formally explored.

For their study, Badre and Laskowski used news and shopping sites to investigate the effects of expression and form borrowing. They constructed news and shopping test sites based on an analysis of the expressions and forms of two popular news and shopping commercial sites. They tested four conditions that included news in a news format (Figure 6.12), news in a shopping format (Figure 6.13; see also Plate 14), shopping in a shopping format (Figure 6.14; see also Plate 15), and shopping in a news format (Figure 6.15).

They compared users' performances and preferences for the four site versions. For performance, they measured the time to complete a task, such as finding on a news site the number of casualties in a Pakistani plane crash. To determine preference, users were asked a set of preference and satisfaction

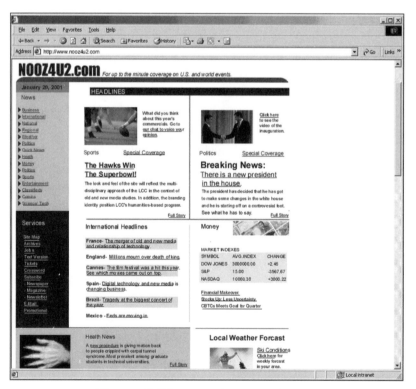

Figure 6.12: *News in a news format*
(Design by Sarah Craighill.)

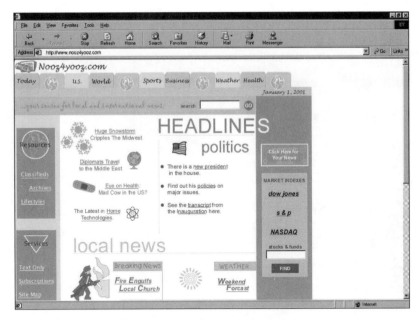

Figure 6.13: *News in a shopping format* (see also Plate 14)
(Design by Sarah Craighill.)

Figure 6.14: *Shopping in a shopping format* (see also Plate 15)
(Design by Sarah Craighill.)

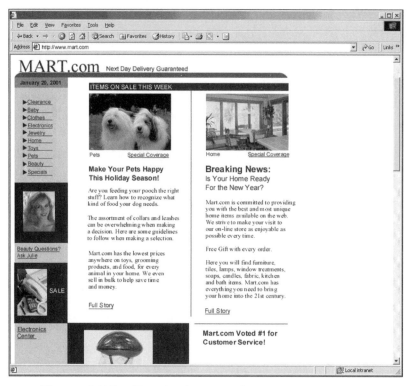

Figure 6.15: *Shopping in a news format* (see also Plate 16)
(Design by Sarah Craighill.)

questions in a Lickert scale format. The preference data showed that users liked the shopping format more than the news format, even for news content. Sixty-seven percent chose news in the shopping format as the most popular site.

The performance data revealed that those who saw only news content sites and preferred news as shopping performed better than those who saw only news content sites and preferred news as news. When it came to performance alone, participants took significantly less time and visited fewer pages to complete a task when the genres were not mixed.

It seems that if the goal is to give the visitor a pleasing experience, perhaps designers should consider mixing genres. If efficiency and speed are of primary importance, however, then mixing is a mistake. Keeping in mind that these results are preliminary, designers and researchers should continue to explore more fully the usability aspects of genre mixing.

7

The Web Site

To visitors, the Web site represents a context with its own constraints for taking actions and fulfilling goals. These constraints are different from the more general constraints of the genre context discussed in Chapter 6 and the more specific factors of the page context covered in Chapter 8. At the site level, there are seven key usability design issues that are particularly important for creating effective Web site interfaces.

- Conceptualizing the site with a visitor-centered focus
- Positioning the content
- Speeding up the response time
- Smoothing the navigation
- Assuring reasonable confidence in site security and privacy
- Making the site visible
- Maintaining quality

These seven constraints supersede any human factor guidelines at the page level with which they conflict.

Conceptualizing the Site with a Visitor-Centered Focus

Depending on the site's genre, which embodies its purpose, the site visitor can be an e-shopper, an information browser, a newsreader, a tourist, a student, a combination of these, or one of many other visitor types. Regardless of the visitor's specialized usage characteristics, which are considered at the genre level, visitor-centered design considerations must be incorporated at this time.

Keep the User in Focus. The designer should start with the question: What do I need to do to target the site's audience? The answer will require not only understanding the user, as discussed in Chapter 4, but also getting specific information on site visitors and what they want. Such information can be gathered effectively through the use of online questionnaires or forms without intruding on user privacy. Figure 7.1 is a sample registration form used by Barnes & Noble to collect information on customers interested in receiving a newsletter.

Focusing on the user also means designing for clients' hardware and software environments. If the user population is likely to use more than one browser, then designers should make sure that their designs work equally well for various desktop browsers as well as for mobile devices. The same attention should be paid to users' network connectivity. If, for example, we determine that most members of the target audience have modems with slow connection speeds, then designing for usability means giving a higher priority to reducing the file size of the graphics on the site.

Site Personalization. It is important to have in place noninvasive tools—those that do not violate privacy concerns—to continually gauge what visitors want. Visitors should have the option of giving the site permission to personalize its services. For example, an e-business site such as Amazon.com can collect information on its customers' habits and use it to send them "relevant" shopping information. In this case, Amazon.com is attempting to be visitor-adaptive by anticipating the needs of the user.

To make personalization totally visitor-centered, the e-business should first find out if the user is comfortable with being tracked to get personalized service. It is not enough to ask the user, "Can we send you information on related items?" or "Can we tailor the presentation of the site to the types of requests you've made in the past?" As part of asking users if they want

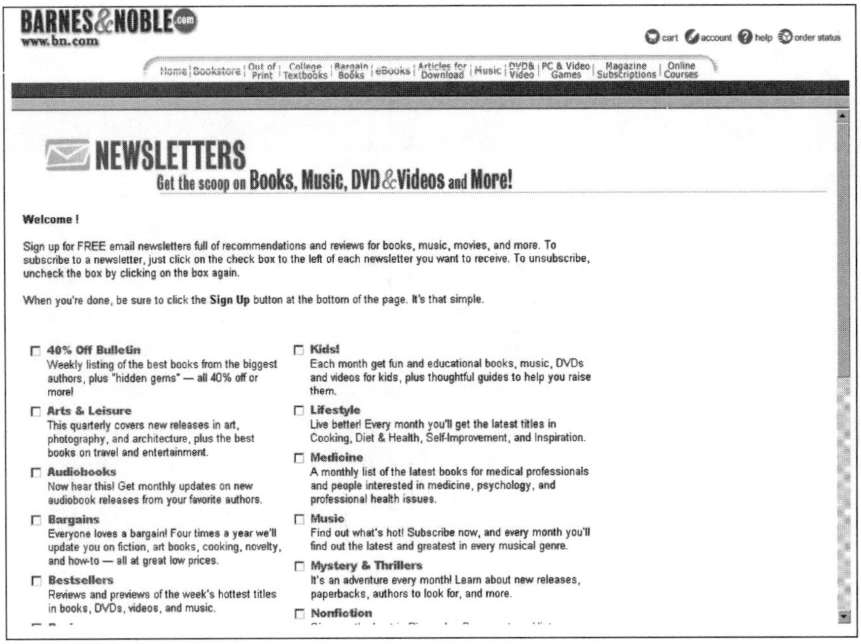

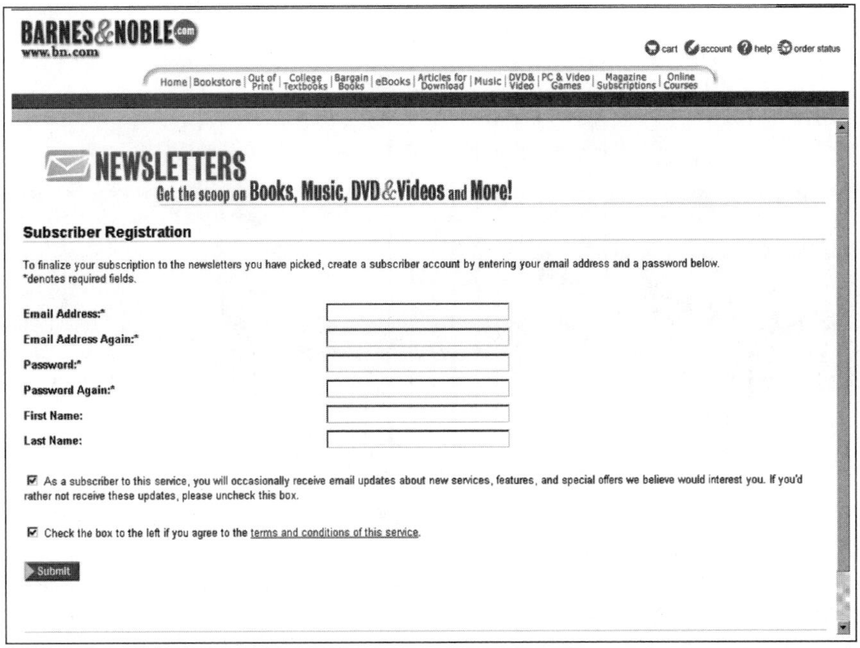

Figure 7.1: *Barnes & Noble registration form*
(© 2001 Barnes & Noble.com. Reprinted with permission.)

personalization, the e-business should explain that it involves constructing user profiles based on tracking the visitors' past site behaviors.

Positioning the Content

Content owners and authors are usually the domain experts. They should be members of the usability design team from the very start. Before the designer can create formats, layout, and pages, the content needs to be specified.

Specifying the Goals. Defining a site's content starts with specifying goals. Making sure that the users' functional goals are met in the site design is paramount. The site's goals and functionality should be clearly marked and visible on the site's home page and on the most likely pages from which the site may be visited. This information can be effectively provided by using buttons or tabs with keywords denoting the primary site functions. As we can see in Figure 7.2, the CNNfn Web pages represent well the subsite's goals as keywords, such as *Deals & Debuts, Retirement, Markets, World Business,* and *News,* on tabs.

Specifying the Tasks. Task analysis to decide what tasks follow from the identified goals is the next step in the process of creating site content. Tasks can range from the general, such as "finding information," to the specific,

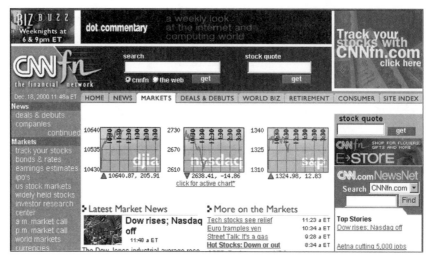

Figure 7.2: *CNNfn Web page*
(Reprinted with permission.)

such as "contact customer service." The designer should not only specify the tasks but also prioritize them. Priority can be determined on the basis of the most to the least important tasks or on the basis of a performance frequency scale. By prioritizing the tasks, the designer can decide on the order of functionality presentation on the site's home page and on the subsites. Furthermore, in defining tasks, the site's title should represent a major task and the site's topics should represent subtasks. Each topic should have a clearly stated goal. The subtasks should also be ordered according to which task is most likely to be performed. Defining the tasks and topics can be done by such methods as structured interviews and focus groups.

Organizing Site and Content. The goal here is not simply to organize information on a single page but to make the site's content coherent. A site that is structured in a coherent manner for the user supports the user's structural and functional mental models of the content. These models should be directly related to the content's goals and tasks discussed earlier. Often a site's content is organized to reflect the internal structure of an organization (Heller and Rivers, 1996) instead of user expectations of the site's topics and tasks.

To ascertain the users' mental models of information organization (after specifying the tasks and topics as described earlier), we can employ the card-sorting technique reported by Nielsen and Sano (1994). Each topic and task is written on a card. Then a sample of users is asked to group the cards according to their relatedness or semantic closeness. The result of this process is a collection of information chunks that designers can use to organize the site. Depending on the size of the site, each topic will have its own page in a task-logical order or, for large sites, its own subsite. Figure 7.2 shows an example of topics within a subsite represented as tabs. Figure 7.3 shows the pull-down menu of the CNN subsites. Titles, labels, and names should be carefully selected with the audience in mind when organizing site content and chunks of information, as well as site and subsite goals. The user should not have to look up the definition of site words to figure out what the site is about.

At this stage, designers begin the task of structuring the information and the tasks into a Web site. They use the resulting chunks of information to organize the site into coherent pages, subsites, and related sites. Subsites organize a body of information that can be used in performing tasks without having to visit other subsites. The subsites of a given Web site are related by a common user interface and a consistent look and feel.

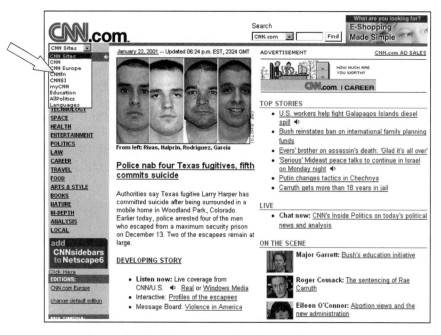

Figure 7.3: *The CNN subsites' pull-down menu*
(Reprinted with permission.)

For example, the CNNfn subsite shown in Figure 7.2 allows the visitor to get all financial news of the day without ever visiting the CNN news home page. But because people who are interested in news are often interested in more than one type of news, the overall structure of a site should permit visitors to get to the home page of any of the subsites from any site page by clicking on the subsites menu. The CNN site allows you to do subsite navigation from only some of the pages. The subsite pull-down menu is not available on every page. It is not even available on every subsite home page. Additionally, where the menu is available, it is not placed in a consistent location. Contrast the home pages of CNNSI.com, CNN.com, and CNN.com Europe. Figures 7.3, 7.4, and 7.5 show that the subsites' pull-down menu is on the left side for CNN.com, on the right side for CNN.com Europe, and not available at all for CNNSI.com.

Once the structure of a site or subsites is established, then the designer should focus on identifying and creating types of pages within a site such as home pages, a log-in page, transaction pages, and feedback pages. Chapter 8 gives a more complete treatment of page selection and design.

Figure 7.4: *The CNN.com Europe subsite pull-down menu*
(Reprinted with permission.)

Figure 7.5: *CNNSI.com page with no subsites pull-down menu*
(Reprinted with permission.)

Speeding Up the Response

System response time has always been an important factor for designers to consider in human computer interaction. From a usability perspective, optimal response time is dependent on several contextual factors, including the task to be performed, user experience level, user expectations, and other related functions to be performed by the user. There are several studies that relate response time to performance. Butler (1983) reports a significant effect of system response time on user action time. The longer the system response time, the longer the user action time. Barber and Lucas (1983) report that shorter response times yield superior performance. Another study, Tobmaugh, et al. (1985), showed that errors increased in a reading task where participants had to read and answer questions, with more errors for slower display rates than for faster display rates.

It is generally accepted that on the Web, people are more satisfied with rapid response times. User surveys (GVU, 1996; Hamilton, 1997) have reported that slow Web response time was the number one problem listed by users. Slow response times include slow downloading and slow Internet connections. Of course, system response times and speed of downloading are not entirely under the control of the designer. Quality of phone lines, server speed, and CPU power are among the factors that ultimately determine response time. However, designers can anticipate speed problems and take preventive measures. In addition, context and expectations make a difference in visitors' reaction to slow times. Sears, et al. (1997) found that visitors who accessed documents containing text and graphics were much less tolerant with the process than when the document contained text only.

To maintain "reasonable" site response times (within ten seconds for modems ranging between 28Kbps and 56Kbps), designers should attend to the following guidelines.

- Make sure there is feedback, indicating delay.
- Keep the total page content to not more than 60KB of text and graphics.
- Keep graphics less than 25KB.
- For five or more graphics per page, keep each graphic at 10KB or less (see Figure 7.5).
- Resort to the use of thumbnails measuring 1″ × 2″ (see Figure 7.6).
- Provide text-only options.

- Avoid the use of animation if at all possible.
- Avoid the use of multimedia and audio clips requiring the download of plug-ins.
- Use progressive rendering, allowing text to download before graphics.

Smoothing the Navigation

Web visitors navigate both on a single site and across sites. They navigate within a single site to find specific information or simply to explore. They navigate the World Wide Web to find a site relevant to their goals or to reach a site related to a currently visited site. In either scenario, the visitor starts with a mental model of a navigation map. In some cases, the map is very primitive and incomplete, consisting primarily of a search engine and some keywords. In other instances, because of experience, the user has in mind a quite well-developed and precise map, as in the case of someone looking for the current DOW numbers on the CNNfn home page.

Human Navigational Strategies. Research on site maps and navigational aids can be useful for designing Web navigational strategies. Let's consider what others have said about human navigational strategies. Wickens (1992) summarizes work by Thorndyke (1980) suggesting that human knowledge acquisition of navigational space progresses along three stages: landmark knowledge, route knowledge, and survey knowledge. To help us navigate, we start by using landmarks present in the environment to find our way and to remind us of how to navigate the same path again. Using distinctive visual clues is the critical attribute of this navigational strategy. In a Web space, titles, labels, link names, and icons can represent landmarks. Route knowledge enables navigators to connect landmarks into a distinctive path, helping them revisit a previously traveled route. Using visual history paths in a Web site can facilitate the acquisition of route knowledge for the visitor. With survey knowledge, navigators form a structural mental model of their navigational space. The inclusion and use of a Web site map would accelerate a visitor's survey knowledge of the site navigational space.

There are at least two different practical ways of presenting paths and site routes on a Web site: linear lists and actual schemata or site maps. Is one more effective than the other as a navigational aid? Bartram (1980) compared the two representations for travelers using the London bus system. In this case, people had to construct a path between two locations from either a list or a map presentation of the route system. The findings indicated that map users made decisions more rapidly than list users. On the other hand, when people were asked by Wetherell (1979) to learn a route from either of the two presentation formats and then actually navigate the route between two locations, the map users made more mistakes. In a Web navigational context, designers need to include both formats. For novices, who are trying to *construct* a path, it is likely that maps are more effective. For experienced people, who are trying to *remember* a path, route lists are probably more effective.

Well-Defined versus Ill-Defined Task Statements. One useful way of classifying navigational tasks is on the basis of the completeness of information that a person perceives as available to perform the task. The key word is "perceives." We call a task statement ill-defined to a user if the information necessary to perform the task successfully is perceived as incomplete by that person (Reitman, 1970; Badre, 1974). A well-defined task statement is one that, in the perception of the user, contains all the information required to perform the task successfully. In addition, one of the following two conditions is true: (1) the task statement explicitly says what is necessary for successful performance, or (2) the user can reconstruct the necessary elements for successful performance from memory when presented with the task statement. For example, consider the word-processing task of moving a block of text from one place to another. To a novice, the task statement is ill-defined because it does not explain the sequence of steps required to perform the task successfully. To the experienced user, the statement implies a sequence of actions, available for retrieval from memory, that when executed will permit a successful completion of the task. The task is well defined to the experienced user. It is ill defined to the novice. The task statement could be made well defined to the novice by making it explicit: "Place pointer at first word in block; press F8 to mark word; press F6 to extend; press F8 again."

More precisely, a task may be defined in terms of the triple $\{I,O,G\}$, where I stands for initial task state, O denotes the set of admissible operators, and G stands for the goal state. An ill-defined task, one likely to be encountered by a novice user, is a task with a statement that, in the perception of the user, is incomplete in at least one of three specifications: (1) a complete description of the initial state; (2) a complete description of goal-state properties; and (3) the set of operators or rules that permit transformation from initial to goal states. When a user is faced with a task where at least one of these three sets is not completely specified in the task statement—and at the same time, the statement does not trigger a set of memory reconstruction rules—then the task is considered ill defined. At that point the user must move to reformulate the task statement by either (a) completing the specification of the incomplete set or (b) identifying the set of rules required to reconstruct the necessary elements for successful task completion.

Navigating in Real-World Environments. When we navigate in real-world environments, we do so either to explore—often for the thrill of discovery—or because we are searching for a specific object. When we explore, we start with very little information about the task and the environment and with no specific object as the goal of our exploration. We are in an ill-defined task environment. As we navigate, we continuously redefine the environment to make it more familiar by keeping a record, even if a mental one, of our path. We like to be able to retrace our steps, visualize a context for our present position, and wonder what we will find if we go around the corner or over the next hill. When we find something that interests us—an antique store or a restaurant—we stop to investigate. As we explore and gain more information, our mental statement of the task environment becomes less ill defined. We are at the least gaining information about paths and landmarks that we can use to retrace our path to go back to where we started.

We also navigate in the real world to search for a specific object. We search in both ill- and well-defined task environments. Searching for a specific object in an ill-stated task environment is similar to exploring because we are learning to construct paths that we can retrace and to notice landmarks that we can use until we find the object of our search. Searching for specific objects in a well-defined environment requires recognizing relevant cues, remembering landmarks, and retracing previously traveled paths.

Navigating in Hyperspace. Navigating in Web hyperspace is not unlike navigating in the real world. Exploring on the Internet requires selecting an environment to explore, an environment that is defined conceptually rather than physically, as in the real world. For example, if we wish to meander into the area of "usability," we can use a search engine to visit that topic. By doing so, we can be said to be exploring the "usability environment" on the Internet. The constituents of the environment are ill defined, and the goal is simply to explore. On the other hand, if we wanted to know the meaning of the term *discount usability,* then we are specifying a target goal in an exploratory environment. Once we find the meaning of discount usability in a document on Jakob Nielsen's site (*http://www.useit.com/papers/web_discount_usability.html*), or we have specific instructions on where to go to find the definition, then we are performing an Internet search in a well-defined environment for a specific object.

Navigational Aids. If users visit a site and find themselves unable to navigate easily and efficiently, they are likely to exit the site and look further for one that meets their navigational goals. How can a designer make a site easier to navigate? We can use several navigational tools to make both exploration and a well-defined search more efficient.

- Links
- Buttons and controls
- Site maps, content lists, and indexes
- Landmarks and history trails
- Keywords and site search engine

Links

Well-designed links show visitors how to navigate most effectively the content of a Web site. Accordingly, what a link says and where it is located relative to other links in a site and on a page are paramount to its effectiveness as a navigation tool. Haine (1998) suggests that to be effective and unambiguous, a link's label should indicate both a unique reason for selecting the link and the expected results of selection. In their study comparing the results of the Edmunds and Disney sites, Spool, et al. (1997, URL) report that one reason visitors did better on the Edmunds site is the superior design of the links. The Edmunds links contained more text describing the results of selecting the links. The Disney links were cryptic and terse. Figure 7.6 shows the Edmunds site with its textual links.

It is important that same-site links be labeled in a way that indicates definite distinctions. Visitors should be able to figure out where links will lead from the labeling. Spool, et al. report that link labeling relates to the time and accuracy of selecting a link. They also report that the greater the number of links on a page, the less efficient the search. Larson and Czerwinski (1998) report in their study of experienced users that site organizations with few links in a broad structure were more effective than sites with deep link structures. On the other hand, as we increase the number of links, the efficiency of access to content decreases. Designers must ensure that link destinations are accurate. The link label, or words used in a link, should be the same as the title of the destination page. In addition, some experts have found that confusion can occur when links are used for destinations within the same

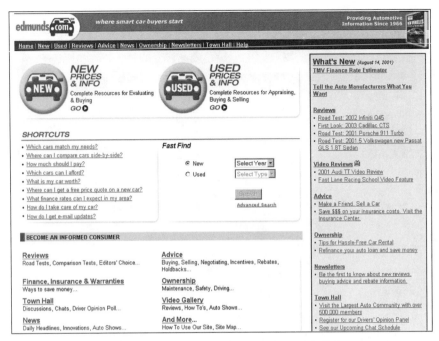

Figures 7.6: *Edmunds.com page with links*
(Reprinted with permission of Edmunds.com, Inc.)

long page (Spool, et al., 1997; Heath, 1998). My recommendation is that same-page links should be labeled as such or put in a category with a title such as "links on this page."

Buttons and Controls

Navigation buttons and controls, such as "back" and "forward," are included in the navigation bar on the browser, and sometimes they are available on the Web site. As designers, should we prefer that navigation controls be available only on the browser or also on Web pages? It is quite important to keep in mind that the browser interface remains constant irrespective of which Web site the visitor navigates. Because most visitors consistently use the same browser, we would expect visitors to become very familiar with the browser's controls and functionality and to use them frequently. This assumption is all the more likely because not all Web sites include navigational controls on their pages. See Figure 7.7 for the Netscape browser buttons.

Evidently, however, the results of this observation are mixed. Various studies (Tauscher and Greenberg, 1997; Cateledge and Pitkow, 1995) have reported that the browser back button is used frequently, in 30 to 40 percent

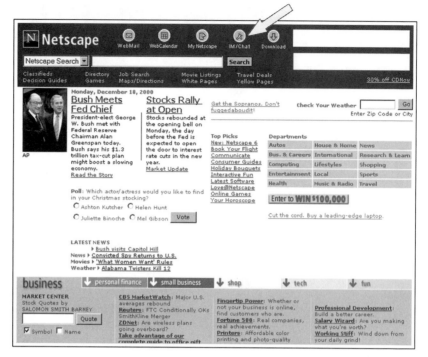

Figure 7.7: *Netscape browser buttons*
(© 2000 Netscape Communications Corporation. screen shot used with permission.)

of all navigation. On the other hand, the "forward" and "home" buttons are seldom used. This inconsistency in the use of browser controls suggests that visitors may be confused about the functionality on the browser and the functionality within the Web site. Therefore, it is preferable that navigation aids, particularly those related to content (Bachiochi, et al., 1997), be placed within the Web site.

Site Maps, Content Lists, and Indexes

Site maps, content lists, and indexes are content-specific navigational aids that are designed and placed intentionally within a Web site. As mentioned earlier, there is evidence that navigation efficiency improves when content navigation aids are placed consistently near the top of a page. In comparing the effectiveness of maps with content lists, McDonald and Stevenson (1998) determined that visitor performance using maps was superior to that of content lists. The use of either navigational aid yielded superior results over a hypertext condition with no navigation aids. See Figure 7.8 for an example of a site map.

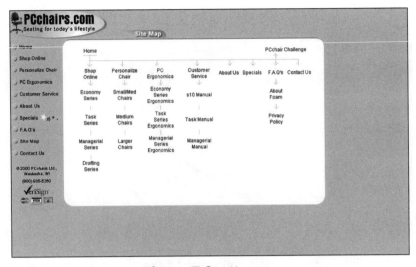

Figure 7.8: *Site map*
(© 2000 PCChairs, Ltd. Reprinted with permission.)

Furthermore, novice participants who were not knowledgeable in the domain relied more extensively on aids than did knowledgeable participants. It was clear, however, that both novice and knowledgeable participants benefited from the use of a map as a navigational aid. The implication for Web design is that designers should include a site map as a minimum navigational aid in their Web site. The general recommendation is that any site with 20 or more pages should have a site map link on every page where the visitor is likely to enter the site. Some investigators (Allison and Hammond, 1989) have suggested that maps are most useful when visitors are first attempting to gain familiarity with content. Finally, it is important to ensure that links in the site map are correctly named and lead to the intended destination.

Landmarks and History Trails

As discussed earlier, we use landmarks for navigating new environments. Accordingly, designers should supply functional placeholders to help the novice traverse the links and navigational buttons of a Web site. Site functions should be marked by unique icons and labels that visitors can remember easily when they return to a site. This means that landmarks or icons should have distinctive features, such as complex and unique shapes, and should be free standing (Vinson, 1999). Objects such as icons should be concrete, depicting real items (Ruddle, et al., 1997). Figure 7.9 (see also Plate 16) shows some uniquely shaped icons.

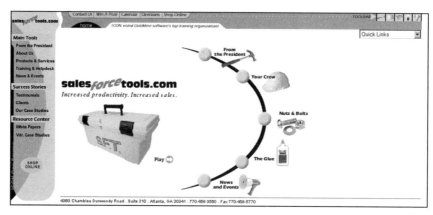

Figure 7.9: *Icons* (see also Plate 16)
(Reprinted with permission of salesforcetools.com.)

Like links, icons should be unique and distinctive relative to other icons and landmarks in the same space. When icons look the same, there is a higher likelihood that navigators will select the wrong one, usually the icon adjacent to the one they want. Darken and Banker (1998) report evidence supporting this navigation error, which they call the "parallel error." The design should also make available a history of pages visited within a site and between sites. Pages should be designed with distinctive and memorable titles. Distinctive titles will help users when surveying a history trail or a list of bookmarks.

Figure 7.10: *Web page with history trail*
(Reprinted with permission.)

Avoid the use of frames, which make bookmarking cumbersome. See Figure 7.10 for an example of a history trail.

Keywords and Site Search Engines

For large sites, 20 or more pages, designers should provide for keyword-based search engines. Spool, et al. (1997) report that when a large site did not have a search engine, visitors gave up on the site. Search engines are most likely to be used by visitors who know what they are looking for but are unfamiliar with the search environment. In such cases, visitors are searching for object(s) or information in an ill-defined environment because the statement of the search problem does not include a specific path or paths to retrace. Figure 7.11 shows the search engine on the upper left of the home page for the Graphic Visualization and Usability Center (GVU) site. Designers should make sure that search engines on large sites appear on the most frequent site-entry pages and that there are multiple search choices. For example, *www.metacrawler.com* in Figure 7.12 gives "any," "all," and "phrase" searches.

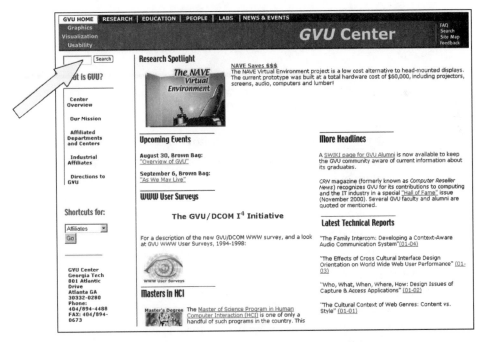

Figure 7.11: *GVU site with search engine*
(Reprinted with permission.)

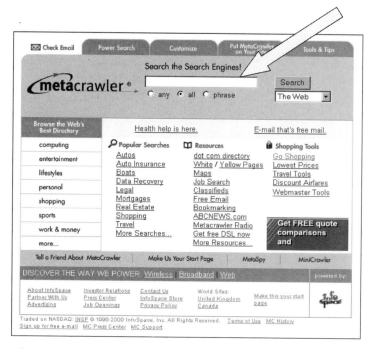

Figure 7.12: *Metacrawler site with multiple search choices*
(© 2001 Infospace, Inc. All rights reserved. Infospace and their designs and related marks
are the intellectual property of Infospace, Inc.)

Assuring Reasonable Confidence in the Site's Privacy and Security

Privacy. If site owners track site visitors and collect personal behavior data, then site design etiquette requires that visitors be told about this from the beginning. Site owners should tell potential visitors about the method that they use to collect site behavior data and how the collected information will be used. For example, if "cookies" or temporary ID numbers are used to personalize, the designer should inform the site visitor by providing a site personalization link prominently on the home page and any other frequently visited pages. (Cookies are files that are created and remain attached to a user's browser.) In some cases, full disclosure by site owners is not just a matter of etiquette but a question of legality. For example, the use of cookies is outlawed in many countries, as we discuss in Chapter 11.

Security. Security is a paramount concern for e-business Web site design. Visitors have more confidence in the security of professional-looking sites. Site performance also reveals the level of security (Bouch, et al., 2000). Security technologies, such as SSL, are crucial, and the availability of a link to a "security practices" page helps to reassure visitors. For transaction pages, designers should provide confirmation pages that are easily print-able and should remind users to print pages as receipts. Contact informa-tion including address, e-mail, and phone number should be prominently displayed. When designing the information needed to complete a trans-action, it is important not to ask for more information than is absolutely necessary.

Making the Site Visible

It is the responsibility of the Web site designer and, later, the Web manager to ensure that the site is visible to the target audience. Visibility is both a design and a marketing task. Marketing strategies include such steps as arranging reciprocal links, submitting pages to popular search engines, and joining a banner exchange program. Our main concern in this book, however, is with design strategies. Designers can enhance site visibility to a target audience in a number of ways, including the following.

- Make sure to use domain-related keywords.
- Do not hide the keywords in the background. Instead, place keywords prominently on top of the target page.
- Compose a site name that thematically reflects the content.
- For brick and mortar companies, use the business name as the domain name.
- In other cases, create a domain name that is easy for the target audi-ence to remember. For example, the name usabilityadvice.com is easy to recall by people looking for usability advice.
- Include a statement on the site's home page reminding visitors to bookmark the page.
- On the most frequently accessed pages of the site, have only internal links that send visitors to other key locations within the site. Links sending visitors away from the site should be placed only on secondary pages.
- Provide multiple languages for a multinational targeted audience.

Maintaining Quality

There is a strong correlation between the actual and the perceived quality of service for Internet commerce (Bouch, et al., 2000). That is, if quality is a design goal, the subjective perception of users will be one of quality. Here is a set of design points that Web owners and designers should consider when their goal is to enhance a site's quality.

- Make sure that contact information is prominently placed.
- Make the customer service button or link highly visible.
- Provide for personalization on the site.
- Ask users to submit feedback and provide user reviews of services and products.
- Make sure that content is frequently updated with date of revision visible.
- Indicate "new" for new information.
- Include a statement guaranteeing the quality of service.
- Base design and service on user testing and market research should be the basis of design and service.
- Make sure that site pages, particularly receipts and confirmations, are easy to print.
- Perform continual reviews to look for and eliminate dangling links.
- Identify and incorporate on a continuing basis relevant new technology.

8

The Web Page

As designers, we should think of a Web page as the entrance to a cove of treasures, be they products, services, or information. If the entrance is clean, appealing, easy to understand, and compatible with the visitor's interests, then the user will venture deeper into the cove. If visitors perceive the entrance to be confusing, irritating, useless, or inefficient, however, then the chances increase that they will leave and try another cove. First impressions are even more important on the World Wide Web than in the real world. In the real world, there are often reasons why customers may not leave a bad situation. For example, in a sales encounter, salespeople who give a bad first impression can recognize their mistake and modify their behavior, prompting a change in the customer's initial unfavorable response. A Web page cannot detect a visitor's negative reaction and then modify its presentation in response to that reaction.

If, after they enter the cove—the Web page—visitors have a pleasant and memorable experience and find the treasures they seek, then they will prolong their visit and return often. The look and feel of different types of Web pages should engender just such a pleasant and memorable experience. A positive experience can happen for many design-related reasons, ranging from good usability to attractive graphics. No matter what formula we use to produce a pleasant experience, a well-designed page is the goal. What are the ingredients of a well-designed page?

147

General Page Design Issues

A Web site can contain several kinds of pages, and associated with each kind is a set of design constraints. Depending on the purpose of a site, a site's pages may include a home page, content pages, and transaction pages. Many of the general usability design criteria that apply to software screen design work equally well for Web page design. Accordingly, I will first review some general, well-accepted design principles and then consider specific design criteria for each type of page.

General principles of good display design include the following areas of concern.

- Consistency
- Coherence
- Information placement
- Information coding
- Color
- Text clarity

Consistency

First, regardless of the type of page, consistency is paramount in Web design. Remember, the ultimate aim of usability design is to make the Web site as easy to use as possible. The need for consistency derives from the reality that people acquire skills through habit and repetition. It is much easier for a person to perform an act by using an already learned skill or behavior than to learn a new technique.

For designing Web pages, both information placement and interaction procedures should be consistent. For example, the tab or button for a site map should be in the same location throughout the site. On a news site, a feature story should always appear in the same Web space, usually front and center, where visitors will look first as a matter of habit. If the visitor clicks a navigation button called BACK on the second page to go back to the first page, it would be confusing if a button with the same purpose were labeled PREVIOUS in another context or on a different page. Also, navigation buttons, tabs, or links should always be placed in the same location throughout the site.

The principle of consistency in page design has its limitations. It may be superseded on occasion by constraints that derive from higher-level contexts (as discussed in Chapter 2). For example, if a Web site is to be designed for two different cultures, French and Arabic, then the constraints of script orientation may make it necessary to place the same information in two different locations—on the right and left sides of the page. Design constraints associated with user context (in this case, user cultural attributes) take precedence over the page design constraint of consistency of information placement.

Coherence

Both the amount of content, or density, and the placement of content on a page will affect coherence—that is, how easily visitors can manage the information and perform the relevant tasks. More density and less organization raise visitors' perception of clutter and lower performance. Density is a measure of the number of characters per screen area. Research has demonstrated that increasing screen density increases both the time it takes to search for information and the error rate (Thacker, 1987; Treisman, 1982; Dodson and Shields, 1978). Clutter occurs when the page content appears haphazard and lacks structure meaningful to the user. A cluttered page can make it difficult for visitors to find information or to navigate.

There are several techniques that designers can employ to achieve an uncluttered page. First, how users expect a page to be organized depends largely on the context and purpose of the page. If, for example, the page is part of a "report," then the expectation is that the target page may be preceded and followed by other pages. One would therefore look for an indication of how to move forward and backward between pages. If the context of a page is a small-sized document, such as a letter that fits on two pages, the user would look first for a scrolling instead of a paging tool.

Moreover, if the target page's purpose is to convey textual content, then the expected structure would include a title and paragraphs, probably organized like familiar print materials. This suggests that the title will be placed at the top middle or top left, and the text will be divided into sections. Furthermore, if the intention is that visitors to the page will scan the text as opposed to reading every word, then part of the expected organization will be the inclusion of keywords and subheads, as well as text lines that are no longer than 35 characters. If the page has different types of content, then an expected meaningful organization would require that each content type be grouped in a separate sector on the screen. By paying attention to expected organization as it relates to context and purpose, a designer using the same content can transform a "busy" page to one that is meaningful and manageable. Figures 8.1 and 8.2 are examples, respectively, of cluttered and well-organized pages.

Figure 8.1: *A cluttered page*

Figure 8.2: *A well-organized page*
(Reprinted with permission.)

A second technique for reducing clutter is to aggressively design to preserve "white," or unfilled, space. Designers should start with the premise that white space is to be preserved at all reasonable costs. The object of the design should be to start with white space and fill as little of it as is possible and still accomplish the page's purpose. Figure 8.3 is an example of a Web page that uses white space effectively.

By focusing on the preservation of white space, the designer reduces the amount of content that the user has to manage on a single page. This reduces the user's information load, the degree to which a person's processing capabilities and working memory are taxed by the volume and presentation of content on a page. A page with relatively little content, structured to contain a number of information chunks within working memory range, results in lower information load than a page with large amounts of content and more than seven chunks of information. A design that lowers the visitor's information load allows the user to both manage the page's content and perform the

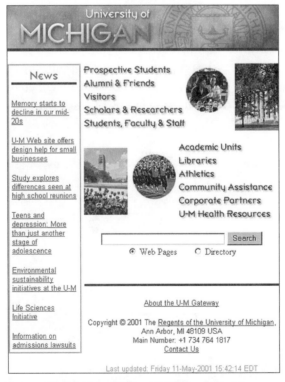

Figure 8.3: *Page with effective use of white space*
(Reprinted with permission.)

intended task more efficiently. The white space approach has the same final goal as Nielsen's (1994) minimalist design guideline, in which the designer minimizes the inclusion of nonrelevant or rarely used content.

A third technique for reducing clutter is the use of progressive disclosure to present the content of a page. This strategy introduces content gradually in the order in which the user needs it. Progressive disclosure is similar to the "training wheels" method introduced by Carroll and Carrithers (1984) for learning how to use a new system. They found that learning efficiency improves when the system is introduced in "layers." For Web page design, this approach means presenting only the content required to perform the task at hand and providing additional content only as it becomes relevant.

Placing content with an eye for closure is a fourth way to reduce clutter and achieve page coherence. In structuring content, we achieve closure of a visual presentation when all the elements are perceived as belonging to the same presentation. Figure 8.4 is an example of page content where closure is not achieved because of the seeming visual disconnect between the field labels and the fields, the buttons and the dialog box, and the title and the content. The visual disconnects are corrected in Figure 8.5, thus achieving a higher level of closure.

A fifth technique is the proper use of labeling. Labeling the contents of a page aids immensely in giving the impression of coherence. We should always provide labels to designate chunks of information, messages, data

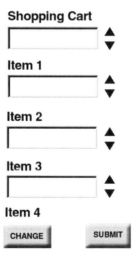

Figure 8.4: *A design that lacks closure*

Shopping Cart

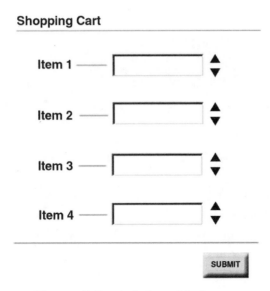

Figure 8.5: *A design with closure*

fields, and groups of data by a thematic word, phrase, title, or subtitle. Labels should be placed next to the information chunks, messages, or data group they describe. For example, if the information is in text form, the title goes on top at the center or to the left; if it is a data field, then the descriptive label should be to the left of the field; if the label is for a column, then it should be on top.

In constructing labels and titles, choose unambiguous words and shapes. A name or a label should convey no more than one salient meaning. Highlighting, shading, or reverse-imaging the label will distinguish it from the data group it designates and will make it easier to scan and recognize. The method of highlighting should be consistent and different from methods used to highlight other types of information, such as error messages and warnings. Avoid labels that might mislead users by suggesting that they must take some action. Example: Do not make a label look like a three-dimensional button, which might prompt the user to press or point/click it.

A sixth technique for organizing information to reduce clutter is to use various coding techniques to designate content and information chunks. We can organize information by spatial grouping, the use of color, highlighting, blinking rates, object size, shapes, and numbers, among others. Here are some guidelines for using Web page coding techniques.

- Use brightness intensity coding to indicate a contrast between adjacently placed items of information. Brightness should not be used with screens of low intensity. Only two levels of brightness should be used for rapid, error-free reaction time.

- Use location encoding to reduce the user's information search time. Icon and symbol encoding can convey a great deal of information in a small space. Use icons and symbols to economize on information transfer. Icons and symbols should resemble as much as possible the object or process they are intended to represent. Furthermore, use icons/symbols that are familiar to the user. The size of symbols or icons may be considered a coding technique. If so, use a maximum of three size levels with no less than 1.5 times in difference between any two consecutive sizes for ease and quickness of differentiation.

- Geometric shapes are effective coding techniques for certain types of tasks. Geometric-shape coding could have a high mnemonic value— that is, it is an aid to memory. For rapid, error-free reaction time, nine shapes are the recommended maximum.

- Length-of-line can be used as a coding technique, particularly when the absolute comparison of quantities is required. No more than three different lengths are recommended. For example, if we use line length to indicate difference in distance on a map display, we should not use more than three lines. Be aware that lines can clutter the display with many signals. We can use width-of-line as a coding technique in line graphs. Have no more than two sizes on a single screen. For example, if we use line width to represent different variables on a graph such as age range, do not use more than two lines. If there are more than two age ranges, use another coding technique, such as symbols or colors. For each successive line length or width, the longer or wider lines should be 1.5 times the shorter or narrower.

- To increase speed and accuracy of pointing to an object, increase the size of the object. Of course, this increase must not occur at the expense of obscuring other objects or decreasing clarity.

- Put an equal amount of space between items of equal status. For example, all buttons in one group should have the same amount of space separating them. All groups of buttons should be separated by a space larger than the space between individual buttons.

Placement of Information

Visitors to a Web page should be able to discern the major components of the page without assistance from learning aids such as "online help" or a "user manual." This should be possible irrespective of whether the page is a site entry page, a transaction page, or an information page. Drawing on people's experience should be paramount in designers' plans.

Designers should start with the question of how people represent the organization of a page. What do people expect to see when viewing a page? They expect to see an advanced organizer such as a caption or statement that introduces the subject material that follows and aids in organizing and comprehending it. They also expect to view, scan, or read screen material in the Western culture's left-to-right reading orientation. The combination of the advanced organizer principle and the left-to-right orientation provides us with an expected thematic starting point on the top left of any page. The upper left corner starting position is recommended by screen design experts (Galitz, 1993) and confirmed by studies of locating visual targets on a screen by Streveler and Wasserman (1984). Megaw and Richardson (1979) also found that in systematic search patterns, the tendency is to start a target search in the upper left corner of the display. As we scan a page of text, our eyes start on the top left of a page and move from left to right and top down in a clockwise direction. Therefore, if all objects on a Web page are equal in presentation, it is likely that the viewer will look first at the top left quadrant of the screen. This means that the designer and content organizer should be sure to place the most important content—the text that should be read first or the function that should be invoked first—in that upper left quadrant.

Another design strategy for providing a clear starting point is to capitalize on the viewer's propensity to notice a stimulus that is radically different from the other stimuli in the same visual space. For example, a large graphic would draw the viewer's eye, as would a highlighted or blinking object. Designers should keep in mind that, to be effective, only one starting-point strategy should be used on a given page. For example, if designers want to use the top left quadrant starting-point strategy, they should not weaken the effect by using a competing strategy such as highlighting, a large graphic, or blinking objects.

Information Coding

Designers can use various object and information coding techniques to draw a viewer's attention to certain aspects of a Web page. First, if there are a number of objects on a page that require the user's attention, it is better to use the same coding technique. For example, encode all relevant spatially separated objects that must be tied together with the same color (Wickens and Andre, 1990). Another possibility is to make them all bold, as in the case, for example, of embedded keywords to help in scanning a document. We can use one of many other coding conventions, always using the same code value—for example, if using color as a code, use the same color, such as red, to draw the viewer's attention.

It is important to minimize the number of code values used to draw attention to objects on a page. The use of multiple values of the same code can have the countereffect of diluting rather than focusing attention. For example, only one color, rather than many, should be used to draw attention to the relevant objects or chunks of information. If we use multiple colors, then we should use another uniquely valued code, such as a single graphic in the midst of text, to draw attention.

There are limits to focused attention, and designers should take into account both what is pleasing and what is annoying to viewers. Too many display cues can lead to a lack of focus. Consider a page where the intent is to read a document but where on one of the page's edges, there is an animated or changing brand advertisement. As one attempts to read, the motion contained in the ad is viewed in the reader's peripheral vision as a blinking item, causing distraction, frustration, and delays in task performance. One solution to animated or continuously changing ads is to limit the time in which they change to the first ten seconds after the page is downloaded.

Color

Color can be used both to organize information on a page and to help focus attention. We should use black and white when designing and developing the Web page for clarity and readability and add color as a supplementary option. The use of color to code targets on a monochrome background is a very effective technique for rapid attention focusing (Christ, 1975). There is a limit, however, to the number of colors that can be used effectively on one screen. To avoid overburdening processing capacity in identifying colors, the convention is to not use more than five or six colors on a screen (Carter and Cahill, 1979). The following are color guidelines for Web page designers.

- Color-coding can be used in many ways. We can use color to differentiate between classes of information and to improve screens with high symbol density. Color-coding is less effective on the periphery of a page because humans do not see color in the periphery of the visual field. Do not code small objects in blue because people do not process blue in the center of the retina. When choosing colors, choose those with high contrast, such as yellow on a black background, for display features that must catch the user's attention.

■ If a Web user's physical environment will be a brightly lit area, avoid color coding with subtle contrasts. High ambient illumination washes out colors.

■ Sensitivity to color is greater at low light levels. Thus, colors that look bright at low light levels look faded at high light levels. If the Web site will be used under a wide range of light intensities, do not encode critical information by color alone. Red is very visible under bright light, but it is not very visible in dim light. Use red for coding only if the application will not be used under dim conditions. If the Web site will be viewed under a wide range of light intensities, such as in a shopping mall or airport, use green and yellow, which are fairly visible in these conditions.

■ For Web sites and applications where the audience age is over 35, provide high-contrast color coding. Color discrimination decreases after the age of 35. In designing with color, be aware that 8 percent of males and 0.5 percent of females have some degree of color blindness. There are two forms of color blindness. The more common type is the inability to distinguish red and green from gray. The less common type is the inability to distinguish blue, yellow, and gray. Because of the real potential for color blindness, design for monochrome and then use color as redundant code.

■ When extending a design from monochrome to color, be aware that sharpness can be lost, and even that the color monitor might be of lower resolution. Reduce the effects of possible lower resolution with high-contrast colors such as yellow and blue. Placing the following pairs of colors side by side can result in visual vibrations and afterimages: red and green, yellow and blue, blue and red, or blue and green.

■ When using multiple colors, make sure to establish adequate hue difference in color coding. Learn to use the color wheel (shown in Figure 8.6; see also Plate 17) to pick combinations that are well established in the culture. Use a complementary color pair for good, eye-pleasing contrasts. Complementary colors are opposite each other on the color wheel. Avoid color combinations that are garish. Garish contrasts are 120 degrees apart on the circle. To indicate relationships or a predominant tone, choose colors that are near each other (30 degrees or less). Make the workspace background the most neutral color, generally white, black, or gray. Avoid color pairs with too little contrast, such as yellow/white, yellow/tan, black/purple, and black/blue. If using five different colors, stay with red, yellow, green, blue, and white. A combination of six colors may include cyan, green, amber, red, magenta, and blue.

- Color codes should transmit information relevant to the task to be performed. For example, if the task is to locate all Middle East news stories on a site, then the color scheme should mark the links to all Middle East stories with one color and links to all other stories with a different color or colors.

- Color can be useful in Web interaction for many different purposes. Designers can use color to give three-dimensional effects, which can be useful for enhancing the realism of an illustration or giving an illusion of motion. We use color for entertainment and/or for aesthetic value in situations where the user is just waiting, such as initialization pages. In a tightly packed screen, designers can use different-colored backgrounds instead of space to indicate area boundaries.

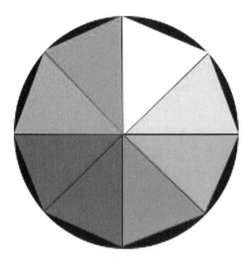

Figure 8.6: *Color wheel* (see also Plate 17)

■ Color coding should be consistent. Use the same color and only that color for the same purpose throughout the entire Web site. For example, if red is used to indicate a warning or error condition in one place, red should mean warning or error condition throughout the site.

■ There are targeted tasks where using color is most desirable. Recall tasks as well as search-and-locate tasks show improved performance with color. Tasks requiring retention of information show better performance with color. Color improves reader comprehension of instructional material, and it also improves performance in tasks that require decisions or judgment. Color is more effective than other coding methods for search tasks when the question being answered is "Where is it?"; for counting tasks when the question is "How many?"; and for comparison tasks when the answer is a "yes/no." For verification tasks when the answer is "true/false," color coding is second in effectiveness to number coding. Use color to discriminate between different areas on the screen, show relationships among objects, both functionally and otherwise, and mark crucial features and locations.

■ The use of color displays improves reaction time over monochrome for pie charts, bar graphs, and tables. Color significantly improves accuracy for pie charts and line graphs. Use different colors to distinguish between different classes of objects. For example, make all active buttons black and all inactive buttons light gray. Use the same color to indicate a relationship between objects of one class. For example, make all keywords the same color. Use color to draw attention to important features. Make an embedded text button a different color (either background or foreground) from the rest of the text.

■ When designing, keep in mind that there are standard cultural associations of color codes. Here are some that are prevalent in Western culture. Cyan is readable as text. Use neutral colors (black, white, gray, brown, bone, tan, and so on) for background on a page. We use blue for nonessential information. It is also used to highlight large symbols, such as labels, and to mark large areas on the screen. Saturated blue is unreadable as text and makes for a poor visual cue. The predominant Web convention is to use nonsaturated blue for links. Green is readable as text, and green also means normal state, go, or ready. We associate red with danger, failure, and error. Flashing red often represents an unacknowledged alarm, but it makes a poor peripheral cue. We use yellow to mean caution, attention required, or warning.

Text Clarity

Phrases, words, titles, and labels, as well as names given to links, fields, and icons, should be selected carefully with the target audience in mind. When creating content, word selection should also be audience sensitive. A single word usually has multiple meanings. If everything else is equal, there is one predominant meaning for a given context of use and audience domain. Psycholinguistic research has demonstrated that if a word is used in a sentence to convey a meaning other than the conventional one for the context and audience, it takes the reader a longer time to process the sentence (Foss, 1970; Cairns and Kamerman, 1975). For example, the word *court* has a different predominant meaning for a community of tennis players than for an audience of lawyers. If text takes longer to read and understand, then the ease of using and interacting with a Web page diminishes.

Using the appropriate character case helps reading speed. Studies by Moskel, et al. (1984) showed that, for screen reading comprehension, mixed-case text was superior to text material presented in upper case or all capital letters. It is postulated that when we read, our first level of processing is to recognize the word by its shape. If we fail, then we go to the next level of semantic processing. Reading time improves if we are able to recognize some of the words by their shape. CAPITAL LETTERS—all the same height and depth—give an identical rectangular shape for all words, thus requiring a longer time to read and comprehend. Uppercase letters are used when the intention is to highlight or draw attention to one or a few words. Titles, subheadings, and captions may be presented in capital letters.

The length of a line of text in a document is determined by how the reader will use the document. For pages intended for scanning, the general recommendation is that the line length should not be more than 35 characters. Pages to be read word for word can have lines up to 75 characters long. Documents to be scanned or browsed should be organized into paragraphs with keyword subheadings. Generally, allow visitors to easily print a page or a document because reading performance is higher for paper over displayed text. Reading speed is significantly lower for screen reading (Gould and Grischkowsky, 1984).

Content providers should pay special attention to the writing style. Brief and simple affirmative sentences using the active voice are easier to

Plate 1 (Figure 3.6)
What Scenario 1 shoppers see
(Photos courtesy of Harris Teeter, Inc.)

Plate 2 (Figure 3.7)
What Scenario 2 shoppers see
(Photos courtesy of Harris Teeter, Inc.)

Plate 3 (Figure 3.8)
What Scenario 3 shoppers see
(Photos courtesy of Harris Teeter, Inc.)

Plate 4 (Figure 3.9)
What Scenario 4 shoppers see
(Photos courtesy of Harris Teeter, Inc.)

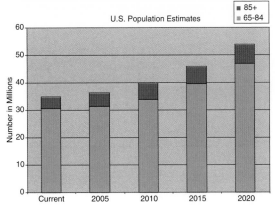

Plate 5 (Figure 5.1)
Projected population estimates
(Source: *http://www.census.gov/population/ www/projections/natsum-T3.html.* Reprinted with permission.)

Plate 6 (Figure 5.2)
Sample home page of a fictitious health Web site
(Source: Mead, Lamson, and Rogers, 2002.)

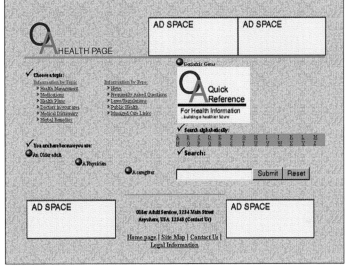

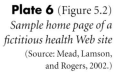

Plate 7 (Figure 5.3)
Redesigned home page from Figure 5.2
(Source: Mead, Lamson, and Rogers, 2002.)

Association for Senior Citizens
2839 West 44th Avenue
Denver, Colorado 80211-1428
Telephone: 303-455-9642   *Fax:* 303-455-2613
Office Hours: 9:00am - 4:00pm
Monday through Thursday

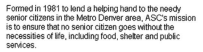

Formed in 1981 to lend a helping hand to the needy senior citizens in the Metro Denver area, ASC's mission is to ensure that no senior citizen goes without the necessities of life, including food, shelter and public services.

The Association for Senior Citizens does not discriminate against staff, board members, or the clientele being served. ASC does not discriminate on the basis of race, religion, color, gender, national origin, sexual orientation, non-disqualifying physical or mental disability or veteran status.

The Association for Senior Citizens is proud to serve the needs of the Senior Community throughout the six Metro area counties: Adams, Arapahoe, Boulder, Douglas, Denver and Jefferson.

Plate 8 (Figure 5.4)
Association for Senior Citizens home page
(Reprinted with permission.)

Plate 9
(Figure 5.6)
Justice Store home page
(Reprinted with permission.)

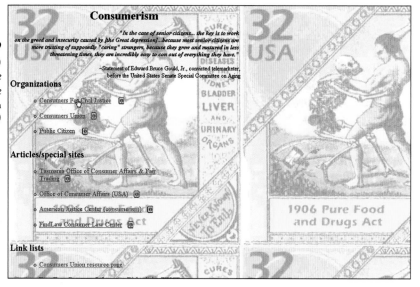

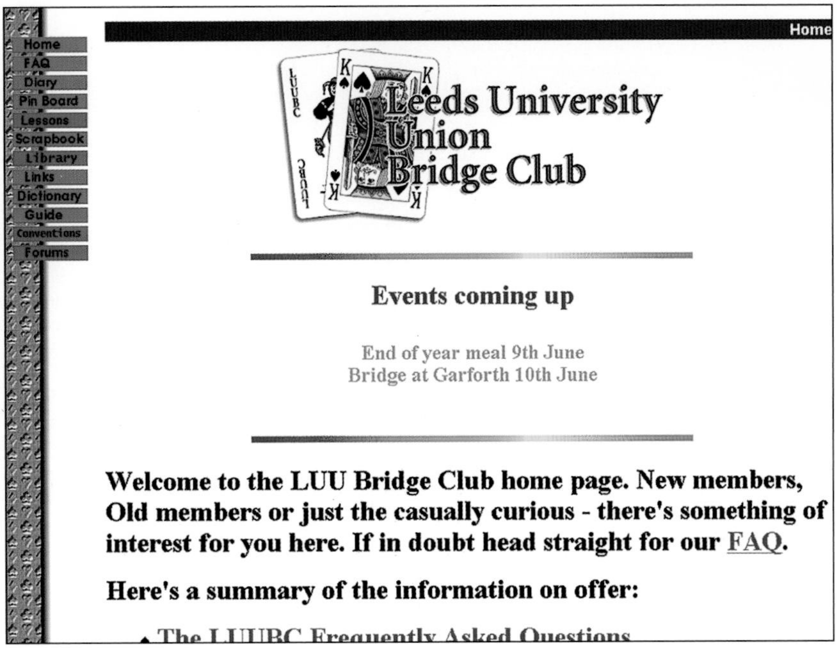

Plate 10
(Figure 6.3)
Leeds University Union Bridge Club home page
(Reprinted with permission.)

Events coming up

End of year meal 9th June
Bridge at Garforth 10th June

Welcome to the LUU Bridge Club home page. New members, Old members or just the casually curious - there's something of interest for you here. If in doubt head straight for our FAQ.

Here's a summary of the information on offer:

• The LUUBC Frequently Asked Questions

Plate 11 (Figure 6.4)
Gambling.com home page
(Reprinted with permission.)

Plate 12
(Figure 6.8)
*E-shopping products
subgenre*
(© 2001 Lands' End, Inc.
Used with permission.)

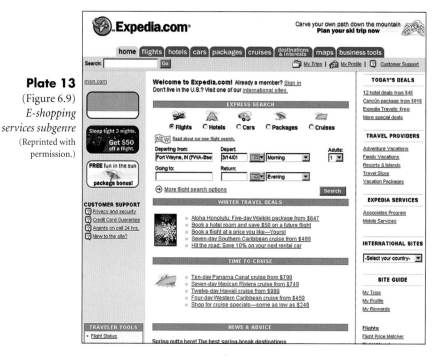

Plate 13
(Figure 6.9)
*E-shopping
services subgenre*
(Reprinted with
permission.)

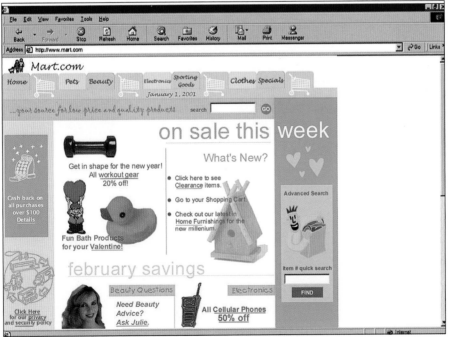

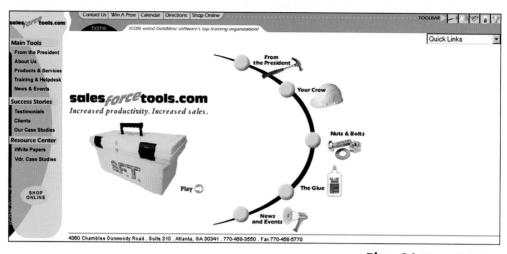

Plate 16 (Figure 7.9) *Icons*
(Reprinted with permission of
salesforcetools.com.)

Plate 17 (Figure 8.6)
Color wheel

Plate 18 (Figure 9.1) *Original home page of a botanical garden site*
(Design by Sarah Craighill from a photograph by Julie Shinabery.)

Plate 19 (Figure 9.2) *High-contrast rendering of botanical garden site*

Plate 20 (Figure 9.3) *Removing the title only*

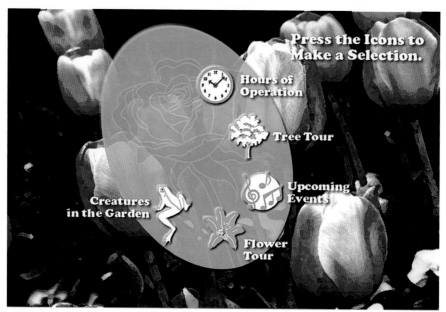

Plate 21 (Figure 9.4) *Removing the title and providing high contrast*

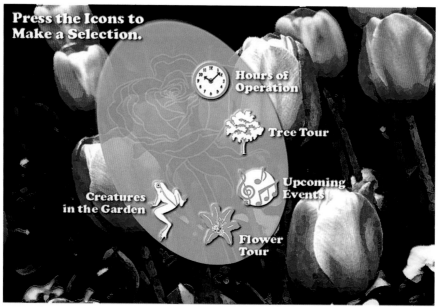

Plate 22 (Figure 9.5) *Further improvement by placing instructions in upper left*

Plate 23 (Figure 9.6) *Reinserting title in lower right of page*

Plate 24 (Figure 9.7) *Positioning icons in left-to-right, top-to-bottom orientation*

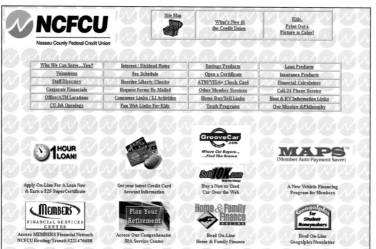

Plate 25
(Figure 9.9)
Page where background interferes with visibility of links
(Reprinted by permission of Nassau Federal Credit Union.)

Plate 26
(Figure 9.14)
Art that gives rise to the wrong interpretation

Plate 27
(Figure 9.15)
Title header that looks like a banner ad

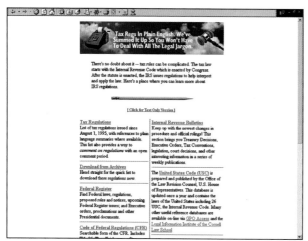

Plate 28 (Figure 10.7) *Université de Savoie home page*
(Université de Savoie [France]: *www.univ-savoie.fr.*)

Plate 29
(Figure 10.11)
*Partial view of the Université
de Savoie home page*
(Université de Savoie [France]:
www.univ-savoie.fr.)

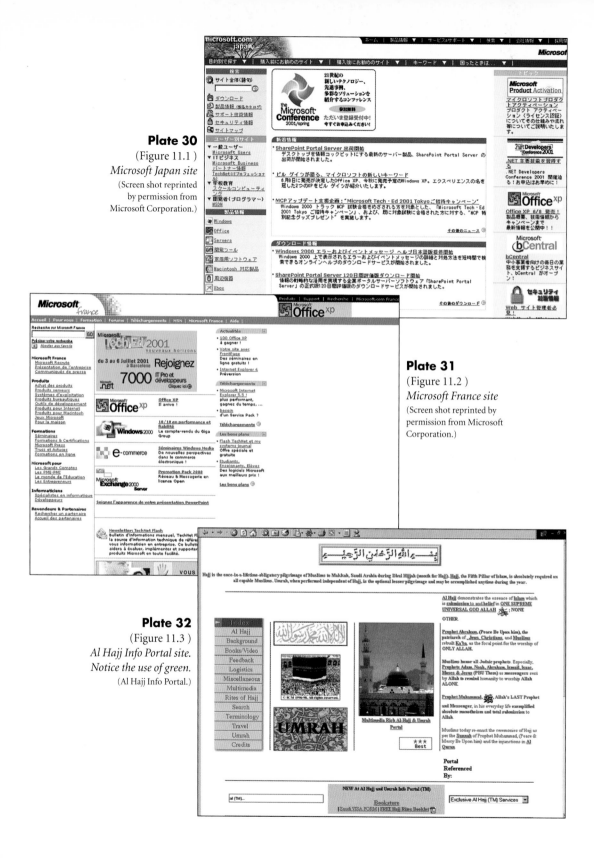

Plate 30

(Figure 11.1)

Microsoft Japan site

(Screen shot reprinted
by permission from
Microsoft Corporation.)

Plate 31

(Figure 11.2)

Microsoft France site

(Screen shot reprinted by
permission from Microsoft
Corporation.)

Plate 32

(Figure 11.3)

Al Hajj Info Portal site.
Notice the use of green.

(Al Hajj Info Portal.)

comprehend than long sentences with multiple clauses. Java-scripts and animated GIFs are not a substitute for meaningful textual content. Text should include audience-tested vocabulary and should be carefully checked for spelling errors. Remember that automatic "spell check" programs do not catch errors if the misspelling results in another word—"he" for "the," for example—nor do they catch usage errors, such as "too" for "two." Content creators should not write text in HTML. Write and edit using a word processing program, then transfer to HTML.

Home, Content, and Transaction Pages

We can divide the pages of a Web site into three types: the home, or entry, page, the content page, and the transaction page. The home page provides an introduction to the site. The visitor uses content, or information, pages to scan or read domain-specific information. Transaction pages are where visitors enter relevant data and receive responses. The design features we have already discussed, such as consistency of information placement, color guidelines, text formatting, and so forth, apply uniformly across page types, but there are a few design issues that are unique to each type.

The Home Page

The home page should establish site identity and give a clear overview of the content. Both topic organization of the site and how to use the site should be communicated by the links, buttons, and tabs on the home page. A Web site should be designed with a hierarchical organization starting with general information on the home page and adding increasingly more specific information as visitors descend to content and transaction pages.

Because some users will not bother to scroll the home page, the important information should fit on one screen. In fact, as a general rule, the home page should be short and nonscrollable. Nielsen's usability studies (1996) suggest that users prefer not to scroll.

The top half of the Web home page is the most crucial area for transmitting the most important information about the site. Regardless of browser type or screen real estate, we can be sure that most visitors will be able to view the top sector of the screen. Because, as pointed out earlier, Westerners scan page information top-down and left to right, the top half of the home page should give the overall purpose and goals of the site. That part of the page has to act as the gate to the rest of the site. Therefore, the goals can be depicted in terms of content-specific descriptive links and/or tabs with clear, unambiguous labels in the upper part of the page. The links on the home page should be to the main parts of the site. Figure 8.7 is an example of a well-designed home page with the most crucial, frequently requested information in the top part of the page. Another example of such a page is the home page of the Interaction Design Institute in Ivrea, shown in Figure 8.8. All the crucial information is in the top one-third of the page. Because of the pull-down menu bar on top, users can go to any location on the site with one click.

For sites of more than 20 pages, it is important to have on the home page an easy-to-find link, button, or tab to a site search facility, such as to a content page, a search function, an index, a site map, or a combination of these. Such reference aids should appear in the top part of the page below the header. They can be in the form of tabs in a utility bar on the upper right or as sublinks in a drop menu or as a link list on either the left or right side, depending on what else is on the page. See Chapter 6 for a discussion of Web site reference aids.

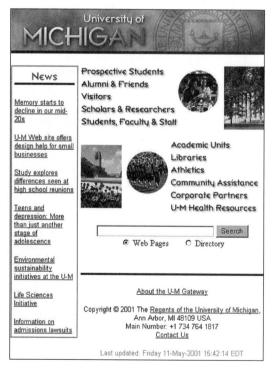

Figure 8.7: *Home page with most requested information at top*
(Reprinted with permission.)

Figure 8.8: *Interaction Design Institute Ivrea page*
(Courtesy of the Interaction Design Institute, IVREA, and designer Chris Downs
with support from Oyster LTS, UK. Reprinted with permission.)

Beyond an introductory statement of purpose, the home page should contain little textual information. Any information not directly related to the organization should be placed outside the body of the page in the header or footer. Headers and footers should be designed so as not to impinge on page content, which could result in potential confusion and delay in finding information. Borges and associates suggest that designers should keep headers at less than 25 percent of a letter-size page so they don't dominate the top part of the home page (Borges, et al., 1998).

When designing the home page, be clear about why users visit the site, and then develop the home page to meet those goals. Make sure that the statement of purpose expresses clearly what the site will accomplish, telling the user what to expect. Then provide the most important goal-oriented links that use words clearly reflecting the target page content.

The Content Page

One very popular reason people visit Web sites is to view, scan, or read the site's content. To keep visitors coming back, that content should be well presented and well organized and of interest to the visitor. Therefore, designs should be such that visitors do not have to expend extra effort to locate the information they want.

Accordingly, the first consideration in designing a Web content page is to place function before form. In other words, the designer's first task is to make the site or application do or offer in an efficient way what users want and need. To capture and maintain user interest, the information provided should be relevant, credible, useful, unique to the site, and up to date.

Designers should conduct content analysis to be clear about the information needs of potential visitors to the site. Content analysis starts with identifying the user tasks to be accomplished on the target page. Tasks can include such things as reading a document, scanning a release, or learning about product features. Identifying the tasks can keep the design process on target. If, for example, the main task on the page is for visitors to locate and identify product features, then the page will be organized to start with the product name(s) followed by a list of features. If the page has only one product, then the features can be accompanied by short definitions. If it is a page showing several products, then the list of features for each product could be links that would open feature boxes. What is important is that the organization is, first, user-relevant; second, task-specific; and third, hierarchical from the general to the specific. Figure 8.9 is an example of a well-designed content page.

After functions, functionality sequencing, and relevant content are determined, then comes the job of laying out and organizing the page. The goal is to establish a consistent, logical screen layout that allows relevant content to be added easily and quickly. The design process should start with establishing a layout grid for all pages that includes consistent placement of titles, headings, links, buttons, graphics, lists, and text. When this basic format is in place as the design foundation, many ad hoc problems can be avoided. The consistency of the design should be predictable to the extent that any designer can pick up and complete an unfinished project with little effort.

In designing the organization of content, our first priority should be speed of managing and locating information. This means we should organize information into small chunks, label the chunks, and start with the most important information. Furthermore, for the greatest clarity, we should write concisely and with proper grammar. To make documents easy to print, we should minimize the use of such elements as frames and make available a print button at both the top and bottom of the page.

Art in Provence

HOME | THE WORKSHOP | THE LOCATION | Nan Hass Feldman MULTIMEDIA | ARTIST BIOS
DATES & DETAILS | RESERVATIONS | CONTACT US

THE DATES & DETAILS

The Painting Workshop consists of 8 painting days and 2 free days. It includes approximately 48 hours of instruction, 11 nights at the hotel, all breakfasts, 8 picnic lunches, 2 cocktail parties, and a farewell dinner. Folding chairs, drawing boards, and easels are supplied. Non-painters are encouraged to join us as guests of painters and are offered a reduced rate, which includes hotel, breakfast, picnics, and parties. Guests may choose to take a cooking workshop.

It is necessary for painters to have their own transportation during the workshop. For those who do not wish to drive, and/or would like to share rental costs, we will make arrangements with other students.

Travel arrangements can be made privately or through our travel agency, Milne Travel/American Express at 800-906-4563. There are quite a few travel options, but many participants fly into Paris and take the train to Montelimar, which is about 12 miles from the hotel.

2001 Painting workshop schedule
Dates refer to the day of arrival at and departure from the hotel. **Please note that in order to arrive in France on the correct day, one must fly from the United States the day before.** There is a cooking workshop which falls within the dates of each painting workshop.

May 14–25(I)	Nan Hass Feldman	June 25–July 6	Frank Francese
May 14–25(II)	Linda Moyer	August 20–31	Hedi Moran
May 28–June 8(I)	Caroline Graham	September 3–14	Patricia Abraham
May 28–June 8(II)	Leslie Parke	September 17–28	Gerald Brommer
June 11–June 22	Hilary Page		

Figure 8.9: *A well-designed content page*
(Courtesy of Art in Provence, LLC.)

Information in documents that require long pages should be chunked with subheads. The subheadings should also be given as links at the top of the document (Janal, 1997). Long pages with links have the advantage over multiple-page documents in that they can be printed more easily. Also, linking within a long page takes less time than linking between pages of the same document. When using the within-page links design solution, we should make sure to distinguish clearly among same-page content links, links to other pages within the site, and links to other sites. All links of the same type should have common depiction characteristics such as shape, color, underlining, and font.

Designers should remember that Web content pages are hyperlinked, allowing users to access them from anywhere on the World Wide Web. Thus, we should design content Web pages as though they may be the first page that a user sees in a given site. It is important, therefore, that content pages have the relevant informative headers and footers as well as a link to the home page of the site. In other words, we should design all our pages to become what Web style guide manuals call "freestanding."

Unlike printed pages in a document, Web pages should have titles. Because they may be accessed from anywhere and can appear in bookmarks and search engines, the titles should be meaningful out of context.

In general, designers should avoid the use of frames on content pages, not only because of printing problems, as mentioned earlier, but also because bookmarking becomes more difficult and load time can increase. Framing often results in exceeding the 30K limit on a page before any content has been added.

To help users establish a context for their Web interactions, it is vital that designers document the site's pages—that is, identify the page's creators and owners and the last update. For example, whenever there is a new feature on the page, the word *NEW* should be placed next to it. Frequent content updating is a manifestation of a "living" site. Making users aware of frequent updating practices is likely to increase the frequency of their visits. Another way of engaging the visitor of the Web content page is to provide a "Frequently Asked Questions" (FAQ) feature and a news release section.

The Transaction Page

Another popular reason for visiting Web sites is to perform a transaction, such as registering for a conference or purchasing airline tickets. Transaction pages differ from the home and content pages in that they invite the user to take action and give feedback in response to that action. Transaction pages are interactive and not static. The user either fills in field data or enters text in response to a prompt or a request. It is this proactivity of the visitor that distinguishes the transaction page from the others. This does not mean that we cannot have a content page that allows the visitor to take action, as in the use of the shopping cart, for example. There are pages, however, that are intended by the Web designer primarily to support transaction activities. These require special design attention to keep the user interested in pursuing the interaction. Figure 8.10 is an example of a Web transaction page.

To promote transactions, designers should pay attention to both sides of the communication flow: facilitating actions by the user and providing feedback to the user's actions. The first rule of transaction facilitating is to inform visitors of what they should do. We should provide clear instructions to accompany well-designed transaction media, such as fill-in forms and tables.

We should provide tables when we anticipate that visitors will want to scan to interpret data quickly. The row-by-column format is simple and

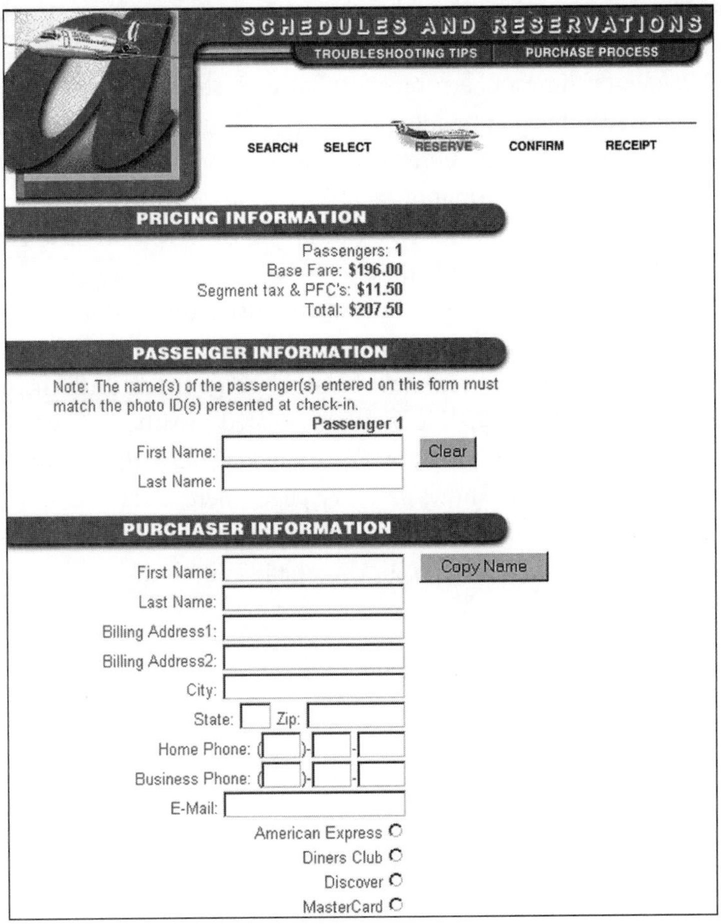

Figure 8.10: *A Web transaction page*
(Reservations page from Airtran.com.)

effective. When presenting tabular alphanumeric data, we should left-justify it as in Figure 8.11a. Numeric data should be right-justified or aligned by decimal point as shown in Figure 8.11b.

Present tabular data in a top-to-bottom and left-to-right format. If tabular data extends vertically over more than one page, then column headings should be identical and consistent on every screen. Fixed-width tables are inflexible and can run afoul of browser idiosyncrasies. If the fixed-width table is wider than the display, users are forced to scroll sideways to view the page. Use relative-width tables because they automatically size themselves to fit the reader's browser window.

Facilitating user actions should also mean paying particular attention to data-entry transactions with the goals of reducing errors and increasing speed of entry. Data-entry time and error performance are superior when the source document or screen text is presented in upper and lower case rather than in all capitals. Furthermore, data-entry performance improves when data to be entered is organized in information chunks that are meaningful to the end user. The user's inspection and verification performance of data entered improves if the screen format is identical to the format of the source document.

We should design the interaction so that users do not have to switch back and forth between different modes of entry, such as point/click and keying. A user should be able to remain within the same mode until the transaction is complete. This guideline is often violated in situations where the user has to enter a password and an ID via the keyboard, then click on the ENTER button. Figure 8.12 shows an entry page where users have to change from keyboard entry to mouse clicking mode as they move from entering the Social Security number and PIN to clicking the ENTER button.

a. Alphanumeric Data	b. Numeric Data	
	Numeric	Decimal
PL7 5341 279	7121	75.21
PL8 5341 280	475	5.2
QS2 7521 21	21	0.123
	2	2.21

Figure 8.11: *Tabular alphanumeric and numeric data presentation*

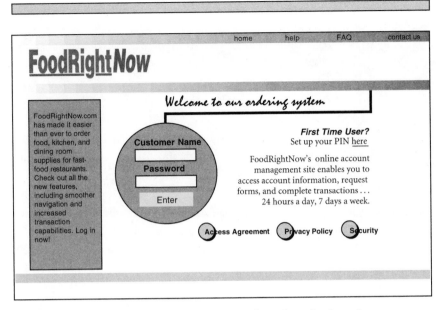

Figure 8.12: *Page that requires switching from keyboard to mouse*

The second facet of communication that we should take into account when designing transaction pages is responding to user action. Communication is a two-way street. Therefore, when a user finishes an activity, such as submitting a request or filling out a form, the Web site should provide immediate feedback, giving users an opportunity to check and modify or confirm their actions. When the user enters any kind of data, the page should show as soon as possible a response indicating that the entry was accepted or rejected or is still being processed. The message should be as detailed as possible. For incorrect input, the response should state specifically what is wrong and what the user should do. At the end of processing, the site should state whether more user action is necessary.

When a user selects a screen item, such as a menu choice, button, data, or field, highlight the chosen item. When giving feedback, if relevant and appropriate, tell the user how to get more detailed information, either online or offline.

In a task where accuracy is more important than speed, designers should provide extensive feedback and error checking, along with prompting, if possible. Such tasks include the preparation of legal documents and fiduciary records.

In a task where speed is more important than accuracy, or where skilled users are the sole users (or where the skill level of the user indicates few errors), designers need provide only a minimum amount of feedback, error checking, and prompting. Such tasks include text entry for skilled typists or casual interactions such as games.

While entering data, users should be able to quit the page, Web site, or Web application and then return easily (with a minimum number of actions) to exactly where they had discontinued their work earlier. Any time the user quits the data-entry mode, a response should verify whether entered data has been or is to be saved. That is, visitors should be required to take action explicitly to ENTER or submit data whenever they finish.

Design the transaction to minimize the need for the user to enter information that is already available to the Web site. For example, do not ask users to enter current time and date if that is already provided to the Web site.

For keyboard data entry, minimize the number of keystrokes required. The probability of errors goes up as the number of keystrokes increases. Provide the user with a default option for records that have identical fields such as date or zip code. With the use of a default option, the system should enter such data automatically. Allow the user to change or initialize defaults as the situation requires.

In a data-entry mode where two or more successively placed records have some fields with identical values, allow the user to invoke a duplicate value with a single keystroke. When new data items are inserted in an already sorted list, such as a list of products, provide for automatic resorting of the list.

Designers should never force the user to enter measurement units if they can be inferred from the task. For example, a user should not have to enter "lbs." after a number in a field for weight or "years" in a field for age. If the units of measure are desired, the system should be designed to add them.

Always place captions over the data-entry field for column-oriented entries and to the left of the entry field for row-oriented entries. If several fields in a screen are to be filled in, arrange for them to be filled from top to bottom by default. The cursor should start at the topmost field, and when that entry is completed, the cursor should move automatically to the next lower field by default.

The use of prompting has its place on transaction Web pages. Designers should use prompting to request additional information from the user and, in response to a user action, to instruct the user to correct or modify entered information. In interactive sessions such as tutorials or orientations, use prompting to tell users what to do next. In addition, prompt users for verification of requests that require extensive and permanent changes to files, records, fields, documents, or data. A prompt message that is a response to user input should appear in a consistent location as close to the line of the input as possible. Prompts that require user input should appear at the beginning of the next line to be typed.

9

The Aesthetic Factor

When designing usable Web sites, designers should pay particular attention to both efficiency and the simplicity of elegance (Mullet and Sano, 1994). To ensure that the visitor has an enjoyable experience, however, there should also be the aesthetic enrichment that comes from the artist's virtuosity of expression. These requirements are not necessarily incompatible, but very often the goals of one supersede those of the other. Such situations occur when we determine that the Web site visitor's purpose and the user experience are better served by emphasizing either the experience of usable efficiency or the experience of artistic enrichment.

The question that Web designers should always have at the top of their list is how best to accommodate the requirement for balance among the emotional, aesthetic, and informational needs of Web site visitors. In the case of a Web store site, for example, is the feeling of being in an actual store important, or is it enough to state that it is a site where visitors can shop from a list of products? The experiment on the effects of enriched environments described in Chapter 3 indicates clearly that the answer depends on what the visitor wants out of visiting the Web site.

Usability and Aesthetics

The Human Computer Interaction community has been unduly conservative when it comes to aesthetic expression considerations in the design of the user interface. Within the HCI community, the attitude toward aesthetics has been, at worst, overtly negative. In describing the design of a museum, Norman (1988), says, "Just don't let the focus on cost, or durability, or aesthetics destroy the major point of the museum: to be used, to be understood," as though to be "enjoyed" should not be one of the "major points" of a museum or is not an important part of the human experience. At best, the HCI community has ignored the role of aesthetics completely, as in the case of many textbooks (Preece, et al., 1994; Dix, et al., 1998; Shneiderman, 1998; Baecker, et al., 1999). A few notable exceptions include recent empirical work showing relationships between aesthetic perception and usability (Kurosu and Kashimora, 1995; Tratinsky, 1997), as well as the treatment of HCI by B. Laurel in her book *Computers as Theater* (1991). In the foreword to Laurel's book, Norman takes a view different from the one he expressed earlier. He asks, "Do you enjoy the experience of using these new technologies? . . . Perhaps it never occurred to you that the concepts of 'enjoy' and 'experience' could apply. . . . After all, the purpose of most of these technologies is to assist in doing our daily activities . . . and we most certainly should enjoy the experience of doing those activities."

As a matter of everyday practice, human interface designers recommend the use of aesthetic expression in the form of enriched graphics, animated graphics, or 3-D graphics only when it enhances the functionality and efficiency of use. Aesthetic expression for the sake of enriching the user's enjoyment is fundamentally absent from design recommendations of user-centered design experts (Meads and Nielsen, 2001).

The fact is that in our daily lives, the art experience awakens in us senses that go beyond the need for efficiency (Dewey, 1934; Maquet, 1986). The human being is a composite of cognitive and affective characteristics that need to be satisfied. Which of these predominate depends on the situation at hand and the task to be undertaken. For example, on government sites where the visitor's focus is on finding information quickly, animation can be annoying, images can be distracting, and large amounts of graphics slow page download time. On the other hand, a site for exploring a zoo would be dull indeed without graphics and even without animation.

The very process of visiting a Web site has its unique aspects and is quite different from using a software application. Visitors to a Web site may decide whether to navigate further into a site based solely on the aesthetic appeal of the home or entry page. If they find the page either unusable or unappealing, they may immediately search for another site that satisfies their needs more completely. On the other hand, software users who would like to invest or have invested in a software application that permits them to perform some specified tasks are more likely to focus primarily, or even solely, on how efficiently they can perform their tasks with the acquired software. If they already have invested in the software, they are more likely to learn to compensate for its poor usability than to invest in another software tool. With the Web, it is much easier and less expensive to discard an unappealing Web site and try another.

When it comes to pages deeper into a Web site, the notion that we should ignore aesthetic enrichment because it might interfere with usability is fundamentally flawed. The designer must take into account the interaction among the emotional, aesthetic, and cognitive needs of site visitors when considering the site visitor's pleasantness of experience in the overall design plan. The reality is that for a good number of Web sites, both simple designs engendered by the requirement for usability and aesthetic enrichment emanating from the artist's free expression hold in some measure, with one slightly superseding the other.

It is just important to remember that it is possible to provide a sophisticated aesthetic expression without violating usability constraints. An example could be a Web site designed not only to educate people about the benefits of visiting a botanical garden in their community but to inspire them to visit. To encourage site visitors to visit the actual garden, it would be helpful to provide visitors a feel for the highlights of a botanical garden and the experience of being there. In this case, it is necessary to go beyond a textual description of what is in the garden. Providing an artist's rendering of the kinds of flowers, trees, and various botanical events available will give visitors a more attractive and enriched experience.

Figure 9.1 (see also Plate 18) shows the home page for a botanical garden site with artwork consisting of flowers in the background and icons representing features of the garden and different topics for further exploration. This page is an example of a presentation that is pleasing to the eye but that violates several usability constraints. For example, placing the instructions in the right corner would delay finding them because in this culture we read from left to right. Also, given our reading orientation, it would seem more appropriate to place the selection icons on the left than on the right of the oval background

Figure 9.1: *Original home page of a botanical garden site* (see also Plate 18)
(Design by Sarah Craighill from a photograph by Julie Shinabery.)

image. Putting the title where the instructions should be is totally useless and further hinders the visitor who is trying to figure out what to do. Additionally, the low contrast between the background and foreground contributes to the impression of display clutter and makes finding an icon more difficult.

We can fix the usability problems of the page in Figure 9.1 and still preserve the artist's depiction. First, by simply increasing the contrast between the foreground and the background, we make it easier for the user to find the icons. Compare Figure 9.1 with Figure 9.2 (see also Plate 19), which is a high-contrast rendering of the same graphic.

Figure 9.3 (see also Plate 20) shows another approach to the problem. By removing the overpowering thematic words "Botanical Gardens, Take The Tour," we significantly reduce the clutter and make it easier to find the icons. Figure 9.4 (see also Plate 21) both removes the thematic statement and provides high contrast, thus considerably improving the usability of the page.

In Figure 9.5 (see also Plate 22) we improve further on the usability by moving the instructions to the spot where the thematic statement was originally. Given the left-to-right reading orientation in Western culture, most people will immediately figure out what they have to do to take an action on this page.

Even though most visitors to this page know in advance that they are visiting the botanical garden site, it is a good idea to have a site thematic statement, both for reinforcement, as well as for the few who encounter the

Figure 9.2: *High-contrast rendering of botanical garden site* (see also Plate 19)

site accidentally. The statement, however, should be provided in a less over-bearing manner than originally shown by reducing its size and/or placing it more discreetly on the page, such as in Figure 9.6 (see also Plate 23).

Another usability improvement that we can make without taking away from the artist's expression is to place most of the icons on the left and top

Figure 9.3: *Removing the title only* (see also Plate 20)

Figure 9.4: *Removing the title and providing high contrast* (see also Plate 21)

sides of the oval image, as shown in Figure 9.7 (see also Plate 24). Visitors will be able to locate them more quickly, again because of the left-to-right, top-to-bottom orientation. Notice that Figure 9.7 shows all the changes we made to improve the page's usability while respecting and preserving the artist's virtuosity of expression.

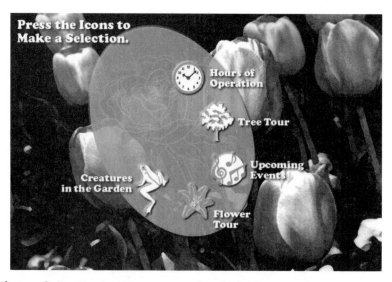

Figure 9.5: *Further improvement by placing instructions in upper left*
(see also Plate 22)

Figure 9.6: *Reinserting title in lower right of page* (see also Plate 23)

We can improve the page's usability still further by making the oval the only patent image and having a neutral background with no graphics. This approach is shown in Figure 9.8. By making these changes, however, we only improve usability slightly at the expense of destroying the aesthetic appeal that provides visitors an enjoyable experience.

Figure 9.7: *Positioning icons in left-to-right, top-to-bottom orientation* (see also Plate 24)

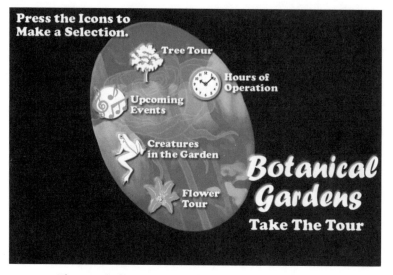

Figure 9.8: *Page with background art removed*

Simplicity and Enrichment

Common performance measures often indicate that users perform tasks more efficiently on sites with simple designs than on those with enriched color-graphics, animation, and 3-D depictions. But when you ask the same users to compare the simple site with one that has features that go beyond the 2-D widget, they tend to rate the enriched one more favorably in some aspects of information interaction (Gonzalez, 1996). As graphics technologies become more elaborate, the opportunities for graphical representations on the Web have become more varied. With these varied opportunities, artists can produce an attractive site while at the same time respecting the need for simplicity.

In the previous section we saw how usability designers can have all the usability constraints without sacrificing the artist's aesthetic expression for sites where enjoyment is as important as function. It is also incumbent upon artists to be aware of how to create art without violating usability and human factor principles of design.

Artistic expressions can be achieved without violating the usability principle of simplicity. Simplicity of page design, which may be treated as the opposite of complexity, can be determined precisely by applying information theory (Tullis, 1981). This method works well for screens that are exclusively alphanumeric character based, where we can locate and count the number of fields and alignment points. For Web pages containing graphics, animations, and 3-D depictions, we need to employ several heuristic rules to achieve artistic expression and at the same time maintain simplicity.

- Art should not interfere with the site's goal and functionality.
- Art should not result in visual noise.
- Art should not allow misinterpretation.
- Art should be consistent with the visitor's Web experience.

Art should not interfere with the site's goal and functionality. Artists should be aware that their art can interfere with functionality by slowing down the rate at which visitors locate what they need on a display or perform the functions required to accomplish their tasks efficiently. One way this could happen is when the background interferes with the visibility of the links. In Figure 9.9 (see also Plate 25), the links are royal blue instead of black or dark blue. As a result, their visibility diminishes against the background. Another way art interferes with functionality is if the page has flashing animation and banner advertisements.

Sometimes sites are done entirely in Flash, and while they are aesthetically pleasing with innovative and interesting graphics, navigation is

Figure 9.9: *Page where background interferes with visibility of links*
(see also Plate 25)
(Reprinted by permission of Nassau Federal Credit Union.)

very difficult. Even though such designs are interesting and attractive, the graphics tend to dominate the page and interfere with functionality. Often the art in these cases is created with no thought to usability of the site.

Most preferable is a page with art that is both good looking and useful. At the very least, the art can be neutral and neither detract from nor enhance the usability of the site. Figure 9.10 is an example of a page where the art is helpful. In Figure 9.10, all the pictures are linked either to the main theme— inviting your friends to a gathering—or to the navigation. Adequate white space and large icons draw the eye to the three main functions: Evite Create, My Evite, and Evite Ideas. Figure 9.11 shows an example of a page where the art reinforces the purpose of the page.

The site in Figure 9.12 is an example of a page where the art is pleasant and neutral. The picture of the president and logos of name brands neither enhance nor take away from the main navigation bar, which is one color and textual. The functionality would be the same if those images were changed or eliminated. Figure 9.13 is another example of art that is both pleasant and neutral. There are only three small icons besides the logo on the upper left. Because the aesthetics are driven by the text and the gridlike design, remov-

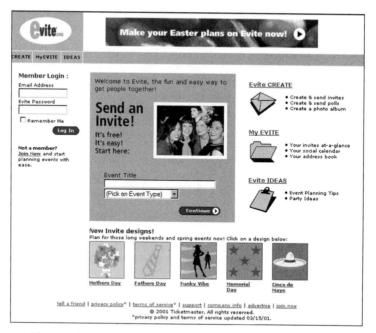

Figure 9.10: *Page where art is helpful to functionality*
(© 2001 Ticketmaster. Used by permission of Ticketmaster.)

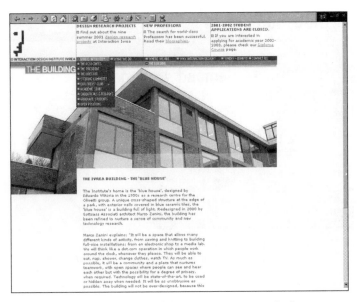

Figure 9.11: *Page where art supports goal of page*
(Courtesy of the Interaction Design Institute, IVREA, and designer Chris Downs
with support from Oyster LTS, UK. Reprinted by permission.)

Figure 9.12: *Page with art that is pleasant but neutral to functionality*

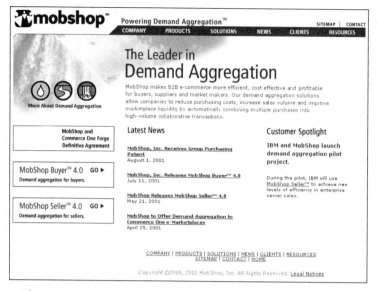

Figure 9.13: *MobShop page with pleasant and neutral art*
(Reprinted by permission.)

ing or changing the icons would not make a difference in navigating the site. The main navigation bar is at the top and does not have graphic elements.

Art should not result in visual noise. Artists who are not paying attention to usability often tend to overdo the number of art elements, resulting in a cluttered screen, or what is known as visual noise. Instead of being aesthetically pleasing, the art impedes the ease of use. Visual noise can happen if we place an excessive number of colorful images or icons on the page. It can also happen with a few instances of flashing, changing, or animated elements on the same page.

Art should not allow misinterpretation. The impact of an image is both strong and immediate. Remember the old phrase "A picture is worth a thousand words"? An image on a home Web page can instantaneously either help visitors understand the purpose of the site or confuse them. An aesthetically pleasing graphic can still either lead or mislead the visitor. Artists should always consider whether their art might allow erroneous interpretations by novice visitors to the site.

Figure 9.14 (see also Plate 26) shows the IRS's page "Tax Interactive, an online 'zine for understanding taxes." The page is aesthetically very pleasing with colorful sectors, words, and images. The problem is with the picture of a yellow taxi in the title header. While cute, this image could be misleading. A visitor coming to this page from a different Web site might get the impression

Figure 9.14: *Art that gives rise to the wrong interpretation*
(see also Plate 26)

that this site is for calling a taxi. Someone browsing from within the IRS Web site might make the initial interpretation that this page provides information for taxi owners and drivers.

Art should be consistent with the visitor's Web experience. Artists are creative individuals who demand free rein in design. However, it is important to realize that when engaged in creating art for a people interaction context, then it is incumbent upon artists to pay attention to the constituents of the context. One of these constituents is the convention to which the people have become accustomed. Therefore, the artists' freedom to create in interaction contexts must be swayed by the accepted practices.

An example of how an artist's depiction is inconsistent with the visitor's expectations is shown in Figure 9.15 (see also Plate 27). Here the IRS title header looks like a banner ad. This banner style header includes a title as well as a tag line for the page. Because of the banner style look, visitors may simply skip over the title, as is often the habit with banner advertisements. Moreover, if the header is animated, then the likelihood is even greater that it and any information in its proximity will be ignored deliberately (Nielsen, 1999;

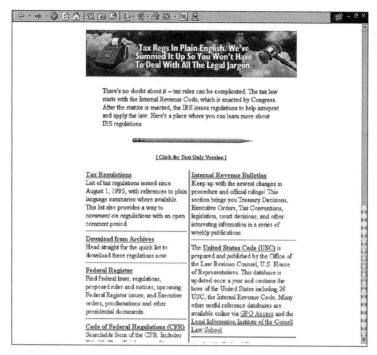

Figure 9.15: *Title header that looks like a banner ad*
(see also Plate 27)

http://www.useit.com/alertbox/99052.html). Again, Figure 9.15 shows an example where the aesthetics are attractive but inconsistent with visitors' interaction habits.

The Use of Graphics

In emphasizing the use of graphics for aesthetic expressions, we shouldn't overlook their equally important use as facilitators in the human processing of information (Haber and Wilkinson, 1982). Graphics, when effectively designed, can be useful tools for information processing. For example, colors can help the visitor to organize chunks of information. A pictorial image can help increase the size of a chunk to be processed, and, indeed, it often may be the most economical way to transmit a complex concept. Here are the main usability guidelines that designers should consider as they incorporate graphics into the design of Web sites.

- Minimize the use of graphics for sites where the purpose is to complete a transaction. Quick system response times are paramount for satisfying visitor interaction experiences, and graphics are too slow to download.

- If graphics must be used, use small images that load quickly, and repeat them if possible. For pages with multiple images, individual images should not be more than 5K in size, with total size of all images not greater than 20K. For a page to download within an acceptable response time rate, the total page size content, including text and images, should not be more than 30K.

- Provide a text-only option, particularly for Web sites when the majority of visitors are dialup users or where the browser or screen real estate is not conducive to graphic displays, such as for some handheld devices.

- When using color graphics, minimize the number of colors that are used in a single image.

- For information coding on a single screen, do not use more than six colors; four are preferable.

- GIFs are smaller than JPEGs and should be used instead of JPEGs for image rendering. In the case where color tonality changes are required, such as in photographs, using JPEGs is recommended.

- Include ALT tags for images. Display alternate text for each image using HTML's ALT feature, and make sure that the text provides a complete description in no more than five words. If a reasonable description cannot be contained within the ALT tag, place the description in the page.

- If images or icons are used as links, provide a redundant text link, particularly if the images are close together. In the case of image maps, provide text links next to the image map.

- Inform the visitor when a link will lead to a page with a large image.

- Clearly identify the active, clickable parts of an image map. For example, make them look like buttons.

- To highlight an item, use coding techniques such as brightness, reverse imaging, and texture rendering. Site visitors will ignore images that look and behave like banner ads or other animated objects.

10

From Desktops to Handhelds

The use of handheld devices such as PDAs (Personal Digital Assistants) and mobile phones has been growing at a steady pace worldwide. These are devices with small-screen "real estate." For PDAs, the low-end devices typically support low-resolution displays with approximately 5″ × 3″ and 160 × 160 pixels. Phones have even lower resolution displays, averaging 1.5″ × 2.5″ and 60 × 96 pixels. Figures 10.1 and 10.2 show a PDA and a phone, respectively. The high-end units are 6.5″ × 3″ and 640 × 240 pixels. It is clear that the technology will continue to improve to allow us to do many of our Internet activities on the move.

A handheld device equipped with a powerful browser and wireless technology will allow users to access a wide range of Internet services such as checking the latest news, stock quotes, travel information, entertainment, flight schedules, and shopping. The technology to support such services efficiently and satisfactorily is still evolving. Nonetheless, we anticipate

---

* This chapter is coauthored by Albert Badre and Kayt Sukel of IXL, Inc.

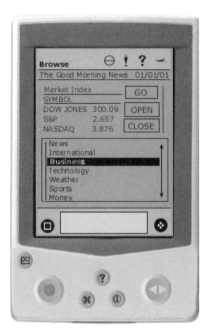

Figure 10.1: *A PDA*
(Design by Sarah Craighill.)

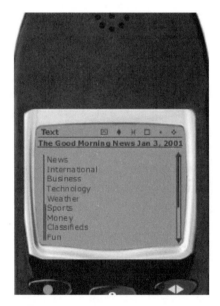

Figure 10.2: *A mobile phone*
(Design by Sarah Craighill.)

technology problems such as small storage capacity, short battery life, and slow CPU speed will be solved eventually.

No matter when these shortcomings are resolved, it is clear that the use of computers with small screens is here for the long haul. Accordingly, usability professionals need to focus on two issues central to end-user performance and satisfaction: first, usability constraints of designing Web sites and Web applications for small screens, and second, designing Web applications and services for mobile contexts. For small screens, designers need to consider the implications of structure, content, and navigation strategies. For a mobile environment, designers must make it easy for end users to tailor relevant applications, services, and tasks to the context of use.

It is important when considering designing for both the PDAs' "small displays" and the mobile phones' "very small displays" to keep in mind that "designing for usability" is tantamount to adopting the principle of user centrality discussed in Chapter 2. This in turn means that we should let what the user requires, wants to do, sees, interacts with, and uses as an Internet service dictate the eventual display size and the appropriate usability designs. If the users' requirements to perform certain transactions necessitate the use of a PDA size display instead of a phone display, then designers should employ the best usability practices for wireless PDAs and implement accordingly. On the other hand, there are certainly Internet activities, applications, and services that are best suited for phone displays. Usability design teams should first identify those activities and then tailor the designs to optimize the user's performance and pleasantness of experience.

The Technology of Wireless Devices

To understand these issues better, let's briefly discuss the technology of wireless devices. Currently, handheld wireless devices are severely constrained in terms of their CPU, memory, battery life, and screen size. Among PDAs, for example, the Jornada, manufactured by Hewlett-Packard, has a screen size of approximately 240×320 pixels. The more popular Palm devices have an even smaller screen size, falling to approximately 160×160 pixels. Mobile telephones, which are expected to hold the higher market share of future wireless users, operate with a minuscule screen size. Usability of wireless devices is also complicated by the constraints of wireless networks, including low bandwidth, high latency, unpredictable stability, and limited availability. To deal with these issues, wireless application developers currently rely on the wireless application protocol (WAP).

Stated simply, WAP is a method for standardizing both data formatting and data transmission for the wireless Web. Wireless device manufacturers have adopted WAP as the industry standard, so businesses interested in developing wireless Web applications can port information to a variety of wireless devices, including cellular phones, PDAs, and wearables.

The WAP programming model, patterned after the World Wide Web's programming model, is optimized to meet the constraints of the wireless networking environment. The wireless application protocol divides HTML pages into well-defined "cards," which are interaction-based units. Cards are delimited by what the user does with a particular page. For example, an existing Web site that allows users to view stock quotes may have separate cards that allow users to enter a stock or to search for a stock. Thus, WAP successfully deals with many wireless issues by creating smaller pages with focused interaction.

WAP delivers content to wireless devices using wireless markup language (WML), a derivative of the extensible markup language (XML), which is the standardized document and data format for the WWW. Defined another way, XML is the method for placing structured data (such as spreadsheets, address books, and so on) into HTML text files. XML interacts with WML in much the same way as it does with HTML, as shown in Figure 10.3. The major difference between WML and HTML is that WML does not assume keyboard or mouse input methods. This distinction is crucial for handheld wireless devices that have alternative input methods, such as the touch-sensitive stylus. You can find more information on WAP and WML at *www.wapforum.org,* a group dedicated to standardizing WAP and the transfer of information from WWW to wireless.

The limitations of WAP and wireless devices raise the usability question of how should standard HTML pages—those with which users have experience (and, thus, most likely a strong mental model)—be divided into meaningful cards? Also, given the lack of standard interactive media (a mouse or a keyboard), how can designers best create applications that can be used easily?

A potential alternative to WAP is the General Packet Radio Service (GPRS). GPRS provides immediacy over WAP because no dialup modem or connection is needed, so information can be sent or received at any time. Furthermore, GPRS supports more robust applications because they are not limited by speed or packet size as WAP currently is. Thus, chat, file transfers, graphics, audio, and collaborative working are all possible over cell phones

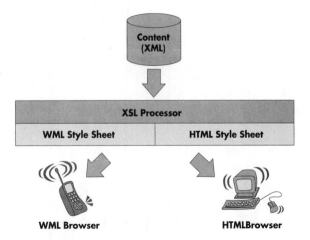

Figure 10.3: *Content development*
(Courtesy of the WAP Forum. Adapted from "Wireless Application
Protocol White Paper," WAP Forum, June 2000.)

using the GPRS protocol. GPRS also works with the wireless protocols used in Europe and Japan, making it a truly global proposition.

Research on the usability of mobile wireless telecommunication devices that provide immediate access to online information is still in its infancy. But there is enough research on small computational devices to identify usability design issues for Internet applications and services on handheld mobile devices. We can explore these issues to generate relevant usability guidelines and to define further studies for "best practices."

The Usability of Wireless Devices

The bulk of wireless research has concerned the improvement of wireless technology, including transmission quality, bandwidth issues, browser compatibility, and standardization of a common format (Buyukkokten 2000a, 2000b; Herstad, et al., 1998). In fact, much of the usability research deals with these ever-changing technological problems. For example, a paper by Chris Johnson (1997) addresses the need for designers to create interfaces that help users compensate for electromagnetic interference, poor interaction, and transmission delays.

Another part of the wireless usability literature exists simply to explain why usability is so important in wireless devices. Peter Johnson (1998) points out that while general human-computer interaction methodology works well in a single, consistent context of use, the wireless world throws out traditional ideas of context. With the increased use of cellular phones and PDAs, we simply do not know who the users are, where they are going to be, or what they are going to want to do. We will not know what types of devices they'll be using or what type of interaction style they prefer. To keep up with this shift in technology, Peter Johnson argues that we need to pay careful attention not only to the context of tasks and the physical context of the user but also to the multitude of choices that users have in terms of wireless device, service, and application.

Several recent studies have managed to surmount the contextual problem through careful analysis and observation. One of the best examples is a study in which MediaOne (now AT&T Broadband) examined the integration of a Web tablet device into household activities. The Web tablet is a wireless computing device with pen-based interaction that is larger and heavier than the average PDA. Researchers took an ethnographic approach to discover how this type of device could be integrated into everyday household activities. MediaOne found that users preferred the tablet to their normal PC because of its portability and the fact that users were able to carry on other household activities while using the tablet (multitasking). However, in the course of their investigation, researchers also found that users had difficulty with extensive data entry, optimal viewing of the display screen, and stylus use. Through ethnographic observation and user input, researchers were better able to understand specific user needs for a Web tablet in the home, the context in which a tablet is used, and how to utilize this information for design improvements (McClard and Somers, 2000).

This study is limited, obviously, because only one device and one location were involved. In the real world, users of wireless Web access could be anywhere and could be using a variety of devices and services. What other design issues are uncovered when we look at the different devices used for the same task?

In fact, to complement the existing research, we did our own simple study of wireless handheld devices. We recruited 16 Xcelerate employees to act as participants. Of these 16 individuals, 8 were current PDA users, and the other 8 were not. All, however, were quite experienced in computer and Web use. Each participant was asked to do four tasks, each on one of four possible devices: the Palm Pilot VII, the NeoPoint NP-1000 SmartPhone, the Hewlett-Packard Jornada 690, and the IBM ThinkPad 600E, which was used as a baseline. All devices accessed the WWW via wireless technology.

The four tasks were based on results from the Graphic, Visualization, and Usability Center's Seventh WWW Survey results. The survey found that the most frequent tasks done on the Web include information gathering, searching, shopping, and browsing. Thus, we created a task for each category. For information gathering, we asked the users to find the price of a particular stock (task 1). For searching, we asked them to search for an arbitrary name on yahoo.com (task 2). For shopping, we asked them to go to amazon.com, find a book, and start the buying process (task 3). For browsing, we asked them to go to a news site and browse the top headlines (task 4). Tasks were counterbalanced with devices so that each participant did each task on a different device, and each task was paired with each device at least once.

Overall, we found no significant differences between either the user groups or the tasks. The biggest differences were among the devices themselves. In terms of time to complete a task and user ratings of a particular device, participants took the most time and had the least favorable impression of the NeoPoint phone, followed closely by the Palm Pilot (see Tables 10.1 and 10.2).

Each of the devices, however, had its usability flaws. Although users preferred the HP Jornada, because it was similar to a laptop computer, most

Table 10.1: *Mean Time to Complete Each Task (in Seconds)*

DEVICE		Palm Pilot	NeoPoint Phone	HP Jornada	IBM ThinkPad
PDA Users	Task 1	67	137	152	69
	Task 2	93	210	135	64
	Task 3	199	361	316	139
	Task 4	151	125	228	46
Nonusers	Task 1	173	208	135	105
	Task 2	232	347	203	38
	Task 3	239	487	223	79
	Task 4	226	148	209	126

Table 10.2: *Mean User Rating (0–5) for Each Device by Task*

DEVICE		Palm Pilot	NeoPoint Phone	HP Jornada	IBM ThinkPad
PDA Users	Task 1	4.8	3.3	3.7	4.2
	Task 2	3.8	2.4	4.1	4.7
	Task 3	2.7	2.3	3.6	5
	Task 4	3.9	3.5	3	5
Nonusers	Task 1	3.7	2.2	3.1	4.3
	Task 2	2.8	2.2	2.8	5
	Task 3	2.4	2.5	4.7	4.9
	Task 4	3.2	3.1	2.6	3.7

participants commented that they disliked having to scroll so much to find a particular part of a Web page. Additionally, many people did not immediately discover the stylus and did not always assume that the screen was a touch screen. They also complained about the lack of a mouse. Concerning the phone, users had difficulty navigating by the various buttons and were unsure of how to find their way back when they made an error. And, since most users in both groups did own cellular phones, they were greatly frustrated when their mental model of phone interaction did not match this particular phone. They found the interaction to be frustratingly time consuming. With the Palm Pilot, users had difficulty locating the keyboard functionality to enter URLs, and, due to their inexperience, they could not get graffiti to work as they would have liked.

These results yield the following important points. First, although different wireless devices may use a similar technology to access the Web, each of these devices is very different and interacts with the user differently. Designers must take these differences into consideration when developing applications that will be usable for multiple devices. Second, users have distinct mental models about how each of these devices should work and what they expect to see on the screen display. These mental models also need to be taken into account when designing wireless Web applications. And finally, participants unanimously voted that they disliked the devices because the users did not see themselves using the devices as a replacement for a desktop computer. They felt that interaction was much too cumbersome for the times they use handheld devices, which, for the most part, was only when they were unable to access a desktop computer. Thus, and most important, it is crucial that designers understand the context in which users will be interacting with wireless devices and the type of information users will want to access given that context.

The Role of Context

The most significant way in which mobile devices differ from fixed-location computers is that their usability is driven by a consideration of their multi-faceted and changing context. Because these devices are by intent mobile, interaction on them is no longer solely a property of the device but rather is strongly related to the context of use. Therefore, when designing for usability on mobile handheld devices, we need to consider the usability constraints associated with the context of use. For example, the changing physical contexts for phone-Web devices suggest that displayed information should be visible under a range of lighting conditions, requiring designs for high-contrast foreground/background combinations.

There are several levels of context that impact the design of interaction for mobile communication and handheld Web devices. Infrastructure, application, location, and physical contexts all have unique usability implications.

Infrastructure Context. Variability in the supporting infrastructure can affect different styles of interaction (Greenberg and Marwood, 1994). For example, disconnection failures, which are highly likely in mobile systems, should be properly reflected visually or by auditory means via interaction between the user interface and the underlying communication infrastructure. Other infrastructure failures should also be properly reported through the Web/application/service interface.

Application Context. Allowing users to personalize applications and services is key to the usability of mobile Web communication devices. How to allow the customer to tailor the transmitted information is an important issue for usability design. For example, items on a menu list might be selected with different frequencies relative to different users. Users might want to have frequently selected commands or links available in a one-click button or pop-up menu. Personalization should make it easy for users to configure and invoke different first pages depending on their interest—for example, cnn.com stock quotations or sports scores.

Location Context. The most fundamental advantage of mobile devices is, obviously, their ability to operate in many locations. Designing for usability should include making it possible in an easy way for the user to tailor the interface to the constituents of the situation. For example, if a person is in New York City when using the phone to access cnn.com, the cnn.com first page should give the relevant local information, such as weather, as a matter of course.

Physical Context. The user interface should be sensitive to environmental conditions, or at least allow the user to easily configure the interface to meet the constraints of the present physical environment. Different physical conditions that affect the design of the device's "look and feel" include lighting, weather, noise, and moving vehicles. This last situation, for example, calls for an auditory rather than a visual presentation to the vehicle's driver.

Small-Size Effects

Small screens impose limitations on design that will affect the user's experience. Three possible effects result from reduction of screen "real estate" space: screen context, constructive synthesis, and partial content.

Screen context effect. The amount of information shown affects how the viewer of the information interprets it. Using the definition of *context* as "that which surrounds," user's interpretations and therefore user's actions can be sensitive to the viewing area of the information. Using the definition of *context* as "that which weaves constituents into a coherent whole," the user's interpretation can be influenced by the objects available for weaving.

A global view is likely to give the user a more accurate picture for interpretation than a localized view. This is true because a global view shows a more complete exposure to the relevant objects and how they relate to each other than does a partial view of the objects. If the size of a display forces a partial view of the intended information, it can certainly lead to a different interpretation than what the designer intends. The examples that follow are given only to illustrate the points of interpreting information on a small-sized screen. They are not given to suggest that the use of pictures and drawings is expected or recommended on small handheld displays.

For a generic example of the effects of context on interpretation, consider viewing artist Rene Magritte's *Le Promenades d'Euclide*. If we were to show the painting on a desktop monitor with high resolution, the viewer would see a completeness of detail with fine distinctions among objects such as buildings, windows, roofs, and streets. As shown in Figure 10.4, this work is a surreal painting of a village view from a window. The village we see shows houses, a coned roof, and a street drawn in perspective in the middle of the village.

Assume now that because of size of display and a resolution of 160×160 pixels, we can show only parts of the painting at lower than full resolution, as in Figures 10.5 and 10.6. Assume further that each of these figures shows the default view before scrolling. In Figure 10.5, we see part of the village at low resolution, so details like buildings and windows are hardly distinguishable, resulting in a clear view of only the coned roof and the street, which, for correctness of perspective, has been drawn narrow on the top and wide at the bottom.

Because of several factors, a viewer unfamiliar with the painting will likely misinterpret the street as another coned roof. First, the low resolution

Figure 10.4: *Painting* Le Promenades d'Euclide *by Rene Magritte*
(The Minneapolis Institute of Arts. The William Hood Dunwoody Fund.
© 2002 C. Herscovici, Brussels/Artists Rights Society [ARS], New York.)

Figure 10.5: *Detail of painting shown at low resolution*
(The Minneapolis Institute of Arts. The William Hood Dunwoody Fund.
© 2002 C. Herscovici, Brussels/Artists Rights Society [ARS], New York.)

Figure 10.6: *Cutting off the curtains removes
the impression of a view from a window.*
(The Minneapolis Institute of Arts. The William Hood Dunwoody Fund.
© 2002 C. Herscovici, Brussels/Artists Rights Society [ARS], New York.)

and the reduction of the viewing area obscure the immediate surroundings of the street. If we scan the picture in the classic Western left-to-right reading pattern, we will see first the coned roof, thus biasing our interpretation of the second shape, the street, as a second coned roof. Even if we do not scan the picture from left to right but focus instead on the two bright objects in the picture, we are likely—given most people's bias for symmetry—to attach the same plausible meaning to the street as we do to the roof. The reason is that interpreting the first bright object as a roof does not require perspective, while interpreting the second bright object as a street requires the clear perception of perspective. Portraying perspective for successful interpretation requires the presence of meaningful surrounds. Again, a viewer can easily misidentify the street as a second coned roof.

Figure 10.6 shows a slightly larger area of the painting incorporating the view of the village and parts of the easel. The curtains suggesting that this is a view from a window are missing. Instead, the focus on what looks like an easel suggests that we are viewing a painted canvas on an easel. Here again, lack of critical detail because of size of display results in misinterpretation. This is not unlike the example in Figure 10.7 (see also Plate 28) of the Université de Savoie home page, showing a university in a scenic setting. The context of the view can lead to different interpretations.

Constructive Synthesis Effect. Viewers of a scene often have to add information based on their experience and memory that is not present in the picture. They have to construct a meaning based on a combination of what data are given and the viewer's stored experience. In fact, experts—people with

Figure 10.7: *Université de Savoie home page* (see also Plate 28)
(Universite de Savoie [France]: *www.univ-savoie.fr.*)

accumulated experience—often interpret the same data differently and more efficiently than novices precisely because they are able to organize information in ways that utilize their previous experience (Schneider, 1982). We call this type of information processing "constructive synthesis."

The classic example of constructive synthesis is illustrated in the picture of a Dalmatian dog that has appeared in many psychology books. The dog is bending with its head down on the left side of the picture. A front limb is also shown, but no hind limbs or rear end is visible. To interpret the picture as that of a Dalmatian, we must pull from our memories a mental depiction of a Dalmatian and use it to construct the rest of the image. Figure 10.8. shows the partially drawn image of a ballerina to which we would have to add information to complete the figure and interpret it as such. Here, constructive synthesis is possible because we are cued, by recognizing part of the dress and the face, as to what information to pull out from memory.

Figure 10.8: *Drawing of ballerina*
(Courtesy of Barbara Badre.)

Recognizing the figure as that of a female dancer is possible because of our learned and stored experience with visual images of ballerinas. It is important to realize that without such experience, we would not have been able to construct the image and interpret it as a ballerina. If, on a small display, we were to show only one-half of the image (see Figure 10.9), there would not be sufficient information for cueing our stored experiences, and we would find it much more difficult to interpret the image as that of a female dancer.

Figure 10.7 of the Université de Savoie home page illustrates the importance of well-learned experience for the interpretation of data. A view of the right half of the page, as in Figure 10.7, allows us to construct the interpretation that this university is in a beautiful, scenic surrounding. Our independent experiences with universities and with picturesque mountain environments allow us to construct the interpretation of "university education in a scenic setting," which is the obvious message intended by the designer without using an explicit statement to that effect. On the other hand, a small display showing one side of the page, as in Figure 10.10 (see also

Figure 10.9: *Only part of the ballerina drawing is visible*
(Courtesy of Barbara Badre.)

Figure 10.10: *Partial view of the Université de Savoie home page*
(see also Plate 29)
(Universite de Savoie [France]: *www.univ-savoie.fr.*)

Plate 29), will be difficult to interpret as the designer intends. It shows only a beautiful mountain setting.

Partial Content Effect. If we are not careful when reducing the size of the display, what is shown on the screen could become useless, misleading, or annoying. A blinking banner ad, even if only in text, can be quite annoying given the size of the ad in relation to the size of the display. Figure 10.11 shows an example of a useless display in which all we can see is the logo of the company. Figure 10.12 shows a graph, and Figure 10.13 shows a boxed area representing a portion of the same graph that might be visible on a small display. Showing only part of the full graph conveys misleading information.

The usability constraints of designing Web sites for small-screen computers are in many ways potentially different from constraints for displays that have larger real estate with greater resolution. There are several design issues that are usability sensitive:

- Effective functionality and task preference
- Information presentation
- Interaction and navigation

Figure 10.11: *Company logo taking up entire display*
(Icon One Source, Inc.: *www.iconinc.com.*)

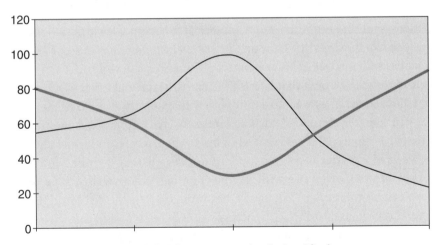

Figure 10.12: *Line graph of scientific data*

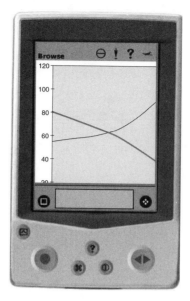

Figure 10.13: *Part of the graph visible on a small display, which can be misleading*

Effective Functionality and Task Preferences

Designers must select from a large number of functions a few priority ones to use with handheld devices. How do we decide which functions to keep? And on what basis do we decide? Device compatibility? Frequency of use? With computer software, and even standard HTML pages, it is crucial to know your users and the tasks that they want to accomplish with that software or Web site.

In user-centric design for the wireless Web, designers can use the old newspaper reporter's "Five W's": who, what, when, where, and why. Who will be using wireless devices? What kinds of devices will they be using, and what sort of browser or service will they be running? Where will they be using these devices most often? When will they want to access the Web? And finally, why (for what tasks) will they be accessing the wireless Web? For each potential application, these questions must be carefully considered to design context-sensitive, usable wireless Web sites.

For example, most functions on mobile phones are rarely used because of the cumbersome way they have to be accessed. Frequently used and important functions should be made available on the first screen by employing the thumbnail approach (Holmquist, 1999). Think of the preceding "where" question. The wireless Web will not replace the use of the WWW on a desktop computer. Chances are a cellular phone user will not be calmly seated at a desk choosing to go through a cumbersome interaction process. The wireless phone user will be on the go, focused on accessing a specific piece of information and then moving on.

In the context of this typical "where" situation, what are the types of tasks that wireless devices best support? Byrne, et al. (1999) suggest that designers should do careful task analysis, or what they term a "taskonomy," for each Web application. This process is even more crucial when designing for the hand Web.

Information Presentation

Users of mobile devices want instant access to information. They do not want to wait until they get back to their fixed-location computer in the office or the home. Hand Web users need data that are easily accessible on a small screen space, can be read or viewed immediately, are presented in cohesive and complete chunks, and are contextually meaningful.

We need to devise solutions for maximizing the use of small-screen space for the user to view textual information. Several strategies can achieve this. First, there is the use of browsers that allow focus + context techniques (Robertson and Mackinlay, 1993; Holmquist, 1997; Fisher, et al., 1997). These techniques employ the notion that as people view content, they need to be able to focus on targeted information in context. This is particularly important for small displays.

Holmquist and Bjork (1998) developed a focus + context technique they call flip zooming. In flip zooming, the display has two components: the target information, which is the object of focus, and contextual information, which is represented as thumbnails. The target information such as a page in a Web site is placed in the middle of the display. All the pages that came before it are represented as thumbnails and placed on the top and to the left of the target page. All the pages that come after the target page are placed as thumbnails at the bottom and to the right of the target page.

Figures 10.14 and 10.15, respectively, show examples of the use of thumbnails in focus + context representations. This technique can also be used for focusing on sections of a page such as paragraphs. This is a particularly attractive usability technique because it provides a practical alternative to scrollbars for reading sections of a long page on small displays. Bjork and Redstrom (1999) found flip zooming to be more effective for providing an overview and searching for specific items than using traditional scrollbars. For Web sites that have more pages than can be accommodated on a small screen, we can indicate "more thumbnails" by using an arrow button. With this technique, a single tap will show a desired page in the immediate vicinity. For pages that are a little farther away, it will take two taps.

On small displays, focusing in a context applies to two presentations: a page in a cluster of pages and the contents of a specific page. In the case of pages traversed, there is evidence that, in Web browsing, people find it problematic when they are unable to find a page, return to it, or organize it relative to other pages (Pitkow and Kehoe, 1996). Providing context such as thumbnails of pages to facilitate page navigation helps enormously.

There are several other design strategies that may be used to accommodate small-screen space. These include, for example, the use of audio instead of visual cues for feedback (Brewster, 1998), a technique already employed by

Figure 10.14: *Phone display of focus + context representation*
using thumbnails
(Design by Sarah Craighill.)

Figure 10.15: *PDA display of focus + context representation using thumbnails*
(Design by Sarah Craighill.)

mobile phones. Another approach is the use of Web clipping. Web clipping is intended to minimize both display and bandwidth usage. The horizontal space content of a regular Web page will take up valuable vertical space on the small screen. Thus, top horizontal icon bars, logos, borders, and so forth should as a general rule be removed on small displays.

For Web pages in general, the first rule of design (as was discussed in Chapter 6) is that form follows function. Ensure that users can do what they want to do quickly, and then worry about formatting the work space. This rule is equally true for small-screen spaces. It is not feasible to make all the functions, links, and so on available on a small screen. The designer needs to decide early what the most important or frequently used functions are and then, once selected, decide how best to present them.

Although we usually recommend hierarchical organization for desktop-size Web designs, this approach may not work on small displays. For small screens, it may be necessary to order what is displayed by the most frequently used information, function, or activity rather than by a logical ordering of the general to the more specific.

Interaction and Navigation

In designing interaction and navigation strategies, it is important for designers to realize that the paradigm for mobile devices is the wristwatch, not the desktop computer. Hand Web users want to be able to interact and navigate almost instantaneously. These users do not have time to read large amounts of text, solve problems, or make hard decisions. They want instant access to information. Speed is of the essence.

On a handheld device, the Internet user should be able to find desired information, such as a stock quote, in a minimum amount of time; to navigate to a Web site, or within a site to a page, with little effort; and to invoke commands quickly. The designer's goals should include designing for fast command execution and quick viewing of information. Fast command execution means that we should distinguish between frequently used commands, links, selections, and buttons and those that are used occasionally. Frequently invoked actions are those that range between several times per hour and several times per week. The design should be such that the most frequently invoked actions can be taken with one tap. Actions that are used with moderate frequency should require no more than two taps, and actions that are very infrequently used can be activated with more than two taps, depending on their level in the frequency hierarchy. Designers can develop a default frequency hierarchy on the basis of task and usage analysis.

Navigation is slower on small devices (Buyukkokten, et al., 2000a, 2000b). To help improve navigation speed, links should be organized so that the most frequently visited links appear on the home page and the most frequently accessed pages. All pages should have a frequent-links button that when tapped will show a page with the most frequently used links.

For presenting and viewing information quickly on mobile displays, an all-text content is the most usable format. Web pages should be designed to communicate content using "cryptic text" such as bullets, short phrases, and keywords. Cryptic text presentations allow the mobile user to view information with quick glances and also reduce download and response times.

Designer's Palette: Guidelines for Hand Web Design

Context of use, mobility of user, and diversity of device integration give rise to a host of usability issues in designing for the hand Web. There are a number of guidelines to assist designers.

- Develop phone Web devices that users can tailor readily and quickly to meet their needs. In cases where tailoring cannot be done automatically, users should be able to easily customize the interface to meet their requirements, the requirements of the physical constraints, and those of the location of use.

- Define patterns of use for phone Web applications or services. For example, is the pattern one user at a time, or does the task require use by two or more people simultaneously?

- Because mobile phones can be shared by groups of people in a public setting (for example, traveling and looking for directions), test a variety of viewing angles of the display to support group viewing. Such designs should include large character sets, display lighting, and high-contrast foreground and background combinations.

- Consider the use of redundant audio output, particularly for situations where visual information acquisition is not convenient, such as while the user is driving a car or is in the dark.

- Allow the user to easily adjust text size to improve viewing and reading in poor lighting conditions.

- Allow users to manipulate and organize presented data quickly according to their individual requirements.

- Make frequently used functionality available on first screens. Minimize the number of display levels to limit the menu surfing required to access frequently used functions.

- Provide command buttons for high-frequency functions.

- Phone Web devices should approximate the quickness associated with voice phone interaction: quick command execution, quick page navigation, and quick data searches.

- Allow users to access and navigate Web pages, sites, and information in more than one designated way.

- Design the functionality to minimize the need for typing or key entry on phone devices.
- Consider the use of voice commands for navigating—for example, "back" and "next" or "up" and "down."
- Keep links short; one word is preferable.
- Choose meaningful words for links; use those that are familiar to the users by selecting them from the audience lexicon.
- Consider the use of voice commands for one-word links.
- Allow users more than one way of marking and highlighting important information, such as boldfacing and changing font.
- Designers should conduct contextual inquiries as part of their usability evaluations to determine what tasks, functions, and habits are prevalent among different types of mobile Web users.
- Provide text and background in high-contrast combinations.
- For data tables, label row and column headers.
- Avoid the use of blinking content as a coding technique.
- Create a style of presentation that is consistent across pages.
- Limit the use of "very small" devices to applications and services where text is the most suitable presentation form.
- Design with speed of access and speed of interaction in mind.
- Upon request, a first page on a phone Web device should come up within a matter of a few seconds.
- The rule that "form follows function" is especially true for very small display devices.
- Because of the small real estate, hierarchical organization is a must.
- Make sure that screen layout is consistent.
- Establish visual identity on the display by using consistent visual elements and style.

11
The Cultural Context

Creating or retrofitting software applications for different cultures requires attention to technical detail that goes beyond mere translation. Designers must understand and incorporate the unique attributes and conventions of targeted cultural communities. For example, how sequential pictorial information is presented and organized for scanning on a display should be related to the script orientation of the user's first language. Therefore, script orientation for a given culture becomes an important consideration for designers even when presenting nontextual information.

It is also important that designers understand the software design and adaptation methods of internationalization and localization. Internationalization is the creation of a modular infrastructure that supports localization, which, in turn, is the process of creating and adapting libraries of attributes to target specific cultures. This chapter delineates the issues that should be considered when creating cultural libraries for the World Wide Web.

Cultural Usability

In recent years, we have witnessed a growing research interest in the cultural context of user interface design. This interest has become even more manifest with the continuing worldwide expansion of the Internet and Web usage. The interest in cultural usability presupposes an operational definition of *culture* that Web designers can use to distinguish between cultures. Culture has been defined in many ways (Yeo, 1996; Hofstede, 1997; El-Shinnawy and Vinze, 1997; Cole, 1997), ranging from "shared values and beliefs" to "collective established patterns of thinking." Bartlett (1932) discussed culture in terms of schemas that were in both the external, material world and the mental world.

For the purpose of designing cultural usability, we will keep the definition simple and operational. We will view culture in terms of attributes belonging to a target audience that distinguish it from other target communities. Therefore, we view culture as the collective of identifiable behaviors, practices, conventions, signs, symbols, artifacts, values, and beliefs that characterize a group. The practice of cultural usability requires that the designer identify the target audience's relevant attributes and design accordingly for them.

The information provided by international respondents to a Cultural Issues Questionnaire administered via the 8th GVU WWW User Survey *(http://www.gvu.gatech.edu/user_surveys/survey-1997-10/)* strongly suggests that there is a need to pay attention to cultural design issues on the World Wide Web. Analysis of the data clearly demonstrates that preferences differ across cultures. For example, Chinese respondents strongly preferred colorful Web pages, whereas German respondents strongly disliked them. English, French, and Spanish respondents indicated a high preference for graphics, whereas German respondents found graphics unappealing. Respondents from Asia and the Middle East were most likely to know people who could not learn to use the Internet due to language barriers.

These self-reporting results of cross-cultural differences in preference are often reinforced by empirical cross-cultural studies of performance between specific cultures. For example, Choong and Salvendy (1998) found that Chinese users performed tasks faster with fewer errors when presented with pictorial icons rather than with alphanumeric ones. The reverse was true for American users. In a study of Italian Web users, Badre (2001) compared the Web search performance for Italian subjects by providing them with either Italian or American navigation icons. The results showed that the performance of Italian Web users was improved when the Web page included Italian navigation icons. The subjects also preferred the Italian icons.

Furthermore, the demography of Internet users in general has been changing dramatically. Years ago, the average Internet inhabitant was more likely to be a young and technologically advanced male and, in most cases, English speaking. But today, the WWW reaches people with a variety of different educational levels and from different cultures.

A number of investigations explored the role of culture in the design of Web interfaces. Marcus and Gould (2000) analyzed the relationships of intangible cultural dimensions as postulated by Hofstede (1997) to Web site design. Evers and Day (1997) reported on how cultural design preferences affect user acceptance of an interface. Analysis of the data collected during the 8th GVU WWW User Survey is representative of this fact. Users from a number of countries differed in their opinions about the meaningfulness of navigation icons, intensity of graphics, use of background color, and use of sound effects for Web sites designed in the United States.

In a cultural usability study, Barber and Badre (1998) identified a number of attributes that are culture-specific. Table 11.1 lists the design markers identified as potential candidates for cultural preference. Some of these cultural markers were used in a study by Sheppard and Scholtz (1999) that showed some performance benefits for users of a given culture when Web sites were designed to include markers from their culture.

Gobbin (1998) considered this problem from a more general point of view—the adaptation of new technological tools. He argued that users have a cultural model of methodology to be employed in a given task and that this model should be taken into consideration when designing technological tools for supporting the task. Gobbin showed that the cultural fitness of a tool in an organizational context played a more important role in the adaptation of a new technology than even its operational advantages by allowing for a faster learning pattern due to knowledge transfer. Bourges-Waldegg and Scrivener (1998) demonstrated the limitations of culturally insensitive design approaches for an international audience.

Table 11.1: *Design Markers List*

Color:	Colors of:	Language:	Motion:	Fonts:
Red	Flag	Native	Animated GIFs	Cursive
Blue	Graphics	Foreign	Advertising	Italics
Green	Pictures	Multiple	Text	Bold
Black	Links		Video	Size
Yellow	Borders			Shading
Gold	Background			Centering
Brown				
Pink				
Purple		**Flag:**	**Sound:**	**Links:**
Teal		National	Music	Color
Background		International	Voice	Internal
		Multiple		External
				Embedded
				Stand alone

(continued)

Table 11.1: *Design Markers List (cont.)*

Regional:	Grouping:	Shapes:	Icons/Metaphors:
Foliage	Symmetrical	Squares	International
Animals	Asymmetrical	Circles	Local
Landscape	Proximity	Triangles	Clock
Water	Alignment	Rectangles	Newspaper
Desert	Boundary	Lines	Book
	Enclosure	Arrows	Pages
	Connection	Sun	House/Home
Geography:			Stamps
Map			Envelopes
Outline			Musical Notes
Globe			
Architecture:	**Human Figure:**		
Slate building	Photograph		
House	Drawing/Cartoon		
Church	Bodyparts		
Office			
Cityscape			

Culture-Specific Designs

Designers of Web sites have started to pay attention to the fact that their designs should be tailored to the cultural communities that make up their target audiences. As a minimum, where it is relevant, the same site appears in the language of the target audience. Contrast, for example, the Microsoft site for Japan and France in Figures 11.1 (see also Plate 30) and 11.2 (see also Plate 31). The most prominent factors differentiating the two sites are the language and layout. There are few other differences deriving from culture. The same is true for other companies' sites, such as Amazon.com, America Online, and Yahoo.

When we examine the cultural design differences among sites of various businesses, such as Amazon and Microsoft, for the same country, we can see that the cultural design markers for the same country differ substantially among the companies' sites. No cultural commonalities stand out. These are examples, however, of attempts to recognize the need to address the varying cultural communities of the World Wide Web.

Figure 11.1: *Microsoft Japan site* (see also Plate 30)
(Screen shot reprinted by permission from Microsoft Corporation.)

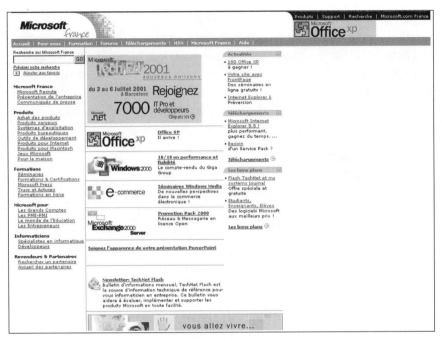

Figure 11.2: *Microsoft France site* (see also Plate 31)
(Screen shot reprinted by permission from Microsoft Corporation.)

The environment in which a Web site is designed is likely to affect the cultural characteristics of the design. For example, a Russian site designed in California will employ design habits that are particularly American and will differ from the same site developed in Moscow. In studying the characteristics of several dozen Web sites originating either in the United States or in the country of the language of the site, Barber and Badre (1998) discovered significant differences in cultural markers as a function of the original design environment. Designs developed in the United States were often burdened with American cultural markers, such as the use of red and blue colors when green is the predominant cultural color of the target audience, or the preponderance of graphics in sites for cultures where the predominant mode of expression is text.

Designing for the Localized Web

Cultural elements for designing localized Web sites derive from the interaction of two contexts: the environment and the user. The environment provides physical cultural attributes such as architecture, regional plants and wildlife, natural and adopted colors, symbols, signs, images, sounds, and scents. The cultural attributes associated with the users include customs, practices, and behaviors that range from conventions, such as how people express date and time, to intangibles, such as power-distance relations and uncertainty avoidance (Hofstede, 1997).

When targeting a cultural community, Web designers should consider foraging for six categories of culture-specific elements.

- Genre-localized attributes
- Behaviors and practices
- Icons, symbols, pictorials, and artifacts
- Conventions and formats
- Intangible values and dimensions
- Preferred content

The process of localizing Web sites consists of exploring and identifying the cultural elements of each of the six categories, incorporating them into the design, then modifying the design with testing and experience.

Genre-Localized Attributes

Genres differ, one genre from another, by a set of basic attributes, as discussed in Chapter 6. These basic attributes of expression and form, however, can differ within the same genre across cultures. Designers should study the physical world equivalents of their genres to identify culturally unique attributes and practices, which they can incorporate into their designs. For example, in studying the newspapers of a given cultural community, the designer of a news site targeting that community may discover that the common front page formatting in one culture is different from the front page formatting in the designer's culture. The newspaper readers of each of these cultures are accustomed to a particular format in the daily newspaper in their respective communities and would expect the same format on a news Web site. Therefore, the designer should use the format prevalent in the newspapers of the target culture.

In Italian popular magazines, for example, articles are often accompanied by summaries or abstracts of the article, but this is seldom done in U.S. magazines. Another example comes from the museum subgenre. Museums in the United States tend to be pedagogical. With many displayed works of art, there are associated explanations of the work or information about the artist or the period. In Italian museums, it is assumed that the museum visitor is already educated and is visiting simply to view and appreciate the artwork. There is no accompanying information. The designer should provide the actual expected museum experience of the target audience. A museum Web site that combined explanatory text with artwork might be considered annoying and cluttered by an Italian audience.

Behaviors and Practices

Designers often use the real world as a model when developing a Web site. It is important to remember, however, that the real world varies drastically in many ways from country to country. This is particularly true when it comes to people's behaviors and practices. An example is the use of a shopping cart on e-shopping Web sites. Shopping carts are well understood in the United States, where they are available at every supermarket and most discount department stores. In many European and Middle Eastern countries, however, shoppers usually bring their own shopping bags to the stores. A shopping bag, not a cart, would be a more appropriate metaphor for these cultures.

For another example, consider the practice of throwing away trash. In some cultures, it is unacceptable to rummage through a trash can to retrieve a discarded item (Nakakoji, 1994, 1996). Yet, the Macintosh interface allows the user to place an item in the trash can and retrieve it before emptying the trash can. A user's expectation as to whether a file placed in the trash can is permanently lost depends on the user's practices in the physical world. Another example of differences in culture-specific practice is the definition of a workweek. In our designs, we often assume that a workweek is Monday through Friday, but this is not true for many other cultures.

Designers should explore target cultural communities to identify relevant behaviors and practices. Here is a sample of markers that should be considered in collecting cultural design requirements.

- Use of shopping carts in shopping sites
- Use of credit cards in shopping sites
- Use of phone cards for communication sites
- Script orientation for sequencing of text and pictorials
- Mailing of letters and packages
- Disposing of trash
- Dining customs

- The making and publicizing of one's mistakes
- Workweek practices

Icons, Symbols, Pictorials, and Artifacts

We use icons, symbols, and pictorials to communicate information, and we often use interface design metaphors of artifacts to express concepts or convey functionality. This practice is fine as long as the designer understands that representation and interpretation of symbols vary around the world. Inappropriate symbols or pictures can inadvertently offend or confuse someone if cultural differences lead to misunderstanding or misinterpretation. For example, as a sports link, the picture of a baseball player will be less meaningful in Greece than a picture of a soccer player. Similarly, on Web sites where the design requires showing people's faces and attire, designers should localize the pictures to show faces and attire of the target cultural community.

Our familiar pictorial of a mailbox to denote sending and receiving e-mail is inappropriate for many cultures. In many countries, the mail is placed in a door slot.

In government, tourism, and education sites, it may be important to show relevant pictures along with text. In these cases, designers should localize the pictures to include regional markers such as colors predominant in the environment, geography, trees, wildlife, flags, and emblems, as the case may require. The use of popular colors and regional colors should be taken into consideration when localizing sites. Notice, for example, that many Web sites originating in Saudi Arabia and the Emirates use a preponderance of the green Islamic colors or the regional desert colors of yellow, brown, and orange. Notice the use of the green color in the Al Hajj Info Portal site in Figure 11.3 (see also Plate 32).

It is important to study the icons, symbols, pictorials, and artifacts to be used in a given culture as a basis for Web design requirements. Here are some icons, pictorials, symbols, and artifacts to consider when localizing Web site interfaces.

- Mailbox icons
- Flags and emblems
- Architecture
- Regional plants, trees, wildlife, foods, geography
- Colors predominant in the environment

- Food pictorials
- Sounds and music
- Custom and attire
- Human faces
- Religious symbols
- Gestures
- The use of abbreviations, jargon, slang

Conventions and Formats

Designers of internationalized and localized Web sites should research the target culture's national and community conventions. These include standards and formats for items such as date and currency, which often are independent of language translation. Consider, for example, the use of numeric values in the decimal systems of various countries. This is of particular importance in Web interface design because numeric representations can affect user input, visual display, and data processing. The United States uses

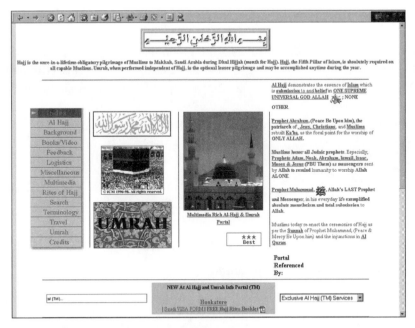

Figure 11.3: *Al Hajj Info Portal site* (see also Plate 32)
(Al Hajj info portal.)

decimal points and commas one way, whereas many European countries use a comma where we would use a decimal point. Some cultures use a period to separate thousands, and others use an apostrophe.

For shopping sites, currency is an issue of cross-cultural concern not only because of the numbers and symbols used but also because of symbol placement. For example, U.S. currency written as $1,500.25 is expressed as 1.500,25 DM in German currency. A Web site interface should allow the user to choose from various symbols such as period, colon, comma, or other currency symbols to be used as decimal separators.

Like currency, time and date formats differ across cultures. For example, most Western countries use the Gregorian calendar. Arab countries use the Islamic and Gregorian calendars. Many other calendars exist that are used locally in different parts of the world. Also, calendar standards should take into account that religious and national holidays can differ across cultures. Variations in calendar types change the display formatting. For example, in the United States Sunday is considered to be the first day of the week, but in Europe the week starts with Monday. Also, in indicating dates, the order of day, month, and year varies across cultures.

Colors often have different meanings in different countries. For example, while red means "danger" and "stop" in the United States, in China it denotes happiness. Green stands for "safety" and "go" in the United States, but in Egypt it denotes fertility and strength, and in France, green means criminality. Designers should attend to these differences, which are often tantamount to cultural standards.

Here are some conventions and formats with which designers should be familiar.

- Date and time

- Currency

- Measurement scales and weight units

- The use of commas and decimals in numerals

- Colors with associated meanings

- Calendars

- Postal addresses

- Telephone numbers
- Temperature
- Punctuation
- Paper sizes
- Collating sequences
- Character sets

Intangible Values and Dimensions

Cultural values are deeply rooted and often transmitted to members of a given community in early childhood. Well-entrenched, strong, and enduring, these values cover a range of fundamental beliefs concerning what is right and wrong and what is acceptable and unacceptable. These intangible cultural values often have an impact on the design of end-user products such as Web sites. For example, clip art, which is often shipped with software to be used in designing Web pages, should be adapted and localized to account for the target cultural community values. The image of a woman as a leader is acceptable in the United States, but in many other countries such a picture would be frowned upon.

Hofstede (1997) postulated several intangible values that distinguish cultural communities. One such value is power-distance, which concerns the relationship between authority and the less powerful in a society. Another concerns the strength of individualism in a society. Other cultural intangibles include male dominance values and uncertainty avoidance. Marcus and Gould (2000) related these values in a very creative way to how they are expressed in the Web site designs originating in various countries. The following is a sample list of intangible cultural values and associated references.

- Individualism vs collective action (Hofstede, 1997; Nakakoji, 1994)
- Time perception (Nakakoji, 1994)
- Procedural vs declarative (Nakakoji, 1994)
- Femininity vs masculinity (Hofstede, 1997)
- Power-distance (Hofstede, 1997)
- Uncertainty avoidance (Hofstede, 1997)
- Universalistic vs particularistic (Nakakoji, 1994)

Preferred Content

Different cultural communities are likely to have different interests and content preferences. Designers should present content in the order of the most relevant to the least relevant to the target cultural community. For example, in an Islamic religious culture, education sites need to present information about gender with respect to classroom venues. Such content is usually irrelevant to educational site audiences in Western European countries.

There may be different levels of interest in sports from one region to another, as well as from one season to another. For example, more U.S. fans will be interested in baseball in the summer than in the winter, whereas sports readers in Portugal in the summer will be interested in soccer. Figures 11.4 and 11.5 are examples of two news sites on the Web with headlines that reflect the different interests of their readers for the same date, August 24, 2001, in the United States and the United Kingdom.

Figure 11.4: The Atlanta Journal-Constitution *Web page*
(Reprinted with permission from *The Atlanta Journal*
and *The Atlanta Constitution*.)

Figure 11.5: Trinity Mirror Digital Media *Web page*
(Reproduced by permission of *Trinity Mirror Digital Media.*
All rights reserved.)

12

Evaluating Web Usability

Usability testing has traditionally meant testing for efficiency of use, ease of learning, and the ability to remember how to perform interactive tasks without difficulty or errors. Testing for Web usability takes on the added emphasis and necessity of testing for a satisfactory user experience. A Web usability test should ascertain that visitors both achieve the goal of their visit efficiently and at the same time have an enjoyable experience.

An "enjoyable experience" depends to a large extent on the context and the purpose of the visit. If, for example, the context is that of a traveler searching for a cheap airfare, then the experience will be enjoyable if the traveler achieves her purpose efficiently, with a minimum number of clicks and in the shortest time. If the inclusion of graphics or animation in this case leads to delays and annoyance, then it is likely that the traveler would not consider the visit "enjoyable." On the other hand, if the visitor wants to shop for a dress, then a site that provides pictures of dresses with colors and styles, and a feature where dresses can be fitted on an animated figure of a specified size and height is likely to produce a positive experience. The experience would probably be less positive if the visitor must simply select from text-based descriptions of dresses.

It is imperative that design speculations, hunches, and conjectures be put through a valid evaluation methodology. In the final analysis, design insights and solutions are only as good as the quality of the methodology used to derive them. This chapter focuses on considering evaluation methodologies for Web design, with an emphasis on optimizing the user experience. After a brief review of traditional usability evaluation, we'll examine how testing for Web user experience may differ and what specific items to include when evaluating the user experience of a Web site. A description of the process of Web evaluation follows. At the end of the chapter, there is a list of frequently asked question about usability evaluation.

Traditional Usability Testing

Usability testing has long been regarded as essential to good iterative design practices in the software world. Traditionally, usability test methods have been used as evaluation techniques for industrial design artifacts and computer software and hardware. These methods include heuristic techniques, such as expert reviews and cognitive walkthroughs, as well as formal user testing, such as usability lab tests, human factors experiments, and prototype testing. In addition, usability evaluators have used ethnography, field evaluation methods, and data collection, using questionnaires and interviews for task and audience analyses. For a detailed discussion of formal usability testing methods, see Nielsen (1997a, 1993) and any of a number of Human Computer Interaction textbooks (Shneiderman, 1992, 1998; Mayhew, 1992; Preece, et al., 1994; Dix, et al., 1998).

We perform usability evaluation to determine how people use systems and where they may encounter difficulty of use. There is ample evidence that development costs are reduced significantly as a result of employing usability techniques (Sun Microsystems, *http://www.sun.com/usability.benefits. html*). Training and support costs are also reduced. Landauer (1995) suggests that user-centered approaches reduce training time by 25 percent. Other investigators support claims that organizations save substantial amounts in redesign and support costs (Bias and Mayhew, 1994). Usability testing is especially helpful when integrated into an iterative design paradigm, including usability inspection methods such as heuristic evaluation and competitive analysis.

Usability Testing for the Web

Traditional usability testing methods apply equally well to evaluating Web usability, but for the Web, it is at least as important to guarantee a good user experience. What currently resides on the Web is not very usable, and visitors often fail when they try to accomplish tasks on the Web (Nielsen, 1998). In fact, Nielsen argues that users have come to expect failure when doing things on the Web. Other researchers agree and present corroborative evidence. Results show that a significantly large number of attempts to make online purchases fail (Rehman, 2000). Web users report lost transactions, an inability to apply for online jobs, and failure to complete (and in many cases, even to find) tasks on various Web sites.

This unsatisfactory state of Web usability exists in large part because Web developers have not been sensitized to usability constraints and to designing for the user experience. Many Web developers come from graphic user interface (GUI) development experiences that often are not optimal for Web environments, even though many of the design principles of GUI software continue to apply to Web design.

Web-Focused Issues and Testing

Web sites and applications are different from (GUI) software in the following fundamental ways, leading to different usability design and testing emphases.

- Device diversity
- User-controlled navigation
- Mental models of Web usage
- Lowered switching costs
- Point of entry
- Distraction
- Personalization
- Primacy of content
- Context of use

Device diversity. In terms of device diversity, Nielsen (1997b) argues that in traditional GUI design, the designer controls all aspects of the user experience—from the overall look and feel to details such as where on the screen a button will be placed. With Web pages, this is not the case. Among different Web browsers, different devices, and different operating systems, the same Web design can look dramatically different. In addition, the Web has serious constraints in terms of modem speeds and monitor sizes, both of which can directly impact the Web experience from user to user. Thus, test plans should include quality assurance across devices, operating systems, browsers, monitors, and modem/LAN connections.

User-controlled navigation. The GUI designer mandates where users can and will go by interacting with the system. In Web design, with Web controls and browser back buttons and the ability of the visitor to enter the site at any page or from bookmarks, it is the users who control their navigation, and they can easily lead themselves astray.

Navigation pitfalls can be a huge barrier to usability. With different types of navigation, such as browser and page controls available, a user can easily become lost if a control does not work the way the user expects. There are also navigational issues in the spawning of new windows or browsers. Have you ever clicked on a link to find that a whole new browser page has opened? Or have you ever gone to a Web site and immediately been bombarded with several new windows popping up? Such experiences not only can confuse users as to where they are within the Web site, but it can also annoy them enough to make them leave the site.

Mental models of Web usage. Nielsen (1997b) argues that users don't recognize separate pages on the WWW. Instead, he states, they see the Web as a whole. Because of this, they form mental models of Web usage and do not want their experience and control to differ dramatically from site to site or page to page. This is unlike user expectations of traditional software applications, each of which may have a distinct and unique mental model for use.

Lowered switching costs. An important point in Web design and testing, which differentiates it from GUIs, is lowered switching cost for the user. That is, if users are unhappy with their experience on a particular Web site, there are a variety of other Web sites available to them with just a click of the mouse. To expand on this idea, Shum and McKnight (1997) argue that the WWW is a "veritable sea" of information. Thus, it is the overall user experience that determines which sites stay afloat.

Point of entry. Another usability issue that needs to be thought out carefully and evaluated is the fact that, unlike when using a GUI, Web visitors do not have to start at one particular page. For example, they may bookmark a particular page of interest and may enter the site from there. Or users may be sent a link that puts them in the middle of the Web site. At whatever point of entry they choose, users should be able to find key information to navigate to other parts of the site or to complete key functions.

Distraction. The Web itself, unlike a GUI application, provides ample opportunity for distraction. Having more pages than a user knows what to do with, animations, advertisements, sounds, spawning windows, required downloads to see certain pages, and distractions can seriously annoy the user.

Personalization. Personalization is much more popular on the Web than with GUI applications. A Web site can be tailored to a particular user's tasks and needs based on a user's profile, including demographic, location, and buying information. Depending on how it is designed, personalization can be a usability pitfall or a usability champion. A usability test should ascertain the ease with which personalization can be achieved and modified.

Primacy of content. Unlike GUI software, a Web site has only a few seconds to let users understand what they can do on a particular site and how they can do it. If it takes any more time than that, the visitor will leave. Nielsen (1999) argues that the value proposition of a site needs to be summarized in no more than two lines to keep the user's attention.

Context of use. Much more than with GUIs, Web site design and testing must take into account the visitor's context of use. That is, what type of task is the visitor trying to accomplish on the page? Do the content and design facilitate that task? Are users finding the types of interactions they expected? A good example of a context of use problem comes with trying to create a user's profile. If on a hardware buying site, the page is asking users for personal information that has nothing to do with buying hardware, they will probably grow wary and leave the site.

Web-Specific Test Plan Issues

When planning a Web usability test, there are certain issues that evaluators should focus on as particularly important. Kantner and Rosenbaum (1997) state that a plan for Web usability testing must include the purpose of the Web site, profiles of target users, and typical scenarios of use. The following other issues must be addressed.

- Types of users to test
- Number of users to test
- Location of test

- Tasks to use in testing
- Simulating the conditions of use

Types of users to test. First and foremost, to see where the usability of a Web site falls short, an evaluator needs to test the right users. As discussed earlier in this chapter, user input can be difficult to analyze, and the Web page may host a variety of different types of users. These difficulties can be overcome, however, by making sure the designer did a user needs assessment prior to design and preceding the usability evaluation. If the designer did not take this important step, there are other ways to pinpoint the types of users to test: polling the owner of the Web page for the type of user that the page was designed for; analyzing profile information, if available, from current Web pages for key similarities and differences; or possibly, buying user information from different sources. These ad hoc techniques are fallible, however, and it is preferable to do careful target audience analysis prior to an iterative design.

Number of users to test. Nielsen (2000) argues, based on simple regression to the mean, that five representative users will provide the evaluator with the bulk of usability problems per test over the course of three tests. Of course, if the Web site being tested has been designed for several distinct user populations, one needs to test five users in each of those groups. Nielsen suggests testing fewer users with more tests, during the course of an iterative design, for best results.

Location of test. In the past, it was preferred that usability testing take place in a formal testing laboratory. However, due to costs, many have taken a less formal approach to testing. In fact, depending on the Web site one is testing, and the number of types of participants to be tested, it may be more beneficial to test users outside of the laboratory. Not only is this type of testing cheaper, but it will also provide the evaluator with an understanding of what type of problems users encounter within their normal context of use.

Tasks to use in testing. The choice of tasks to test will vary widely from Web site to Web site. What kind of tasks and functionality does the Web page support? What tasks do we want users to be able to easily complete? Because we may not be able to test every possible usage scenario, it is important to prioritize what areas of the site need to be usable for the sake of business or user loyalty or other reasons. The top seven to ten of these tasks should be featured in a usability test.

Simulating the conditions of use. Testing environments and conditions should approximate the actual situation in which visitors to a Web site are likely to find themselves. For example, if the plan is to test user experience on a shopping site, then the participants should be given a reasonable amount of money with which to actually purchase a product that they can keep. To test the user experience, one can consider designing two versions of a site, one with graphics and another with only text lists of products. If given $200, would visitors spend the money on the site that takes more time but provides graphics of the actual products, or would they spend it on the version with faster transaction times but only a textual list of products? Simulating the real conditions of using the site and observing performance are more informative than simply asking visitors which sites they prefer or having them search for the products without purchasing and keeping them.

Web-Specific Evaluation Issues

Evaluators should pay attention to certain issues that are unique to Web design. In formulating a test plan, Web usability evaluators should take account and test for the following questions.

- Does the home page of the Web site act as a gateway? Do users immediately understand the purpose of the Web site and understand how and where to proceed to complete key tasks?

- Are mental models of usage consistent across the Web site, the types of tasks the Web site supports, and the target audience?

- Are evaluators testing the Web site with all items that will appear on it once it is published, including animations, special effects, and advertisements? Are users lost or frustrated by the amount of information on the page? Are they able to still complete tasks despite the distraction?

- Is the overall user experience pleasant and intuitive for the user?

- Does user performance change across different browser and platform types? Across different modem speeds and monitor sizes?

- Is all major functionality visible above the line of scroll on each page?

- Is content organized in such a way that users can easily find the information they are looking for?

- In terms of personalization, is it clear to the user why you are asking the questions you do for their profile? Do they understand what will be done with their information? Has the benefit of personalization been explained to them? Can users easily "de-personalize" the site?

- Do you use standardized terminology? Is this terminology consistent across the Web site?

- Are users provided with feedback about where they are in the site?

- Do error messages make sense to the user?

The Process of Web Evaluation

We perform an evaluation to make a judgment about whether what we have designed or built meets our goals and expectations. For Web usability design, this implies that the process of Web evaluation begins with defining goals and expectations that are user-centered. Furthermore, "performing an evaluation" implies using a method or applying a process, and the credibility of the outcome of the evaluation depends critically on the validity of the process used.

The process of Web usability evaluation consists of four stages, each of which corresponds to one of the phases in the userview iterative design process discussed in Chapter 2. This four-stage process assumes that the design phase of audience and task analyses as described in Chapters 2 and 4 has been completed. The four stages are:

- Usability evaluation goal setting

- Early paper testing

- Storyboard testing

- Interactive prototype testing

For the most credible evaluation outcome, I recommend that evaluators implement all four stages. However, these are four mutually exclusive stages, each of which can be carried out independently. If it is necessary that the evaluators streamline the usability evaluation process for reasons such as tight time schedules or lack of resources, my recommendation is that they reduce the process to defining the usability evaluation goals and performing interactive prototype testing. Within interactive prototype testing, evaluators may want to streamline the process further by using heuristic expert reviews (see following) rather than lab usability tests. What follows is a description of each stage in the Web usability evaluation process.

Usability Evaluation Goal Setting

Before undertaking any kind of evaluation, the first step is to define the goals of the evaluation. Two kinds of goals can be set with respect to Web site evaluation: absolute and relative. An absolute goal is one based on usability performance or satisfaction criteria that designers select for their Web site. In this case, the achieving of the defined goals is judged without regard to competitive sites. An example of an absolute goal for an airline Web site might be "Find the page to make reservations in two or fewer clicks."

A relative goal is one that takes into account other Web sites. An example of a relative goal might be "Make reservations on the designed airline Web site in at most 85 percent of the time it takes on competitor Web sites." The specific goals defined for a given Web usability evaluation should be related to the purpose of the site, the needs and requirements of the users, and the context of usage.

Both absolute and relative goals should be defined behaviorally and measurably, not in terms of abstract concepts. The statement of the goal should include behavioral and/or measurable criteria. It should be possible to judge whether users met the stated goal by observing the users or by measuring their performance or responses. For example, the goal statement "The Web site should be easy to use" is not measurable because it is abstract. The statement "The user should perform the task without asking questions" is concrete and measurable.

Early Paper Testing

In the paper-testing stage, we are interested in gauging the extent to which our initial designs reflect the purpose of the site. We want to know that the designed page can be recognized as belonging to the genre or that the user can recognize the purpose of the page or the site simply by viewing it. We also want to know at this early stage whether the initial designs are clear and aesthetically pleasing.

The testing here is of two to four potential users. Each user will be asked to perform one of several tasks. The tasks will require that the users see either one designed page at a time or two or more designs of the same page so they can compare them. What is important is that at this stage, the users are not allowed to see the full site or a large segment of it. They will only see isolated pages.

A prototypical task at this stage would be to present a page to the user, ask one of several questions, and measure the time it takes the user to answer the question. The criterion time is set as part of the goal definition. Here are some potential questions for the early paper testing stage.

- What is the purpose of this page?
- From viewing this page, what is the purpose of the site?
- From viewing the page, can you tell me to what kind of site this page belongs?
- In viewing those two designs of the same page, which is more pleasing to you?
- Please find a given item on this page.

Storyboard Testing

While early testing focuses on the Web page, the purpose of storyboard testing is to help improve the design of the Web site. Storyboard testing is also done as a form of paper testing. The storyboard should mimic the site map in showing a graph of all possible pages and the connection between them. It should go beyond the site map by showing each page fully laid out in its complete design details, including a side table stating all possible actions or navigation on that page. For Web pages that require scrolling, fold the page so that only the part that can be viewed without scrolling is visible. The part that needs to be scrolled to be visible should be folded back.

We perform storyboard testing using both expert reviewers and potential users. There should be about five participants, including two or three experts and the rest potential users. The evaluator constructs tasks that are intended to address the goals and functionality of the site. As an example, for an airline site, a task might be "Find the time a scheduled flight will arrive at destination." Participants are pointed to an entry page and asked to perform the task. While performing the task and traversing the pages, they are asked to comment on site-related questions. Here is a sample of such questions.

- Can you identify the purpose of this site?
- Can you name some other tasks you can perform on this site?
- Can you tell where you are in the site?
- Do you need to perform an action that is not available on the page?
- Are the textual links self-explanatory?
- Can you perform the task in three or fewer clicks starting from any page?
- Can you tell which are the on-site and which are the off-site links?

Participants may also be asked to verbalize what they are thinking about as they traverse the storyboard. The evaluator should record key behaviors such as points in performing the task where participants indicate frustration; words, links, or icons that participants state they don't understand or that confuse them; or folded pages that participants have to unfold to continue with or complete the task.

Interactive Prototype Testing

Interactive prototype testing differs from storyboard testing in that the purpose of the evaluator is to test and determine the ease of navigation and the flow of the Web site interface. To do so, evaluators plan for one of two types of tests that permit them to identify important problems and bottlenecks that are likely to be encountered by potential users of the Web site or application: expert reviews and usability lab tests.

Expert reviews can be either comprehensive, covering every relevant usability guideline, or heuristic, limited to a select number of high-level rules (Molich and Nielsen, 1990). One or more experts perform comprehensive reviews. The experts evaluate the Web site using detailed design rules and guidelines, such as consistency of layout and the providing of feedback, to guide their judgments. The best reviews are performed by those who are experts in both Web usability design and are also domain experts (Nielsen, 1992). It is therefore recommended that whenever possible, a committee of usability experts and reviewers with subject-matter expertise perform the reviews.

In heuristic reviews, the evaluator focuses on a select number of usability issues that are of particular relevance to the Web site. For example, if the Web site is intended for use by schoolchildren, then the reviewer will focus on usability issues that are of particular relevance to children.

Another type of interactive prototype testing is to conduct structured observations of potential users in a usability lab or to test against the goal(s) specified early in the goal-setting stage. In both of these lab-testing formats, the participants are given a task to perform. In the structured observations test, the evaluator looks for and records potential problems, frustrations, difficulties, and bottlenecks encountered by the participant. In testing against a specified goal, the evaluator measures the time, number of clicks, errors, or other quantifiable variable to determine the extent to which the participant has met the goal.

For situations where time schedules and resources are limited, an effective method, called "discount usability," developed by Nielsen (1989) is highly recommended. Discount usability combines heuristic reviews using a few general guidelines with limited informal observational usability testing. The participants are observed performing one or two tasks based on a single scenario most relevant to the Web site's purpose. Not more than three participants are tested using the "think aloud" technique, in which subjects talk about what they are doing as they are performing the task. Their verbal protocols are audio recorded and analyzed for usability issues that relate to their thoughts about their activities.

Frequently Asked Questions about Usability Evaluation

To summarize a number of traditional usability testing issues, here are sets of related issues preceded by topical questions.

How should usability objectives be set?

- Set usability objectives early in the design process. If possible, set them in the paper design phase.
- Set usability objectives for measurable criteria, not for abstract concepts.
- Set actual numbers in terms of percentage of users expected to meet the goal, or number of errors, or length of time, or whatever factor is relevant.
- Objectives should target improvements on performance in the marketplace of existing and competing products.
- If more than one class of user is expected to use the system, develop usability objectives for each class.

What are the measures of usability?

- Learning time: This is the amount of time a person spends learning how to perform a task on the system.
- Time to perform: This can be the amount of time it takes a person to perform a single action as well as time to complete a task. Remember that the user, not the system, is being measured.
- Errors: This is the number and types of errors the user makes.

- Ease of remembering and amount remembered: This measure includes both the length of time a person will retain relevant information and the amount of information a person will retain over a unit of time.

- Subjective measures: These include user satisfaction, preferences, opinions, and attitudes.

When is each measure of usability appropriate?

- Measure learning time in the following situations.

   a. User will have to begin working on a system right away, without the benefit of an extended training session.

   b. Users will only use the system occasionally or a few times.

   c. Users are discretionary users. Whenever users decide for themselves whether or not to use a system, the initial learning phase is extremely important.

   d. Users will be introduced to a new interface.

- Measure performance time in the following situations.

   a. Users will be interacting with the application over a long period of time. Even a small performance cost adds up with extended use.

   b. Speed is important to the user.

   c. It is important to relate the time it takes between two actions and the interface context in which the actions are performed.

- Measure error rates whenever possible. It is preferable to design the interface so that human errors are minimized. An example is direct manipulation interfaces where syntactic errors are not possible. Remember that an interface where an error cannot occur is better— all other things being equal—than one where errors can occur.

- Measure retention when use will be intermittent.

- Measure attitudes, opinions, and preferences in the following situations.

   a. In the early stage of design when trying to ascertain population characteristics and user requirements.

   b. For discretionary users.

   c. To confirm a positive user experience.

Combine measures of usability whenever possible to obtain the most information at the least cost.

How should usability evaluation fit into the iterative design process, and what procedures should be followed in a usability test?

- Generate an initial interface through user/task analysis.

- Begin early testing of an interface by creating a set of storyboards—paper representations of typical screens. Give the beginning screen and a task to some typical users, and allow each to say what their action would be. Then show the appropriate screen as response to the users' stated action. Encourage the user to comment on screens, and use the comments as well as the mistakes to further refine the design.

- In the early stages of design, discuss the design (either in the abstract or with storyboards) in an informal setting where users feel comfortable and undisturbed.

- After a paper design has been completed, create an online interactive prototype. Give the prototype to some typical users along with some tasks. Encourage the users to speak aloud. Record their comments and actions. Refine the design to eliminate common errors, usually by changing the interface or clarifying the instructions.

- When a prototype is actually being run, provide the user with as close a simulation of the actual environment as possible. In general, a video camera or cameras to record users' actions and comments should be available. Make sure to use screen-capture software. If paper documents are being used, then the camera should record the page the user is looking at. The computer should unobtrusively log all user input. All recorded data should be time-stamped. In general, the evaluator should not be present in the room. Instead, an intercom should be available for participants' questions and problems.

- Repeat the refine-test cycle with the prototype until user performance is at an acceptable level. This level of performance (also known as a usability objective) is usually determined in the earliest stage of design.

- After the actual application has been written, give it to users in the field to see if any problems with actual performance arise. Ask users to record their comments either on paper or online, and send them back to the evaluator/designer. Make any necessary changes.

What are some problems with each measure of usability, and how can they be fixed or ameliorated?

- One problem with measuring learning time is knowing when learning has occurred. To resolve this, evaluators often run a pilot study first to observe how long it usually takes participants to reach a plateau. That plateau becomes the preset measure of performance that participants in the usability test must reach.

- Time to perform as a measure of usability may also include errors (inclusion, detection, and correction). Thus, the evaluator may not be measuring performance of the given task so much as recovery from a particular error. One way to avoid including error time in a performance-time measure is to watch carefully for errors and to subtract error time from the total performance time. Another approach is to ignore the fact that errors occur. This solution is easy to implement but renders the test conclusions much less accurate.

- A problem with any usability test is that sometimes participants may not complete a task, either because they just give up and stop or are totally confused about what to do next. The evaluation in these cases is very tricky. If these participants are left out, the evaluation will be less accurate. If they are included, their results are difficult to analyze statistically. If these results are evaluated separately, they may be misleading. One way to manage the problem of not completing tasks is to give those participants in-depth interviews to determine why they did not finish and use those comments to direct further investigation.

- Errors are the most difficult to determine of the usability measures. The evaluator must decide what counts as an error and also identify the type of error. One solution to determining the type of error in a usability test is to identify and count the number of wrong or misdirected actions—that is, actions that do not lead to accomplishment of the intended or specified task goal. Then define each action as it relates to other interface contextual elements. Another solution is to examine all the data after the test and then classify errors by similarities that appear at that time.

- Collecting attitudes, preferences, and opinions as measures of usability entail several problems.

a. People often do not know the answer to the question and will make up something.

b. Participants may interpret questions differently from the evaluator.

c. Participants may slant their answers (consciously or subconsciously) to match what they think the evaluator wants.

d. Surveys, questionnaires, and interviews are hard to develop and validate.

- To minimize the effects of these problems, use the following guidelines for developing surveys, questionnaires, and interviews.

How should users be selected to participate in usability testing?

- The closer the participants are to actual users, the better and more accurate the information from them will be.

- Choose actual users whenever possible.

- If actual users are not available, then choose people who were not involved in the design of the software. They bring fresh perspective to the design. If these users come from within the company but not the design group, the cost and security risk are both low.

- Choose participants in a stratified way to represent the target audience. If the purpose of a usability study is to identify problems, Nielsen (1993) has argued that using six participants will allow the evaluator to identify the majority of important problems. More recently, this figure has been disputed in studies done by Spool and Schroeder (2001). In the final analysis, what is important is to do stratified sampling based on the audience characteristics as determined in the audience analysis phase.

- If no other participants are available, have the project designers try to act as typical users and work the system. Although they are less likely to know what the end user wants and needs, they may still benefit from seeing the system in action and as a whole.

What precautions can be taken to make the results of usability testing as generalized as possible?

- Make the storyboard/simulation/prototype as realistic as possible.

- Simulate the actual setting.

- Select a stratified sample of participants based on audience characteristics.

- Give participants appropriate motivation.
- Select tasks that are actual, normal tasks for users to perform.
- Keep a time-stamped log of user and system actions. A combination of camera and computer recording is recommended. Use this log to help evaluate the reasons for user actions as well as to obtain measurements.

How should questions in a survey, questionnaire, or interview be phrased?

- Ask several different questions about the same topic and then take a consensus.
- Ask questions that do not have an obviously right answer.
- Ask questions that are unambiguous.
- Ask open-ended questions to obtain suggestions about unanticipated problems or desired changes.
- Ask open-ended questions when the range of possible answers is very large or unbounded.
- Ask open-ended questions to discover issues that have not been identified by the evaluator.
- Ask a limited number of open-ended questions. Otherwise, the respondent will become fatigued.
- Design each question to obtain as much information as possible.
- Ask questions with a limited number of answers for easy evaluation.
- If a limited number of answers is provided, make sure that the answer list is exhaustive but not overlapping. Occasionally, this means including an answer such as "not applicable" or "don't know."
- One type of question with a limited number of answers is a multiple-choice question.
- Another type of question with a limited number of answers is a rating scale.
- Use a rating scale to determine the direction and degree of an opinion.
- With a rating scale, be sure not to give a larger or smaller number of choices than the respondent can actually discriminate among. As a rule of thumb, five to seven choices are an accepted number.
- Another type of question with a limited number of answers is a ranking scale. A respondent is asked to order a list of items by some criteria.

Sometimes to do the sorting, numbers are assigned. Other times, it is done by physically shuffling the items. Ranking questions have the advantage of yielding more complete information than a multiple-choice question or a checklist question.

- Another type of question with a limited number of answers is a semantic differential question. The respondent is asked to rate a topic on a number of scales, where a pair of adjectives anchors each scale. Make sure the anchoring adjectives of a semantic differential are true opposites. Semantic differential questions are good for rating how objects are similar to each other.

- Another type of question is a checklist. Checklists do not give as much information as a rating scale, but they do give more information than a multiple-choice question. If the evaluator is not trying to order the information, a checklist provides useful information rapidly.

- Rating scales represent another type of question. One technique for giving a score on an entire set of items is a Thurstone scale. Judges rate each question as having a value with regard to some topic. Then the respondents are given a score based on the average value of the items they agreed with. These scales are difficult to create.

- Another technique for assigning a single score to an entire set of items is a Lickert scale. All items are assigned a positive or negative value. Each item has a range of responses, such as from "strongly agree" to "strongly disagree." Positive items assign values to each answer in descending sequence. The final score can be either the sum or the average. Lickert scales are easier to construct than Thurstone scales.

- Both Lickert and Thurstone scales attempt to avoid the problem of having a single question address a complex problem, while still being able to assign a single number to each participant's response.

- When constructing questions, constructors should adhere to the following guidelines.

  a. All items should be grammatically correct.

  b. All items should be expressed as neutrally as possible.

    c. Items should be worded in positive rather than in negative terms (except when both negative and positive versions of an item are included in a questionnaire or survey).

    d. Do not ask embarrassing or self-incriminating questions.

    e. Avoid compound questions. Instead break them into multiple questions.

    f. Keep questions simple and short.

How should a questionnaire or survey be formatted?

- Put a title at the top center of the questionnaire or survey, and keep the instructions as short as possible.

- Put items dealing with the same topic together.

- Ask broad questions before narrow ones.

- Ask questions in order of logical progression.

- Ask some easy, nonthreatening questions first to build the respondent's confidence.

- Order the choices in a question with a limited number of answers in a logical fashion if a logical organization is obvious.

- If choices have no logical order, put the choices for a question with a limited number of answers in a random order. This serves to avoid order biases.

- Be consistent in the ordering of choices for a question with a limited number of answers.

- Put alternatives such as "not applicable" or "all of the above" in the last place in the list of choices for a question with a limited number of answers.

- Arrange multiple-choice answers vertically under the questions.

- Place graphic rating scales horizontally under the questions.

- In general, restrict to not more than 30 minutes the time it takes to answer a questionnaire. If the questionnaire relates to an activity a respondent has just finished or material just learned, restrict the response time to 15 minutes or less.

When is an interview better than a survey or questionnaire, and vice versa?

- Use an interview when sufficient personnel and time are available to interview participants and process the responses.

- Use an interview in which answers are automatically recorded—usually taped—when a large number of open-ended questions are asked.

- To give participants a measure of anonymity, use a questionnaire or survey when the material covers sensitive or potentially embarrassing situations.

- Use interviews to develop and test a questionnaire or survey.

Bibliography

Allen, R. B. (1982). Cognitive Factors in Human Interaction with Computers. In A. Badre, and B. Shneiderman (eds.), *Directions in Human/Computer Interaction*, 1–26. Norwood, NJ: Ablex.

Allison, L., and Hammond, N. (1989). A learning support environment: The hitch-hiker's guide. In R. McAleese (ed.), *Hypertext: Theory into Practice*. Oxford: Intellect.

Anderson, J. R. (1983). *The Architecture of Cognition*. Cambridge, MA: Harvard University Press.

Anderson, J. R., and Bower, G. H. (1973). *Human Associative Memory*. Washington, DC: Winston.

Andriole, S. A. (1988). Storyboard prototyping for requirements verification. *Large Scale Systems*, 12, 231–247.

Ashcraft, M. H. (2002). *Cognition*, Third Edition. Upper Saddle River, NJ: Prentice Hall.

Atkinson, R. C., and Shiffrin, R. M. (1968). Human memory: A proposed system and its control processes. In K. W. Spence and J. T. Spence (eds.), *Advances in the Psychology of Learning and Motivation Research and Theory*, Second Edition. New York: Academic Press.

Bachiochi, D., Brestene, M., Chouinard, E., Conlan, N., Danchak, M., Furey, T., Neligon, C., and Way, D. (1997). Usability studies and designing navigational aids for the World Wide Web. *Proceedings of the Sixth World Wide Web Conference*, Santa Clara, CA.

Baddeley, A. D. (1992). Working memory. *Science*, 255, 556–559.

Baddeley, A. D., and Hitch, G. (1974). Working memory. In G. H. Bower (ed.), *The Psychology of Learning and Motivation.* New York: Academic Press.

Badre, A. N. (1974). The effects of hypothesis shifting on the solving of insight problems. *Information Utilities Proceedings of the 37th American Society for Information Science Annual Mtg.,* Atlanta.

Badre, A. N. (1980). Human cognitive factors in front-end interaction. *COMPCON 80 Proceedings (Twenty-first IEEE Computer Society International Conference),* Washington, DC.

Badre, A. N. (1982a). Selecting and representing information structures for visual presentation. *IEEE Transactions on Man, System, and Cybernetics.* Vol. SMC-12(4), 495–504.

Badre, A. N. (1982b). Designing chunks for sequentially displayed information. In A. Badre and B. Shneiderman (eds.), *Directions in Human/Computer Interaction.* Norwood, NJ: Ablex.

Badre, A. N. (1984). Designing transitionality into the user computer interface. In G. Salvandy (ed.), *Human Computer Interaction.* Amsterdam: Elsevier Science Publishers.

Badre, A. N. (2001). The effects of cross-cultural interface design orientation on World Wide Web user performance. *Tech Report GIT-GVU-01-03.*

Badre, A. N., and Jacobs, A. (1999). A museum on the Web: Book index representation vs. spatial metaphor. *IEEE Multimedia Conference Proceedings.* Florence, Italy.

Badre, A. N., and Laskowski, S. (2001). The cultural context of Web genres: Content vs. style. *Proceedings of the 6th Conference of HFWeb.* Minneapolis, MN.

Badre, A. N., and Shneiderman, B. (Eds.) (1982). *Directions in Human Computer Interaction.* Norwood, NJ: Ablex.

Baeker, R. M., Grudin, J., Buxton, W., and Greengerg, S. (1999). *Human-Computer Interaction: Towards the Year 2000.* San Francisco, CA: Morgan Haufmann.

Ball, K., and Owsley, C. (1991). Identifying correlates of accident involvement for the older driver. *Human Factors, 33,* 583–595.

Barber, R. E., and Lucas, H. C. (1983). System response time, operator productivity, and job satisfaction. *Communication of the ACM, 26, 11,* 972–986.

Barber, W., and Badre, A. N. (1998). Culturability: The merging of culture and usability. *Proceedings of the 4th Conference on Human Factors and the Web.* Morristown, NJ.

Bartlett, R. A. (1932). *Remembering.* Cambridge, UK: Cambridge University Press.

Bartram, D. J. (1980). Comprehending spatial information: The relative efficiency of different methods of presenting information about bus routes. *Journal of Applied Psychology,* 65, 103–110.

Bias, R. G., and Mayhew, D. J. (1994). *Cost-Justifying Usability.* Boston, MA: Academic Press.

Bjork, S., and Redstrom, J. (1999). An alternative to scroll bars on small screens. *Extended Abstracts of CHI'99.* New York: ACM Press.

Borges, J., Morales, I., and Rodríguez, N. (1998). Page design guidelines developed through usability testing. In C. Forsythe, E. Grose, and J. Ratner (eds.), *Human Factors and Web Development.* Mahwah, NJ: Lawrence Erlbaum Associates.

Bouch, A., Kuchinski, A., and Bhatti, N. (2000). Quality is in the eye of the beholder: Meeting users' requirements for Internet quality of service. *Proceedings of ACM CHI 2000.* The Hague, Netherlands.

Bourges-Waldegg, P., and Scrivener, S. A. R. (1998). Meaning, the central issue in cross-cultural HCI design. *Interacting with Computers,* 9(3), 287–310.

Brewster, S. A. (1998). The design of sonically-enhanced widgets. *Interacting with Computers,* 11(2), 211–235.

Broadbent, D. E. (1952). Speaking and listening simultaneously. *Journal of Experimental Psychology,* 43, 267–273.

Broadbent, D. E. (1963). Flow of information within the organism. *Journal of Verbal Learning and Verbal Behavior,* 2, 34–39.

Brown, J. S., and Duguid, P. (1994). Borderline issues: Social and material aspects of design. *Human-Computer Interaction,* 9, 3–36.

Butler, T. W. (1983). Computer response time. *Proceedings of CHI '83.* Boston, MA.

Buyukkokten, O., Garcia-Molina, H., Paepcke, A., and Winograd, T. (2000a). Efficient Web browsing for PDAs. *http://www.diglib.stanford.edu/diglib/WP/PUBLIC/DOC268.pdf.*

Buyukkokten, O., Garcia-Molina, H., Paepcke, A., and Winograd, T. (2000b). Power browser: Efficient Web browsing for PDAs glimpses of the future. *Proceedings of ACM CHI 2000 Conference on Human Factors in Computing Systems 2000.* The Hague, Netherlands.

Byrne, M., John, B., Wehrle, N., and Crow, D. (1999). The tangled web we wove: A taskonomy of WWW use. In M. Williams and M. Altom (eds.), *Human Factors in Computing Systems: CHI 99, the CHI is the Limit, Conference Proceedings.* New York: ACM Press.

Cairns, H. S., and Kamerman, J. (1975). Lexical information processing during sentence comprehension. *JVLVB,* 14, 170–179.

Card, S. K., Moran, T. P., and Newell, A. (1980). The keystroke level model for user performance time with interactive systems. *Communications of the ACM,* 23, 396–410.

Card, S. K., Moran, T. P., and Newell, A. (1983). *The Psychology of Human Computer Interaction.* Hillsdale, NJ: Lawrence Erlbaum Associates.

Card, S. K., Moran, T. P., and Newell, A. (1987). Computer Text-Editing: An Information Processing Analysis of a Routine Cognitive Skill, in R. M. Baecker and W. A. S. Buxton (eds.), *Readings in Human-Computer Interaction,* Morgan Kaufmann Publishers, Los Altos, CA: 219–240.

Carroll, J. M., and Carrithers, C. (1984). Blocking learner error states in a training-wheels system. *Human Factors,* 26(4), 377–389.

Carroll, J. M., and Olson, J. R. (1988). Mental models in human-computer interaction. In M. H. Helander (ed.), *Handbook of Human-Computer Interaction.* Amsterdam: North-Holland.

Carroll, J. M., Mack, R. L., and Kellogg, W. A. (1988). Interface metaphors and user interface design. In M. H. Helander (ed.), *Handbook of Human-Computer Interaction.* Amsterdam: North-Holland.

Carter, R. C., and Cahill, M. C. (1979). Regression models of search time for color-coded information displays. *Human Factors,* 21, 293–302.

Cateledge, L., and Pitkow, J. (1995). Characterizing browsing strategies in the World Wide Web. *Proceedings of the Third World Wide Web Conference,* Darmstadt, Germany.

Charness, N., and Bosman, E. A. (1990). Human factors and design for older adults. In J. E. Birren and K. W. Schaie (eds.), *Handbook of the Psychology of Aging,* Third Edition. San Diego: Academic Press.

Chase, W. G., and Simon, H. A. (1973). Perception in chess. *Cognitive Psychology, 4*, 55–81.

Cherry, E. C., and Taylor, W. K. (1954). Some further experiments on the recognition of speech with one and two ears. *Journal of the Acoustical Society of America, 26*, 554–559.

Choong, Y. Y., and Salvendy, G. (1998). Design of icons for use by Chinese in mainland China. *Interacting with Computers, 9*(4), 417–430.

Christ, R. E. (1975). Review and analysis of color-coding research for visual displays. *Human Factors, 17*, 542–570.

Cole, M. (1997). *Cultural Psychology.* Cambridge, MA: Harvard University Press.

Collins, A. M., and Loftus, E. F. (1975). A spreading activation theory of semantic processing. *Psychological Review, 82*, 407–428.

Collins, A. M., and Quillian, M. R. (1969). Retrieval time from semantic memory. *Journal of Verbal Learning and Verbal Behavior, 8*, 240–247.

Collins, A. M., and Quillian, M. R. (1972). Experiments on semantic memory and language comprehension. In L. W. Gregg (ed.), *Cognition in Learning and Memory.* New York: Wiley.

Coutaz, J. (1989). UIMS: Promises, failures, and trends. In A. Sutcliffe and L. Macaulay (eds.), *People and Computers V: Proceedings of the Fifth Conference of the British Computer Society on Human Computer Interaction.* Cambridge, UK: Cambridge University Press.

Craik, F. I. M., and Jennings, J. M. (1992). Human memory. In F. I. M. Craik and T. A. Salthouse (eds.), *The Handbook of Aging and Cognition.* Hillsdale, NJ: Erlbaum.

Craik, F. I. M., and Lockhart, R. S. (1972). Levels of processing: A framework for memory research. *Journal of Verbal Learning and Verbal Behavior, 11*, 671–684.

Craik, F. I. M., and Salthouse, T. A. (2000). *The Handbook of Aging and Cognition.* Mahwah, NJ: Erlbaum.

Darken, R. P., and Banker, W. P. (1998). Navigating in natural environments: A virtual environment training transfer study. *Proceedings of IEEE Virtual Reality Annual International Symposium,* IEE Computer Society. Atlanta, GA.

Davis, A. M. (1993). *Software Requirements: Objects, Functions, and States.* New Jersey: Prentice Hall.

Dewey, J. (1934). *Art as Experience.* New York: Berkley Publishing, Perigree Books.

Dix, A., Finlay, J., Abowd, G., and Beale, R. (1998). *Human-Computer Interaction.* New Jersey: Prentice Hall.

Dodson, D. W., and Shields, N. J. (1978). Development of user guidelines for ECAS display design. *Report No. NASA-CR-150877.* Essex Corp.

Echt, K. V. (2002). Visual considerations and design directives. In R. W. Morrell (ed.), *Older Adults, Health Information, and the World Wide Web.* Mahwah, NJ: Erlbaum.

El-Shinnawy, M., and Vinze, A. S. (1997). Technology, culture, and persuasiveness: A study of choice shifts in group settings. *International Journal of Human-Computer Studies, 47*(3), 473–496.

Ellis, R. D., Jankowski, T. B., and Jasper, J. E. (1998). Participatory design of an Internet-based information system for aging services professionals. *The Gerontologist, 38,* 743–748.

Ellis, D. E., and Kurniawan, S. H. (2000). Increasing the usability of on-line information for older users: A case study in participatory design. *International Journal of Human Computer Interaction, 12,* 263–276.

Eriksen, L., and Ihlstrom, C. (2000). Evolution of the Web news genre—The slow move beyond the print metaphor. *Proceedings of 33rd Hawaii International Conference on System Sciences.*

Evers, V., and Day, D. (1997). The role of culture in interface acceptance. In S. Howard, J. Hammond, and G. Lindegaard (eds.), *Human Computer Interaction, INTERACT'97.* Chapman and Hall, London. *http://www-iet.open.ac.uk/pp/v.evers/htmlfiles/home/interact97.htm.*

Fisher, B., Agelidis, M., Dill, J., Tan, P., Collaud, G., and Jones, C. (1997). CZWeb: Fish-eye views for visualizing the World Wide Web. *Proceedings HCI International '97.* Amsterdam: Elevier.

Flanders, V., and Willis, M. (1998). *Web pages that suck: Learn good design by looking at bad design.* San Francisco: Sybex.

Flesch, R. (1975). *The Art of Readable Writing.* New York: Harper and Row.

Foley, J. D., and Van Dam, A. (1982). *Fundamentals of Interactive Computer Graphics.* Reading, MA: Addison-Wesley.

Foley, J. D., and Wallace, V. L. (1974). The art of graphic man-machine conversation. *Proceedings of the IEEE,* 62, 462–471.

Foley, J. D., Kim, W. C., Kovacevic, S., and Murray, K. (1989). Defining interfaces at a high level of abstraction. *IEEE Software,* January, 25–32.

Foss, D. J. (1970). Some effects of ambiguity upon sentence comprehension. *Journal of Verbal Learning and Verbal Behavior,* 9, 699–706.

Fry, E. (1977). Fry's readability graph: Clarifications, validity, and extensions to level 17. *Journal of Reading,* 21, 241.

Galitz, W. O. (1993). *User Interface Screen Design.* New York: Wiley.

Gehrke, D., and Turban, E. (1999). Determinants of successful website design: Relative importance and recommendations for effectiveness. In R. Sprague (ed.), *Proceedings of the 32nd Annual Hawaii International Conference on System Sciences.*

Gilbreth, F. B. (1911). *Motion Study: A Method for Increasing the Efficiency of the Workman.* New York: Van Nostrand.

Gobbin, R. (1998). The role of cultural fitness in user resistance to information technology tools. *Interacting with Computers,* 9(3), 275–286.

Godden, D. R., and Baddeley, A. D. (1975). Context-dependent memory in two natural environments: On land and underwater. *British Journal of Psychology,* 81, 465–469.

Gonzalez, C. (1996). Does animation in user interfaces improve decision making? *Proceedings of the ACM CHI '96 Conference.* Vancouver, BC.

Gould, J. D. (1981). Composing letters with computer-based text editors. *Human Factors,* 23, 593–606.

Gould, J. D. (1988). How to design usable systems. In M. H. Helander (ed.), *Handbook of Human Computer Interaction.* Amsterdam: North-Holland.

Gould, J. D., and Grischkowsky, N. (1984). Doing the same work with hard copy and with cathode-ray tube (CRT) computer terminals. *Human Factors,* 26, 757–789.

Gould, J. D., and Lewis, C. H. (1985). Designing for usability: Key principles and what designers think. *Communication of the ACM,* 28, 300–311.

Gould, J. D., Boies, S. J., and Ukelson, J. (1997). How to design usable systems. In M. G. Helander, T. K. Landauer, and P. V Prabhu (eds.), *Handbook of Human Computer Interaction.* Amsterdam: North-Holland.

Greenberg, S., and Marwood, D. (1994). Real time groupware as a distributed system; concurrency control and its effect on the interface. *Proceedings of CSCW'94.* New York: ACM Press.

Greenspoon, J., and Raynard, R. (1957). Stimulus condition and retroactive inhibition. *Journal of Experimental Psychology,* 53, 55–59.

Grose, E., Forsythe, C., and Ratner, J. (1998). Using Web and traditional style guides to design Web interfaces. In C. Forsythe, E. Grose, and J. Ratner (eds.), *Human Factors and Web Development.* Mahwah, New Jersey: Lawrence Erlbaum Associates.

GVU's Fifth WWW User Survey. (April 1996). *http://www.gvu.gatech.edu/ user_surveys/survey-04-1996/.*

GVU's Ninth WWW User Survey. (April 1998). *http://www.gvu.gatech.edu/ user_surveys/survey-1998-04/.*

GVU Tenth WWW User Survey. (October 1998). *http://www.gvu.gatech.edu/ user_surveys/survey-1998-10/.*

Haber, R. N., and Wilkinson, L. (1982). Perceptual components of computer displays. *IEEE Computer Graphics and Applications,* 2(3), 23–35.

Haine, D. (1998). Five most serious Web design errors. *E-business Magazine. http://hpcc920.external.hp.cpm/Ebusiness/webdesign.html.*

Hamilton, A. (1997). Avoid the # 1 sin: Slow-loading pages. *http://www4. zdnet.com/anchordesk/story/story_1244.html.*

Heath, J. (1998). Pointers on how to create Web sites that work. *http://www. iinet.net,au/~heath.*

Heller, H., and Rivers, D. (1996). So you wanna design for the Web. *Interactions,* 3(2), 19–23.

Herstad J., Thanh, D. V., and Kristoffersen, S. (1998). Wireless markup language as a framework for interaction with mobile computing communication devices. *GIST Technical Report G98-1, May 1998. Proceedings of the First Workshop on Human Computer Interaction with Mobile Devices.*

Hofstede, G. (1997). *Cultures and Organizations: Software of the Mind.* New York: McGraw-Hill.

Holmquist, L. E. (1997). Focus + context visualization with flip zooming and the zoom browser. *Extended Abstracts of CHI'97*. Atlanta, GA: ACM Press.

Holmquist, L. E. (1999). When will baby faces grow up? *Proceedings of HCI International '99*. Munich, Germany.

Holmquist, L. E., and Bjork, S. A. (1998). A hierarchical focus + context method for image browsing. *SIGGRAPH '98*. New York: ACM Press.

http://www.census.gov/population/www/socdemo/age.html.

Hurst, M. (2000). Special report: Design usability, getting past go. *Internet World*, December. *http://www.internetworld.com/121500/12.15.00 feature4long.jsp.*

Janal, D. (1997). *Online Marketing Handbook—How to Promote, Advertise, and Sell Your Products and Services on the Internet*. New York: John Wiley & Sons, Inc.

Johnson, C. (1997). The impact of time and place on the operation of mobile computing devices. *Proceedings of the HCI'97 Conference on People and Computers XII*. Bristol, UK.

Johnson, P. (1998). Usability and mobility: interactions on the move. *Proceedings of the First Workshop on Human Computer Interaction with Mobile Devices*. Glasgow, Scotland.

Johnston, W. A., and Heinz, S. P. (1978). Flexibility and capacity demands of attention. *Journal of Experimental Psychology: General*, 107, 420–435.

Kantner, L., and Rosenbaum, S. (1997). Usability studies of WWW sites: Heuristic evaluation vs. laboratory testing. *ACM 15th International Conference on Systems Documentation*. Salt Lake City, UT.

Kehoe, C. M., Pitkow, J. E., Sutton, K., Aggarwa, G., and Rogers, J. (1999). Results of the tenth World Wide Web user survey. *http://www.cc.gatech. edu/gvu/user_surveys/survey-1998-10/tenthreport.html.*

Kline, D. W., and Scialfa, C. T. (1997). Sensory and perceptual functioning: Basic research and human factors implications. In A. D. Fisk and W. A. Rogers (eds.), *Handbook of Human Factors and the Older Adult*. San Diego, CA: Academic Press.

Kubeck, J. E., Miller-Albrecht, S. A., and Murphy, M. D. (1999). Finding information on the World Wide Web: Exploring older adults' exploration. *Educational Gerontology*, 25, 167–183.

Kurosu, M., and Kashimora, K. (1995). Apparent usability vs. inherent usability. *Proceedings of CHI '95 Conference Companion.* Denver, CO.

Landauer, T. K. (1995). *The Trouble with Computers.* Cambridge, MA: MIT Press.

Landauer, T. K. (1997). Behavioral research methods in human-computer interaction. In M. G. Helander, T. K. Landauer, and P. V. Prabhu (eds.), *Handbook of Human Computer Interaction.* Amsterdam: North-Holland.

Larson, K., and Czerwinski, M. (1998). Web page design: Implications of memory, structure, and scent for information retrieval. In C. Karat, A. Lund, J. Coutaz, and J. Karat (eds.), *Making the Impossible Possible: Human Factors in Computing Systems, CHI 98 Conference Proceedings.* New York: ACM Press.

Laurel, B. (1991). *Computers as Theater.* Reading, MA: Addison-Wesley.

Licklider, J. C. R. (1960). Man computer symbiosis, IRE transactions on human factors and electronics. *HSE-1 (1), Institute of Radio Engineers,* 4–11.

Locke, J. (1690). *An Essay Concerning Human Understanding.* Reprinted by Everyman's Library, London, 1961.

Lumsden, C., and Wilson, E. (1983). *Promethean Fire.* Cambridge, MA: Harvard University Press.

Mackay, J. M., and Lamb, C. W. (1991). Training needs of novices and experts with referent experience and task domain knowledge. *Information and Management,* 20, 183–189.

Manning, H., McCarthy, J. C., and Souza, R. K. (1998). Why most Web sites fail. *Technology Series,* 3(7).

Maquet, J. (1986). *The Aesthetic Experience: An Anthropologist Looks at the Visual Arts.* New Haven: Yale University Press.

Marcus, A., and Gould, E. W. (2000). Crosscurrents: Cultural dimensions and global Web user-interface design. *ACM Interactions,* 7(4), 32–46.

Mayhew, D. J. (1992). *Principles and Guidelines in Software User Interface Design.* NJ: Prentice Hall.

McClard, A., and Somers, P. (2000). Unleashed: Web tablet integration into the home. *Proceedings of ACM CHI 2000 Conference on Human Factors in Computing Systems, Beyond the Workplace.* The Hague, Netherlands.

McDonald, S., and Stevenson, R. J. (1998). Navigation in hyperspace: An evaluation of the effects of navigational tools and subject matter expertise on browsing and information retrieval in hypertext. *Interacting with Computers,* 10, 129–142.

Mead, S. E., Lamson, N., and Rogers, W. A. (2002). Human factors guidelines for Web site usability: Health-oriented Web sites for older adults. In R. W. Morrell (ed.), *Older Adults, Health Information, and the World Wide Web.* Mahwah, NJ: Erlbaum.

Mead, S. E., Sit, R. A., Rogers, W. A., Jamieson, B. A., and Rousseau, G. K. (2000). Influences of general computer experience and age on library database search performance. *Behavior and Information Technology,* 19, 107–123.

Mead, S. E., Spaulding, V. A., Sit, R. A., Meyer, E., and Walker, N. (1997). Effects of age and training on World Wide Web navigation strategies. *Proceedings of the Human Factors and Ergonomics Society 41st Annual Meeting.* Santa Monica, CA: Human Factors and Ergonomics Society.

Meads, J., and Nielsen, J. (2001). Usability is not graphic design. *Developer.netscape.com/viewsource/meads_usb.htm.*

Megaw, E. D., and Richardson, J. (1979). Target uncertainty and visual scanning strategy. *Human Factors,* 20, 611–632.

Miller, G. A. (1956). The magical number seven, plus one minus two: Some limits on our capacity to process information. *Psychological Review,* 63, 81–97.

Molich, R., and Nielsen, J. (1990). Improving a human-computer dialogue. *Communications of the ACM,* 33(3), 338–348.

Morrell, R. W., Mayhorn, C. B., and Bennett, J. (2000). A survey of World Wide Web use in middle-aged and older adults. *Human Factors,* 42, 175–182.

Moskel, S., Erno, J., and Shneiderman, B. (1984). Proofreading and comprehension of text screens and paper. *University of Maryland Computer Science Technical Report.*

Mullet, K., and Sano, D. (1994). *Designing Visual Interfaces: Communication Oriented Interfaces.* Palo Alto, CA: Prentice Hall PTR/Sun Microsystems Press.

Nakakoji, K. (1994). Crossing the cultural boundary. *BYTE,* June, 107–109.

Nakakoji, K. (1996). Beyond language translation: Crossing the cultural boundary. *IEEE Software,* 13, 42–46.

Netcraft. (2000). *www.netcraft.com.*

Nielsen, J. (1989). Usability engineering at a discount. In G. Salvendy and M. J. Smith (eds.), *Designing and Using Human-Computer Interfaces and Knowledge-Based Systems.* Amsterdam: Elsevier.

Nielsen, J. (1992). Finding usability problems through heuristic evaluation. *CHI'92 Proceedings.* New York: ACM Press.

Nielsen, J. (1993). *Usability Engineering.* New York: Academic Press.

Nielsen, J. (1994) Heuristic evaluation. In J. Nielsen and R. L. Mack (eds.), *Usability Inspection Methods.* New York: Wiley.

Nielsen, J. (1996). Top ten mistakes in Web design. *http://www.useit.com/ columns/alertbox/9605.html.*

Nielsen, J. (1997a). Usability testing. In G. Salvendy (ed.), *Handbook of Human Factors and Ergonomics.* New York: Wiley.

Nielsen, J. (1997b). Alertbox, the difference between Web design and GUI design. *http://www.useit.com/9705a.html.*

Nielsen, J. (1998). The Web-usage paradox: Why do people use something this bad? *http://www.useit.com/alertbox/980809.html.*

Nielsen, J. (1999). *http://www.useit.com/alertbox/99052.html.*

Nielsen, J. (2000). Alertbox, why you only need to test with 5 users. *http://www.useit.com/alertbox/200000319.html.*

Nielsen, J. (2001). Top ten mistakes revisited three years later. *www.useit. com/alterbox/990502.html.*

Nielsen, J., and Sano, D. (1994). SunWeb: User interface design for Sun Microsystem internal Web. *Proceedings of the Second World Wide Web Conference: Mosaic and the Web.* Urbana-Champaign, Illinois.

Nielsen, J., and Tahir, M. (2001) Building Web sites with depth. *Web-techniques,* February. *http://www.webtechniques.com/archives/2001/ 02/nielsen.*

Norman, D. A. (1968). Toward a theory of memory and attention. *Psychological Review,* 75, 522–536.

Norman, D. A. (1970). *Models of Human Memory.* New York: Academic Press.

Norman, D. A. (1986). Cognitive engineering. In D. Norman and S. Draper (eds.), *User-Centered System Design.* Hillside, NJ: Lawrence Erlbaum Associates.

Norman, D. A. (1988). *The Psychology of Everyday Things.* Hillside, NJ: Lawrence Erlbaum Associates.

Park, D. C., and Schwartz, N. (2000). *Cognitive Aging: A Primer.* Philadelphia: Psychology Press.

Pitkow, J. E., and Kehoe, C. M. (1996). Emerging trends in the WWW user population. *Communications of the ACM, 37*(7), 68–71.

Preece, J., Rogers, Y., Sharp, H., Benyon, D., Holland, S., and Carey, T. (1994). *Human-Computer Interaction.* Reading, MA: Addison-Wesley.

Rehman, A. (2000). Holiday 2000 e-commerce: avoiding $14 billion in silent losses. *http://www.ismnet.com/CreativeGood/cg-holiday2000.pdf.*

Reisner, P. (1977). Use of psychological experimentation as an aid to development of a query language. *IEEE Transactions on Software Engineering,* SE-3, 218–229.

Reitman, J. S. (1976). Skilled perception in GO: Deducing memory structures from inter-response times. *Cognitive Psychology,* 8, 336–377.

Reitman, W. R. (1970). The uses of experience: Open statements, ill-defined strategies, and intelligent information processing. In J. Hellmuth (ed.), *Cognitive Studies,* 1. New York: Brunner/Meazel, Inc.

Robertson, G. G., and Mackinlay, J. D. (1993). The document lens. *Proceedings of UIST '93.* New York: ACM Press.

Rogers, W. A. (2000). Attention and aging. In D. C. Park and N. Schwarz (eds.), *Cognitive Aging: A Primer.* Philadelphia: Psychology Press.

Ruddle, R. P., Payne, S. J., and Jones, D. M. (1997). Navigating buildings in desk-top virtual environments: Environmental investigations using extended navigational experience. *Journal of Experimental Psychology: Applied,* 3(2), 143–159.

Schaeffer, B., and Wallace, R. (1969). Semantic similarity and the comparison of word meanings. *Journal of Experimental Psychology,* 82, 343–346.

Schank, R. C., and Abelson, R. (1977). *Scripts, Plans, Goals and Understanding.* Hillsdale, NJ: Lawrence Erlbaum Associates.

Schneider, B. A., and Pichora-Fuller, M. K. (2000). Implications of perceptual deterioration for cognitive aging research. In F. I. M. Craik and T. A. Salthouse (eds.), *The Handbook of Aging and Cognition.* Mahwah, NJ: Erlbaum.

Schneider, M. L. (1982). Models for the design of static software user assistance. In A. Badre and B. Shneiderman (eds.), *Directions in Human/Computer Interaction.* Norwood, NJ: Ablex.

Sears, A., Jacko, J. A., and Borello, M. S. (1997). Internet delay effects: How users perceive quality, organization, and ease of use of information. *Proceedings of the ACM CHI '97 Short Talks.* Atlanta, GA.

SeniorNet. (1998). Research on seniors' computer and Internet usage: Report of a national survey. *http://www.seniornet.org/research/rsch 0998.html.*

Sheppard, C., and Scholtz J. (1999). The effects of cultural markers on Web site use. *Proceedings of the 5th Conference on Human Factors and the Web. http://www.nist.gov/hfweb/proceedings/sheppard/index.html.*

Shiffrin, R. M., and Schneider, W. (1977). Controlled and automatic human information processing. *Psychological Review,* 84, 127–190.

Shneiderman, B. (1978). Improving the human factors aspects of data base interactions. *ACM Transactions on Data Base Systems,* 3(4), 417–439.

Shneiderman, B. (1982). The future of interactive systems and the emergence of direct manipulation. *Behavior and Information Technology,* 1, 237–256.

Shneiderman, B. (1983). Direct manipulation: A step beyond programming languages. *IEEE Computers,* 16, 57–69.

Shneiderman, B. (1997). Designing information-abundant sites: Issues and recommendations. *International Journal of Human-Computer Studies,* 47.

Shneiderman, B. (1987), (1992), (1998). *Designing the User Interface: Strategies for Effective Human-Computer Interaction.* Reading, MA: Addison-Wesley.

Shum, S., and McKnight, C. (1997). World Wide Web usability: Introduction to this special issue. *International Journal of Human-Computer Studies,* 47(1).

Siebert, J. L., Hurley, W. D., Cheng, Y., and Bleser, T. W. (1989). An object centered user interface management systems architecture. *Proceedings of International Conference on Computer-Aided Design and Computer Graphics.* Beijing, China.

Smith, E. E., Shoben, E. J., and Rips, L. J. (1974). Structure and process in semantic memory: A featural model for semantic decision. *Psychological Review,* 81, 214–241.

Smither, J. A. (1993). Short term memory demands in processing synthetic speech by old and young adults. *Behavior and Information Technology,* 12, 330–335.

Spool, J., Scanlon, T., Snyder, C., DeAngelo, T., Schroeder, W. (1997). *Web Site Usability: A Designer's Guide.* New York: Morgan Kaufmann Press. *http://world.std.com/~uieweb/webusability.*

Spool, J., and Schroeder, W. (2001). Testing Web sites: Five users is nowhere near enough. *Proceedings of the ACM CHI '01 Conference.* Seattle, WA.

Squire, L. R. (1993). The organization of declarative and non-declarative memory. In T. Onto, L. R. Squire, M. E. Raichle, D. I. Perrett, and M. Fukuda (eds.), *Brain Mechanisms of Perception and Memory: From Neuron to Behavior.* New York: Oxford University Press.

Sternberg, R. J. (1996). *Cognitive Psychology.* Fort Worth, TX: Harcourt Brace.

Streveler, D. J., and Wasserman, A. I. (1984). Quantitative measures of the spatial property of screen design. *Proceedings of Interact '84 Conference on Human Computer Interaction.* England.

Sun Microsystems. *http://www.sun.com/usability.benefits.html.*

Tauscher, C., and Greenberg, S. (1997). How people revisit Web pages: Empirical findings and implications for the design of history systems. *International Journal of Human-Computer Studies,* 47, 97–138.

Thacker, P. (1987). Tabular displays: A human factors study. *GSTG Bulletin,* 14(1), Human Factors Society, 13.

Thomas, J. (1977). Psychological issues in data base management. *Proceedings of the Third International Conference on Very Large Data Bases.* Tokyo, Japan.

Thomas, J., and Carroll, J. M. (1979). The psychological study of design. *Design Studies,* 1, 5–11.

Thomson, D. M., and Tulving, E. (1970). Associative encoding and retrieval: Weak and strong cues. *Journal of Experimental Psychology,* 86, 255–262.

Thorndyke, P. W. (1980). Performance models for spatial and locational cognition. *Technical Report R-2676-ONR.* Washington, DC: Rand.

Tobmaugh, J., Arkin, M. D., and Dillon, R. F. (1985). The effect of video text-presentation rate on reading comprehension and reading speed. *Proceedings of CHI'85.* New York: ACM Press.

Tratinsky, N. (1997). Aesthetics and apparent usability: Empirically assessing cultural and methodological issues. *Proceedings of the ACM CHI '97 Conference.*

Treisman, A. (1960). Contextual cues in selective listening. *Quarterly Journal of Experimental Psychology,* 12, 252–248.

Treisman, A. (1982). Perceptual grouping and attention in visual search for features and for objects. *Journal of Experimental Psychology: Human Perception and Performance,* 8, 194–214.

Tullis, T. S. (1981). An evaluation of alphanumeric, graphic and color information displays. *Human Factors,* 23, 541–550.

Tulving, E. (1972). Episodic and semantic memory. In E. Tulving and W. Donaldson (eds.), *Organization of Memory.* New York: Academic Press.

Tun, P. A., and Wingfield, A. (1997). Language and communication: Fundamentals of speech communication and language processing in old age. In A. D. Fisk and W. A. Rogers (eds.), *Handbook of Human Factors and the Older Adult.* San Diego, CA: Academic Press.

U.S. Department of Commerce. (2000). Falling through the net: Toward digital inclusion: A report on Americans' access to technology tools. *http://www.ntia.doc.gov/ntiahome/digitaldivide/.*

Vercruyssen, M. (1997). Movement control and speed of behavior. In A. D. Fisk and W. A. Rogers (eds.), *Handbook of Human Factors and the Older Adult.* San Diego, CA: Academic Press.

Vincente, K. J., Hayes, B. C., and Williges, R. C. (1987). Assaying and isolating individual differences in searching a hierarchical file system. *Human Factors,* 29, 349–359.

Vinson, N. (1999). Design guidelines for landmarks to support navigation in virtual environments. *ACM Proceedings of CHI '99.* Pittsburgh, PA.

Vora, P. (1998). Human factors methodology for designing Web sites. In C. Forsythe, E. Grose, and J. Ratner (eds.), *Human Factors and Web Development*. Mahwah, NJ: Lawrence Erlbaum Associates.

Walker, N., Millians, J., and Worden, A. (1996). Mouse accelerations and performance of older computer users. *Proceedings of the Human Factors and Ergonomics Society 40th Annual Meeting*, Philadelphia.

WAP (2000). Wireless Application Protocol White Paper. *Wireless Internet Today*, June. *http://www.wapforum.org/what/WAP_white_pages.pdf*.

Waugh, N. C., and Norman, D. A. (1965). Primary memory. *Psychological Review*, 72, 89–104.

Wetherell, A. (1979). Short-term memory for verbal and graphic route information. *Proceedings of the 23rd Annual Meeting of the Human Factors Society*. CA: Human Factors Society.

Whiteside, J., Bennett, J., and Holtzblatt, K. (1988). Usability engineering: Our experience and evolution. In M. H. Helander (ed.), *Handbook of Human Computer Interaction*. Amsterdam: North-Holland.

Wickens, C. D. (1992). *Engineering Psychology and Human Performance*, Second Edition. New York: Harper Collins.

Wickens, C. D., and Andre, A. D. (1990). Proximity compatibility and information display: Effects of color, space, and objectness of information integration. *Human Factors*, 32, 61–171.

Wickens, C. D., Andre, A. D., and Haskell, I. (1990). Compatibility and consistency in crew station design. In E. J. Lovesey (ed.), *Contemporary Ergonomics 1990*. London: Taylor & Francis Ltd.

Weise, E. (2000). Online express lane hard to find. *USAToday.com*. Dec. 5, 2000. *http://www.usatoday.com/life/cyber/bonus/1200/cb002.htm*.

Worden, A., Walker, N., Bharat, K., and Hudson, S. (1997). Making computers easier for older adults to use: Area cursors and sticky icons. *Human Factors in Computing Systems '97 Proceedings*. Atlanta, GA.

Yeo, A. (1996). World wide CHI: Cultural user interfaces—a silver lining in cultural diversity. *SIHCHI Bulletin*, 28(3), 4–7.

Index

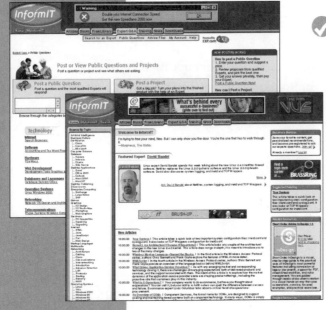

Register Your Book

at www.aw.com/cseng/register

You may be eligible to receive:
- Advance notice of forthcoming editions of the book
- Related book recommendations
- Chapter excerpts and supplements of forthcoming titles
- Information about special contests and promotions throughout the year
- Notices and reminders about author appearances, tradeshows, and online chats with special guests

Contact us

If you are interested in writing a book or reviewing manuscripts prior to publication, please write to us at:

Editorial Department
Addison-Wesley Professional
75 Arlington Street, Suite 300
Boston, MA 02116 USA
Email: AWPro@aw.com

Visit us on the Web: http://www.aw.com/cseng

Addison-Wesley